ERRATUM

SHORT-TERM ECONOMIC INDICATORS: TRANSITION ECONOMIES, 2/1996.

INDICATEURS ÉCONOMIQUES A COURT TERME : ÉCONOMIES EN TRANSITION, 2/1996.

(07 96 02 3) ISBN 92-64-04745-X

Pages 42-43: **INDUSTRIAL PRODUCTION**
Original series were inadvertently shown with 1992 as 100, while seasonally adjusted series were shown as indicated, with 1990 as 100. For greater clarity both original and seasonally adjusted series are shown below with 1990 as 100.

Pages 42-43 : **PRODUCTION INDUSTRIELLE**
Les séries non ajustées ont été présentées par inadvertance en base 100 en 1992, cependant les séries corrigées des variations saisonnières ont été présentées, comme indiqué, en base 100 en 1990. Pour une plus grande clarté, les séries corrigées et non corrigées des variations saisonnières sont présentées ci-dessous en base 100 en 1990.

HUNGARY   **HONGRIE**

			1993	1994	1995	1994 Q1	Q2	Q3	Q4	1995 Q1	Q2	Q3	Q4	1996 Q1			
INDUSTRIAL PRODUCTION															**PRODUCTION INDUSTRIELLE**		
Total		*1990=100*	76.6	84.0	88.1	81.0	80.6	81.4	92.9	88.6	86.3	84.6	93.0		Total		*1990=100*
	sa	*1990=100*				81.8	82.2	87.1	85.1	88.2	88.5	89.9	86.6			*cvs*	*1990=100*
Manufacturing		*1990=100*	74.7	81.6	86.1	76.2	78.4	80.7	91.3	84.4	84.6	83.8	91.5		Industries manufacturières		*1990=100*
	sa	*1990=100*				79.2	78.9	84.3	83.8	86.7	86.1	87.2	84.8			*cvs*	*1990=100*
Mining		*1990=100*	72.5	60.9	51.7	76.2	46.0	55.5	65.8	53.8	44.2	48.3	60.5		Industries extractives		*1990=100*
	sa	*1990=100*				68.1	53.0	62.2	57.9	48.4	51.9	54.2	52.9			*cvs*	*1990=100*
Electricity and gas		*1990=100*	81.8	83.1	84.7	98.2	75.4	63.7	95.2	100.4	75.5	67.3	95.5		Électricité et gaz		*1990=100*
	sa	*1990=100*				85.0	83.4	82.3	81.4	86.1	83.3	87.3	82.9			*cvs*	*1990=100*

HUNGARY   **HONGRIE**

			1995 Apr	May	Jun	Jul	Aug	Sep	Oct	Nov	Dec	1996 Jan	Feb	Mar			
INDUSTRIAL PRODUCTION															**PRODUCTION INDUSTRIELLE**		
Total		*1990=100*	77.4	87.6	93.9	79.1	86.1	88.7	89.9	97.3	91.9				Total		*1990=100*
	sa	*1990=100*	84.1	95.6	85.8	90.0	91.0	88.7	90.4	87.0	82.4					*cvs*	*1990=100*
Manufacturing		*1990=100*	72.0	87.7	94.3	77.0	84.2	90.1	90.5	94.7	89.4				Industries manufacturières		*1990=100*
	sa	*1990=100*	80.8	94.2	83.3	87.5	87.4	86.5	89.1	85.1	80.0					*cvs*	*1990=100*
Mining		*1990=100*	41.9	45.0	45.7	52.0	47.0	45.8	52.6	77.7	51.0				Industries extractives		*1990=100*
	sa	*1990=100*	51.8	51.5	52.4	51.4	58.1	52.9	58.2	55.4	45.2					*cvs*	*1990=100*
Electricity and gas		*1990=100*	89.4	66.4	70.8	64.4	70.3	67.3	76.9	96.1	113.4				Électricité et gaz		*1990=100*
	sa	*1990=100*	80.9	86.8	82.3	89.3	84.5	88.3	79.5	86.0	83.3					*cvs*	*1990=100*

INDICATEURS ÉCONOMIQUES
A COURT TERME :
ÉCONOMIES EN TRANSITION

Ce bulletin trimestriel, qui vient compléter les ***Principaux indicateurs économiques de l'OCDE*,*** est aussi disponible sur disquette.

L'abonnement annuel comprend des données rétrospectives depuis 1980, des mises-à-jour trimestrielles et un supplément annuel (imprimé) sur les Sources et Méthodes.

FF 2 500   £275 $US455   DM 755

Les données sont fournies, dans un format spécifique de l'OCDE, sur des disquettes 3 pouces 1/2, pour les micro-ordinateurs IBM ou compatibles. Les disquettes incluent un programme simple pour effectuer le transfert des données dans un format DIF, SYLK ou LOTUS WKS. Les données peuvent ainsi être facilement utilisées avec des logiciels tels que LOTUS 1-2-3, EXCEL, SYMPHONY et MULTIPLAN.

Pour tout abonnement ou tout renseignement complémentaire veuillez contacter l'OCDE à Paris à l'adresse ci-dessous, un des Centres des Publications et de l'Information à Bonn, Mexico, Tokyo ou Washington, ou le distributeur OCDE dans votre pays.

PUBLICATIONS OCDE
Éditions électroniques
2, rue André-Pascal, 75775 Paris Cedex 16, France

....

* ***Principaux indicateurs économiques de l'OCDE***

Cette publication est une source indispensable pour les statistiques de court terme des pays Membres de l'OCDE. Elle fournit une image complète et à jour des changements les plus récents intervenus dans les économies des pays Membres de l'OCDE et les situe dans un contexte international. Les disquettes correspondantes contiennent dix ans de données mensuelles ou trimestrielles pour ces indicateurs, documentées électroniquemement et faciles à sélectionner pour votre propre analyse.

FF 7 000   £775 $US1 270   DM 2 120

CENTRE FOR CO-OPERATION WITH THE ECONOMIES IN TRANSITION
CENTRE POUR LA COOPÉRATION AVEC LES ÉCONOMIES EN TRANSITION

SHORT-TERM ECONOMIC INDICATORS TRANSITION ECONOMIES

◆

INDICATEURS ÉCONOMIQUES A COURT TERME ÉCONOMIES EN TRANSITION

ORGANISATION FOR ECONOMIC CO-OPERATION AND DEVELOPMENT
ORGANISATION DE COOPÉRATION ET DE DÉVELOPPEMENT ÉCONOMIQUES

ORGANISATION FOR ECONOMIC CO-OPERATION AND DEVELOPMENT

Pursuant to Article 1 of the Convention signed in Paris on 14th December 1960, and which came into force on 30th September 1961, the Organisation for Economic Co-operation and Development (OECD) shall promote policies designed:

– to achieve the highest sustainable economic growth and employment and a rising standard of living in Member countries, while maintaining financial stability, and thus to contribute to the development of the world economy;
– to contribute to sound economic expansion in Member as well as non-member countries in the process of economic development; and
– to contribute to the expansion of world trade on a multilateral, non-discriminatory basis in accordance with international obligations.

The original Member countries of the OECD are Austria, Belgium, Canada, Denmark, France, Germany, Greece, Iceland, Ireland, Italy, Luxembourg, the Netherlands, Norway, Portugal, Spain, Sweden, Switzerland, Turkey, the United Kingdom and the United States. The following countries became Members subsequently through accession at the dates indicated hereafter: Japan (28th April 1964), Finland (28th January 1969), Australia (7th June 1971), New Zealand (29th May 1973), Mexico (18th May 1994), and the Czech Republic (21st December 1995). The Commission of the European Communities takes part in the work of the OECD (Article 13 of the OECD Convention).

THE CENTRE FOR CO-OPERATION WITH THE ECONOMIES IN TRANSITION

The Centre for Co-operation with the European Economies in Transition (CCEET) was created in March 1990, as the focal point for co-operation between the OECD and the countries of Central and Eastern Europe. In 1991, the activities of the Centre were expanded to include the New Independent States of the Former Soviet Union and, the following year, Mongolia. In 1993, the Centre was renamed Centre for Co-operation with the Economies in Transition (CCET) to reflect its wider geographic coverage. Since 1991, the Centre has operated a "Partners in Transition" Programme for the purpose of providing targeted assistance to the countries more advanced in introducing market-oriented reforms and which desire to become Members of OECD. The "Partners" are now Hungary, Poland and the Slovak Republic.

ORGANISATION DE COOPÉRATION ET DE DÉVELOPPEMENT ÉCONOMIQUES

En vertu de l'article 1er de la Convention signée le 14 décembre 1960, à Paris, et entrée en vigueur le 30 septembre 1961, l'Organisation de Coopération et de Développement Économiques (OCDE) a pour objectif de promouvoir des politiques visant :

- à réaliser la plus forte expansion de l'économie et de l'emploi et une progression du niveau de vie dans les pays Membres, tout en maintenant la stabilité financière, et à contribuer ainsi au développement de l'économie mondiale ;
- à contribuer à une saine expansion économique dans les pays Membres, ainsi que les pays non membres, en voie de développement économique ;
- à contribuer à l'expansion du commerce mondial sur une base multilatérale et non discriminatoire conformément aux obligations internationales.

Les pays Membres originaires de l'OCDE sont : l'Allemagne, l'Autriche, la Belgique, le Canada, le Danemark, l'Espagne, les États-Unis, la France, la Grèce, l'Irlande, l'Islande, l'Italie, le Luxembourg, la Norvège, les Pays-Bas, le Portugal, le Royaume-Uni, la Suède, la Suisse et la Turquie. Les pays suivants sont ultérieurement devenus Membres par adhésion aux dates indiquées ci-après : le Japon (28 avril 1964), la Finlande (28 janvier 1969), l'Australie (7 juin 1971), la Nouvelle-Zélande (29 mai 1973), le Mexique (18 mai 1994) et la République tchèque (21 décembre 1995). La Commission des Communautés européennes participe aux travaux de l'OCDE (article 13 de la Convention de l'OCDE).

LE CENTRE POUR LA COOPÉRATION AVEC LES ÉCONOMIES EN TRANSITION

Le Centre pour la Coopération avec les Économies Européennes en Transition (CCEET) a été créé en mars 1990 pour être l'axe de la coopération entre l'OCDE et les pays d'Europe centrale et orientale. Les activités du Centre ont été étendues aux nouveaux États indépendants issus de l'ex-Union soviétique en 1991 et à la Mongolie l'année suivante. En 1993, l'appellation du CCEET a été modifiée pour tenir compte du fait que les activités du Centre couvrent désormais une aire géographique plus large : le CCEET est devenu le Centre pour la Coopération avec les Économies en Transition (CCET). Depuis 1991, le Centre met en œuvre un Programme «Partenaires pour la transition» qui est destiné à apporter une aide ciblée aux pays qui sont les plus avancés dans la voie des réformes axées sur le marché et qui souhaiteraient devenir Membres de l'OCDE. Actuellement, les pays «Partenaires» sont la Hongrie, la Pologne et la République slovaque.

FOREWORD

The development of reliable statistics, which are oriented towards the requirements of a market economy, is one of the priority activities that the Centre for Co-operation with the Economies in Transition (CCET) is supporting in its programme for the transition economies. Activities on statistics include providing advice on the practical implementation of western statistical systems by focusing on areas where the OECD possesses internationally-recognised expertise (e.g. national accounts, price and volume measures, short-term economic indicators and business surveys); organising training workshops for statisticians; and establishing a data base of key economic statistics to monitor economic and social developments.

This quarterly Centre publication presents data on a range of short-term indicators for those transition economies in Central and Eastern Europe and the New Independent States (NIS) that are adapting their statistics to meet international standards and the needs of market economies. It thus constitutes an invaluable source of information for analysing short-term economic developments in individual transition economies and for undertaking comparative analysis of these developments.

This publication, produced by the Statistics Directorate, complements the OECD's *Main Economic Indicators* and, as far as possible, the choice and presentation of statistics are the same in both publications.

These statistics are published on the responsibility of the Secretary-General of the OECD.

Salvatore Zecchini
OECD Deputy Secretary-General
Director of the CCET

AVANT-PROPOS

Le développement de statistiques fiables et adaptées aux exigences d'une économie de marché, est l'une des activités prioritaires que le Centre pour la coopération avec les économies en transition (CCET) soutient dans son programme pour les économies en transition. Les activités dans le domaine des statistiques incluent: le conseil pour la mise en œuvre pratique de systèmes statistiques de type occidental surtout dans les domaines dans lesquels l'OCDE jouit d'une compétence internationalement reconnue (par exemple, les comptes nationaux, les mesures de prix et de volume, les indicateurs économiques à court terme et les enquêtes de conjoncture); l'organisation de séminaires à l'intention de statisticiens; l'établissement d'une base de données des indicateurs économiques essentiels pour le suivi de l'évolution économique et sociale.

Cette publication trimestrielle du Centre présente une série d'indicateurs à court terme se rapportant aux pays en transition de l'Europe centrale et orientale et aux Nouveaux États Indépendants (NEI) qui mettent en conformité leurs statistiques avec les normes internationales et les adaptent aux impératifs d'une économie de marché. Elle constitue donc une source d'information irremplaçable pour analyser les développements économiques à court terme dans chaque économie en transition et pour entreprendre des analyses comparatives.

Cette publication, effectuée par la Direction des Statistiques, vient compléter les *Principaux indicateurs économiques* de l'OCDE avec, dans la mesure du possible, un choix de statistiques et une présentation comparables dans les deux publications.

Ces statistiques sont publiées sous l'autorité du Secrétaire général de l'OCDE.

Salvatore Zecchini
Secrétaire général adjoint de l'OCDE
Directeur du CCET

TABLE OF CONTENTS — TABLE DES MATIÈRES

TABLE OF CONTENTS — TABLE DES MATIÈRES

(continued — suite)

CONVENTIONAL SIGNS — SIGNES CONVENTIONNELS

In tables:			*Dans les tableaux:*
.	Decimal point	.	Point décimal
|	Break in continuity of series	|	Rupture de continuité dans la série
. .	Data not available	. .	Donnée non disponible

ABBREVIATIONS — ABRÉVIATIONS

sa	Series adjusted for seasonal variations	**cvs**	Série corrigée des variations saisonnières
PP=100	Index where the previous period equals 100	**PP=100**	Indice ayant pour base 100 la période précédente
SP85=100	Index where the same period of 1985 equals 100	**PC85=100**	Indice ayant pour base 100 la période correspondante de 1985
SPPY=100	Index where the same period of the previous year equals 100	**PCAP=100**	Indice ayant pour base 100 la période correspondante de l'année précédente
balance	Difference between the percent of respondents giving positive and negative replies	**solde**	Différence entre le pourcentage de personnes ayant donné une réponse positive et ayant donné une réponse négative
'000	Thousand	**'000**	Milliers
mln	Million	**mln**	Millions
bln	Billion (thousand million)	**mrd**	Milliards
'000 bln	Thousand billion	**'000 mrd**	Milliers de milliards
% p.a.	Percent per annum	**%p.a.**	Pourcentage par an
per. ave.	Period average	**moy. pér.**	Moyenne de période
end per.	End of period	**fin pér.**	Fin de période
US$	U.S. dollar	**$É-U**	Dollar des États-Unis
sq km	Square kilometre	**km^2**	Kilomètre carré
publ. sector	Public sector	**sect. publ.**	Secteur public

IN THIS ISSUE _____

The Czech Republic has become the 26th Member country of the OECD, formally joining the Organisation on December 21st, 1995. Data for the Czech Republic were included in the last issue and have since been progressively incorporated in statistical publications for OECD countries. They will therefore not continue to be published here.

Business Surveys Annex

Complete results from harmonised business surveys in Manufacturing, Construction and Retail Trade, first published in SEI number 2/95, are again published here in the Annex. Included for the first time are results from the Manufacturing survey for Belarus and results from the Retail Trade survey for Latvia.

New or revised series

- **Hungary**
  Export order books series refer to "Western export order books" only.

- **Lithuania**
  Retail sales volume has been revised from January 1995. New CPI for Clothing and Footwear is included.

- **Poland**
  Series in zlotys are now referred to as being expressed in either old zlotys or zlotys (see also the footnote on the country page).

- **Romania**
  The index of industrial production is no longer presented seasonally adjusted (see also the footnote on the country page).

- **Slovak Republic**
  New series: US$ end-of-period exchange rate. Employment and earnings series revised from 1993.

- **New Independent States**
  Sub-annual industrial production indices have been suppressed pending verification by the OECD Secretariat. For further details see the note under the industrial production subject table.

  Revised series:

  - Foreign trade series for most NIS have been revised for 1994 and onwards based on data from customs declarations.
  - Commodity output, employment and earnings series have been revised for 1994 based on data from annual reports.
  - Personal deposits, retail trade volumes and some consumer price series have also been revised for 1994 and later periods for a number of NIS.

  New series: for Tajikistan, Earnings in manufacturing expressed in tajik roubles.

New publication

Sources and Definitions released with this issue: contains over 300 pages of methodological notes and comparative methodological tables, corresponding to series included in this quarterly publication and diskettes.

La **République tchèque est devenue le 26e pays Membre de l'OCDE, en adhérant formellement à l'Organisation le 21 décembre 1995. Les données relatives à la République tchèque étaient encore incluses dans la dernière édition de cette publication, mais ont depuis été progressivement intégrées dans les publications statistiques des pays de l'OCDE. Dorénavant, elles ne seront donc plus publiées ici.**

Enquêtes de conjoncture

Les résultats complets des Enquêtes de conjoncture harmonisées dans l'industrie manufacturière, la construction et le commerce de détail, publiés pour la première fois dans le SEI 2/95, sont mises à jour et publiés à nouveau dans l'Annexe. Sont inclus pour la première fois les résultats tirés de l'enquête dans l'industrie manufacturière pour la Bélarus, et les résultats tirés de l'enquête dans le commerce de détail pour la Lettonie.

Séries nouvelles ou révisées

- **Hongrie**
  Les carnets de commandes à l'exportation se réfèrent aux carnets de commandes à l'exportation "à l'Ouest" uniquement.
- **Lituanie**
  La série de ventes de détail en volume est revisée depuis janvier 1995. Nouvel IPC pour l'habillement et chaussures.
- **Pologne**
  Les séries en zlotys sont maintenant exprimées soit en anciens zlotys soit en zlotys (voir aussi la note de bas de page pays).
- **Roumanie**
  L'indice de production industrielle n'est plus présenté corrigé des variations saisonnières (voir aussi la note de bas de page pays).
- **République slovaque**
  Nouvelle série : taux de change du $É-U fin de période. Les séries d'emploi et de gains mensuels sont revisées depuis 1993.
- **Nouveaux États Indépendants**
  Les indices mensuels et trimestriels de la production industrielle ont été supprimés en attente d'une vérification par le Secrétariat de l'OCDE. Pour plus de détails, voir la note sous le tableau sujet de la production industrielle.

  Séries révisées:

  - Les séries du commerce extérieur pour la plupart des NIS ont été revisées pour 1994 et au delà, à partir des déclarations douanières.
  - Certaines séries de quantités produites, emploi et gains mensuels ont été revisées pour 1994 à partir de rapports annuels.
  - Certaines séries des dépôts personnels, ventes de détail en volume et prix à la consommation ont été revisées pour 1994 et au delà pour certains des NIS.

  Nouvelle série : pour le Tadjikistan, gains mensuels dans les industries manufacturières en roubles tadjiks.

Nouvelle publication

Sources et Définitions publiée avec cette édition : contient plus de 300 pages de notes méthodologiques et tableaux méthodologiques comparatifs, qui correspondent aux séries de cette publication trimestrielle et de la disquette.

TRANSITION COUNTRIES

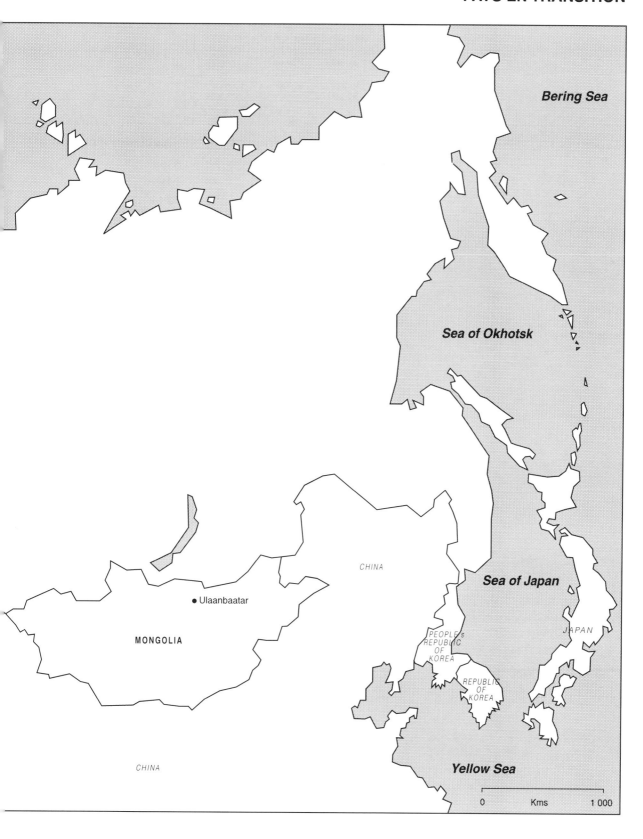

Bering Sea

Sea of Okhotsk

CHINA

Sea of Japan

Ulaanbaatar

MONGOLIA

JAPAN

PEOPLE'S
REPUBLIC
OF
KOREA

REPUBLIC
OF
KOREA

CHINA

Yellow Sea

0   Kms   1 000

BASIC STATISTICS / STATISTIQUES DE BASE

	Population *millions* Population *millions*	Area *1000 sq km* Superficie *100 km²*	Infant mortality *per 1000* Mortalité infantile *pour 1000*	Population per doctor *persons* Population par médecin *personnes*	Population per hospital bed *persons* Population par lit d'hôpital *personnes*	
Central and Eastern Europe						**Europe Centrale et Orientale**
Bulgaria	8.4	110.9	14	318	104	Bulgarie
Estonia	1.5	45.1	16	255	105	Estonie
Hungary	10.3	93.0	15	330	97	Hongrie
Latvia	2.5	64.5	14	281	83	Lettonie
Lithuania	3.7	65.3	13	233	83	Lituanie
Poland	38.5	312.7	15	450	179	Pologne
Republic of Slovenia	1.9	20.3	8	490	169	République de Slovénie
Romania	22.7	237.5	23	536	127	Roumanie
Slovak Republic	5.3	49.0	12	286	105	République slovaque
New Independent States						**Nouveaux États Indépendants**
Armenia	3.5	29.8	21	261	120	Arménie
Azerbaijan	7.5	86.6	28	256	96	Azerbaïdjan
Belarus	10.4	207.6	16	232	79	Bélarus
Kazakstan	17.0	2717.3	29	253	75	Kazakstan
Kyrgyz Republic	4.6	198.5	34	310	94	République kirghize
Republic of Moldova	4.4	33.7	25	253	81	République de Moldova
Russian Federation	148.0	17075.4	21	222	78	Fédération de Russie
Tajikistan	5.8	143.1	47	434	97	Tadjikistan
Turkmenistan	4.0	488.1	56	278	85	Turkménistan
Ukraine	51.9	603.7	16	224	76	Ukraine
Uzbekistan	22.3	447.4	40	281	105	Ouzbékistan
OECD average			7.6	464	176	**Moyenne OCDE**

Population figures refer to mid-year 1994 revised estimates.

Infant mortality figures refer to 1993.

Population per doctor figures and population per hospital bed refer to 1988-1993, depending on the country.

Sources: OECD, World Bank, United Nations, national sources.

Les données sur la population sont des estimations révisées du milieu de l'année 1994.

Les données de la mortalité infantile sont de 1993.

Les données de la population par médecin et de la population par lit d'hôpital sont de 1988-1993, selon le pays.

Sources : OCDE, Banque mondiale, Nations unies, sources nationales.

OECD
OCDE
SHORT-TERM ECONOMIC INDICATORS
OECD/CCET © April 1996

14

INDICATEURS ÉCONOMIQUES À COURT TERME
OCDE/CCET © avril 1996

RECENT TRENDS — TENDANCES RÉCENTES

INDUSTRIAL PRODUCTION
PRODUCTION INDUSTRIELLE

(Rates of change / Taux de variation)

	1-year rate of change Variation sur 1 an			12-month rate of change Variation sur 12 mois								
				1995				1996			
	1993	1994	1995	Sep	Oct	Nov	Dec	Jan	Feb	Mar	
Central and Eastern Europe											**Europe Centrale et Orientale**
Bulgaria	-7.0	3.9		-1.4	7.9	2.8	-15.8	4.6	-8.4	-9.2	Bulgarie
Estonia[1]		-2.2	4.6	9.4	16.4	7.7	-4.4	5.2	4.9	2.9	Estonie[1]
Hungary	3.9	9.6	5.0	2.5	4.6	0.7	-4.3				Hongrie
Latvia	-38.1	-9.4	-6.5	-1.6	-4.8	-2.4	-6.6	0.4	0.0	-5.8	Lettonie
Lithuania	-34.7	-29.7	0.8	5.8	7.8	8.7	5.7	17.3	14.7		Lituanie
Poland	5.6	12.2	10.3	7.2	14.1	9.6	1.5	9.5			Pologne
Republic of Slovenia	-2.8	6.4	2.0	-0.2	-0.1	0.4	-5.6	-4.9	-4.0		République de Slovénie
Romania		3.1	9.5	10.2	14.7	10.4	5.2	8.4	7.0		Roumanie
Slovak Republic	-3.8	4.8	8.3	12.3	12.7	9.9	2.7	14.4	12.2		République slovaque

Note: Monthly industrial production data is collected from enterprises located in member countries of the CIS on a cumulative basis from the beginning of each year. This methodology can lead to the introduction of distortions in the distribution of reported production throughout the year, exacerbating the reporting by enterprises of higher levels of production in the final quarter of each year, for example. The methodology significantly impacts on the ability of the resulting monthly Indices of Industrial Production to reflect the actual distribution of industrial production throughout the year.

The OECD Secretariat is currently assessing the Indices of Industrial Production previously published, and evaluating alternative methods of presentation etc., to minimise the impact of cumulative monthly reporting in order enhance the ability of the series to reflect actual production throughout the year.

Note : Les données mensuelles relatives à la production industrielle sont collectées auprès des entreprises des pays membres de la CEI de façon cumulative à partir du début de chaque année. Cette méthodologie peut introduire des distorsions dans la distribution de la production notifiée tout au long de l'année. Elle accentue par exemple le fait que les entreprises déclarent des niveaux de production plus élevés lors du dernier trimestre de chaque année. Les indices mensuels de la production industrielle censés refléter la distribution réelle de la production industrielle au cours de l'année sont significativement affectés par cette méthodologie.

Le Secrétariat de l'OCDE examine actuellement les indices de la production industrielle précédemment publiés. Des méthodes alternatives de présentation et autres sont envisagées de façon à minimiser l'impact d'une notification mensuelle cumulée et à produire des séries reflétant au mieux la production réelle au long de l'année.

(1) This series has been estimated by the OECD Secretariat.

(1) Cette série a été estimée par le Secrétariat de l'OCDE.

INDUSTRIAL PRODUCTION – PRODUCTION INDUSTRIELLE
Seasonally adjusted - Corrigée des variations saisonnières

Index 1990 = 100 – Indice 1990 = 100

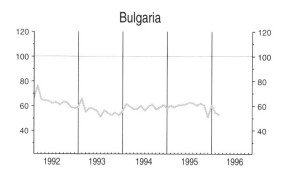

Bulgaria

Hungary

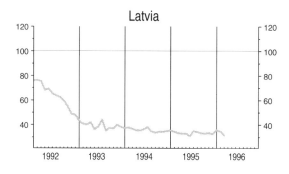

Latvia

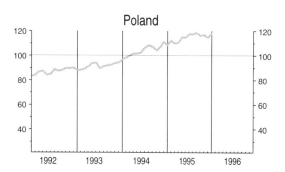

Poland

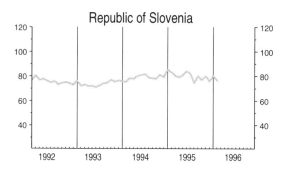

Republic of Slovenia

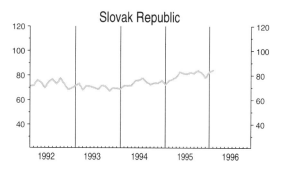

Slovak Republic

BUSINESS SURVEYS, MANUFACTURING
ENQUÊTES DE CONJONCTURE, INDUSTRIES MANUFACTURIÈRES

	1995			1996	1995			1996			
	Q2	Q3	Q4	Q1	Oct	Nov	Dec	Jan	Feb	Mar	
Production: future tendency				*Balance - Solde*							**Production : perspectives**
Bulgaria	32	32	35	33	32	39	35	28	36	36	Bulgarie
Estonia	16	10	5	52							Estonie
Hungary	30	31	22	50							Hongrie
Latvia	17	15	5	15							Lettonie
Lithuania	10	6	-9		-6	-16	-4	14	27		Lituanie
Poland	25	27	13		21	7	10	20	40		Pologne
Romania	38	27	31	32							Roumanie
Slovak Republic	20	43	26	57	34	13	32	50	56	64	République slovaque
Belarus	-16	-23	-7	-3							Bélarus
Russian Federation	-6	5	-7	4	-4	-13	-5	-1	6	6	Fédération de Russie
Stocks of finished goods: level											**Stocks de produits finis : niveau**
Bulgaria	10	10	-4	-7	-1	-7	-5	-7	-8	-5	Bulgarie
Estonia	18	13	12	16							Estonie
Hungary	18	4	8	17							Hongrie
Latvia	14	5	-8	2							Lettonie
Lithuania	7	4	12		13	11	12	13	19		Lituanie
Poland	-1	-4	-3		-1	-2	-5	0	1		Pologne
Romania	11	4	1	0							Roumanie
Slovak Republic	22	25	25	34	29	23	22	39	46	17	République slovaque
Belarus	33	34	20	23							Bélarus
Russian Federation	11	6	19	24	13	19	26	28	22	22	Fédération de Russie
Capacity utilisation				*Percent - Pourcentage*							**Utilisation des capacités**
Bulgaria	60	61	63	63							Bulgarie
Estonia	57	59	59	53							Estonie
Hungary	76	78	79	77							Hongrie
Latvia	51	50	51	52							Lettonie
Lithuania	44	44	45								Lituanie
Poland	69	69	71		71	71	71	69	67		Pologne
Slovak Republic	75	74	76	78	76	76	76	78	78	79	République slovaque
Belarus	51	46	50	47							Bélarus
Russian Federation	47	47	46	44							Fédération de Russie

Note: Average of monthly data for series not originally quarterly.

Note : Moyennes mensuelles pour les séries non trimestrielles à l'origine.

BUSINESS SURVEYS, MANUFACTURING
ENQUÊTES DE CONJONCTURE, INDUSTRIES MANUFACTURIÈRES
Balance — Solde

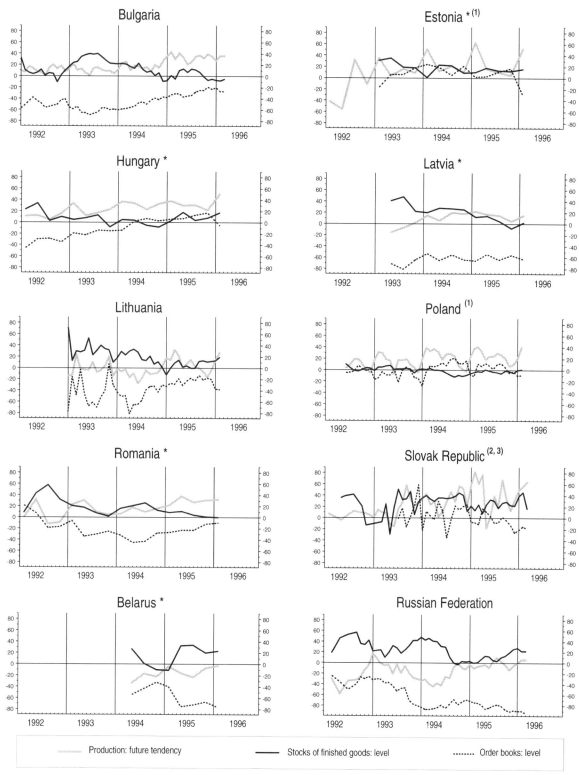

	Production: future tendency		Stocks of finished goods: level		Order books: level

* Quarterly observations are shown in the midmonth of the quarter.

(1) Demand tendency rather than order books level.

(2) Domestic demand tendency rather than total order books level prior to Jan. 95.

(3) Prior to Jan. 1995, total industry; since then, manufacturing sector only.

* Les observations trimestrielles sont affectées au deuxième mois du trimestre.

(1) Demande en tendance à la place de carnets de commandes en niveau.

(2) Demande intérieure en tendance à la place de carnets de commandes totales en niveau avant jan. 95.

(3) Avant jan. 1995, secteur de l'industrie ; ensuite, industries manufacturières seulement.

BUSINESS SURVEYS, CONSTRUCTION
ENQUÊTES DE CONJONCTURE, CONSTRUCTION

	1995			1996	1995			1996			
	Q2	Q3	Q4	Q1	Oct	Nov	Dec	Jan	Feb	Mar	
Business activity: tendency				*Balance - Solde*							**Activité de l'entreprise : tendance**
Bulgaria	-10	3	-1	-29	6	-2	-8	-12	-32	-42	Bulgarie
Estonia	34	49	-8	-28							Estonie
Hungary[1]	3	1	-6	-10							Hongrie[1]
Latvia	-4	-12	-34	-61							Lettonie
Poland	29	31	9		22	9	-4	-33	-25		Pologne
Slovak Republic	35	20	8	4	10	17	-3	-1	-6	20	République slovaque
Orders: level											**Commandes : niveau**
Bulgaria	-47	-36	-34	-42	-33	-34	-35	-38	-41	-46	Bulgarie
Estonia	-26	-4	-20	-41							Estonie
Hungary	-5	-12	2	-36							Hongrie
Latvia	-70	-72	-65	-88							Lettonie
Poland[2]	20	27	4		19	2	-10	-28	-6		Pologne[2]
Slovak Republic	-44	-53	-36	-33	-45	-42	-20	-20	-51	-28	République slovaque
Orders: future tendency											**Commandes : perspectives**
Bulgaria	13	12	-3	7							Bulgarie
Estonia	35	0	-2	54							Estonie
Hungary	-21	-31	-2	21							Hongrie
Latvia	45	-30	-41	-38							Lettonie
Poland	47	27	1		5	-3	2	43	58		Pologne
Romania	69	56	14	-17							Roumanie
Slovak Republic	19	1	-23	1	-36	-23	-11	-32	9	26	République slovaque
Russian Federation	12	-8	-64	-39							Fédération de Russie

Note: Average of monthly data for series not originally quarterly.

Note : Moyennes mensuelles pour les séries non trimestrielles à l'origine.

(1) Appreciation of level of business activity rather than tendency.
(2) Demand tendency rather than order books level.

(1) Activité de l'entreprise en niveau et non en tendance.
(2) Demande en tendance à la place de carnets de commandes en niveau.

BUSINESS SURVEYS, CONSTRUCTION
ENQUÊTES DE CONJONCTURE, CONSTRUCTION

Balance — Solde

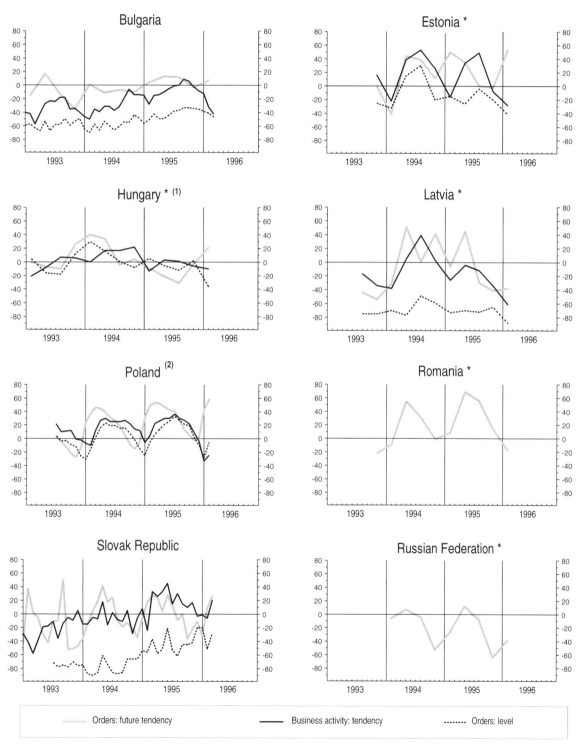

Bulgaria

Estonia *

Hungary * (1)

Latvia *

Poland (2)

Romania *

Slovak Republic

Russian Federation *

——— Orders: future tendency ——— Business activity: tendency ········· Orders: level

* Quarterly observations are shown in the midmonth of the quarter.

(1) Appreciation of level of business activity rather than tendency.

(2) Demand tendency rather than order books level.

* Les observations trimestrielles sont affectées au deuxième mois du trimestre.

(1) Activité de l'entreprise en niveau et non en tendance.

(2) Demande en tendance à la place de carnets de commandes en niveau.

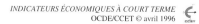

BUSINESS SURVEYS, RETAIL TRADE
ENQUÊTES DE CONJONCTURE, COMMERCE DE DÉTAIL

	1995			1996	1995			1996			
	Q2	Q3	Q4	Q1	Oct	Nov	Dec	Jan	Feb	Mar	
Business situation: future tendency				*Balance - Solde*							**État des affaires : perspectives**
Bulgaria	19	20	22	4	13	27	25	12	-1	2	Bulgarie
Estonia	20	20	29	43							Estonie
Hungary	-3	3	-7	7							Hongrie
Latvia				17							Lettonie
Poland	41	26	-10								Pologne
Romania	0	44	58	9							Roumanie
Slovak Republic	25	25	23	28	49	31	-10	-7	51	40	République slovaque
Intentions of placing orders											**Commandes : intentions**
Bulgaria	14	13	20	12	14	31	16	18	13	4	Bulgarie
Estonia	10	26	9	49							Estonie
Hungary	-26	-2	-38	-13							Hongrie
Latvia				3							Lettonie
Poland	30	26	-10								Pologne
Romania	58	57	65	14							Roumanie
Slovak Republic			2	26	9	-15	12	4	37	36	République slovaque
Stocks: level											**Stocks : niveau**
Bulgaria	-34	-32	-44	-41	-34	-48	-49	-38	-41	-43	Bulgarie
Estonia	7	6	-2	-2							Estonie
Hungary	38	31	18	38							Hongrie
Latvia				-10							Lettonie
Poland	18	16	13								Pologne
Romania	2	3	-2	2							Roumanie
Slovak Republic	4	8	10	1	10	13	8	9	-3	-2	République slovaque

Note: Average of monthly data for series not originally quarterly.

Note : Moyennes mensuelles pour les séries non trimestrielles à l'origine.

BUSINESS SURVEYS, RETAIL TRADE
ENQUÊTES DE CONJONCTURE, COMMERCE DE DÉTAIL

Balance — Solde

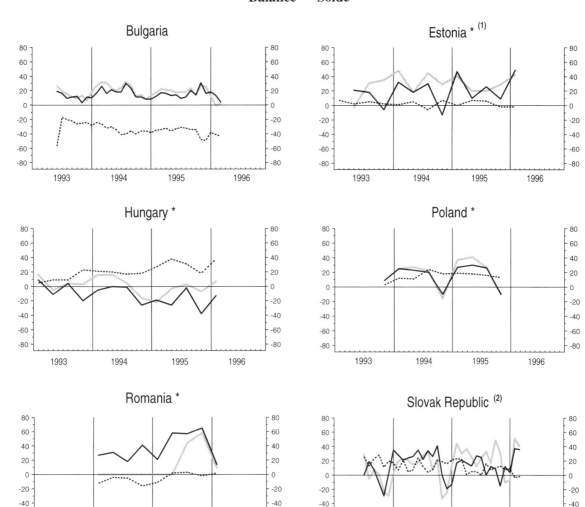

Business situation: future tendency   Intentions of placing orders: future tendency   Stocks: level

* Quarterly observations are shown in the midmonth of the quarter.

(1) Prior to fourth quarter of 1994, refers to domestic orders only.

(2) Prior to October 1995, refers to domestic orders only.

* Les observations trimestrielles sont affectées au deuxième mois du trimestre.

(1) Avant le quatrième trimestre de 1994, se réfèrent aux commandes intérieures seulement.

(2) Avant octobre 1995, se réfèrent aux commandes intérieures seulement.

RETAIL SALES VOLUME
VENTES DE DÉTAIL EN VOLUME

(Rates of change / Taux de variation)

	1-year rate of change Variation sur 1 an			12-month rate of change Variation sur 12 mois							
				1995				1996			
	1993	1994	1995	Sep	Oct	Nov	Dec	Jan	Feb	Mar	
Central and Eastern Europe											**Europe Centrale et Orientale**
Bulgaria[1]	-14.0	-0.3	4.3	9.5	3.0	3.3	11.8	17.0			Bulgarie[1]
Estonia		-2.5	23.8	30.1	30.0	28.8	7.0	10.0	8.9		Estonie
Hungary	3.3	-8.9	-11.2	-12.3	-14.1	-11.6	-13.9	-6.4	-5.1		Hongrie
Latvia	-23.4	-2.4	-7.8	0.0	-11.1	-11.1	-15.0	-6.7	-6.3	0.0	Lettonie
Lithuania	-43.3	-15.8	0.7	12.6	9.3	2.5	2.9	7.7			Lituanie
Poland[1]	9.3	-15.4	18.2	8.8	13.5	12.6	10.1	6.7	11.1		Pologne[1]
Republic of Slovenia	5.1	6.0		6.8							République de Slovénie
Romania		-2.1	9.4	2.6	22.9	22.3	0.6	15.6	8.7		Roumanie
Slovak Republic[1]	9.2	2.0	9.0	8.1	4.7	4.2	22.6	9.2	11.6		République slovaque[1]
New Independent States											**Nouveaux États Indépendants**
Armenia	-41.4	-37.0	26.7	24.5	108.0	100.0	29.1	22.2			Arménie
Azerbaijan	-48.8	-51.0	-9.5	-18.6	-9.9	-6.3	4.2	-1.3			Azerbaïdjan
Belarus	-21.2	-21.7	-25.8	-21.4	-24.4	-27.0	-27.5	-17.2			Bélarus
Kazakstan	-24.8	-49.9	-22.5	-19.1	-5.7	-8.9	-3.0	-6.0			Kazakstan
Kyrgyz Republic	-18.5	-11.9	-16.3	-8.6	-16.5	-18.7	-24.3	-15.6			République kirghize
Republic of Moldova	-32.9	-39.1	-4.3	-3.8	5.6	9.1	6.2	-4.2			République de Moldova
Russian Federation[2]	1.9	0.1	-7.2	-10.0	-7.8	-3.3	-3.5	2.9			Fédération de Russie[2]
Tajikistan	-27.3	-31.5	-76.1	-67.9	-79.8	-85.7	-85.4	-79.5			Tadjikistan
Turkmenistan	-14.7	-56.5									Turkménistan
Ukraine	-35.0	-13.6	-13.2	-12.1	-21.5	-21.3	-6.1	-1.2	1.5		Ukraine
Uzbekistan	9.6	-18.1	-17.5	7.2	-10.8	-8.1	-6.3				Ouzbékistan

(1) Fixed base volume indices are not supplied by these countries. They have been estimated by the OECD Secretariat by deflating value series with appropriate price indices.
(2) Series including estimates of sales by non registered enterprises and private persons in informal markets.

(1) Ces pays ne fournissent pas d'indices de volume en base fixe. Ces indices ont été estimés par le Secrétariat de l'OCDE en corrigeant de l'incidence des prix, à l'aide de l'indice des prix approprié, les séries en valeur.
(2) Série comprenant les ventes effectuées par les entreprises non inscrites au registre du commerce et par les personnes privées sur les marchés informels.

RETAIL SALES VOLUME[(1)] – VENTES DE DÉTAIL EN VOLUME[(1)]

Index 1993 = 100 – Indice 1993 = 100

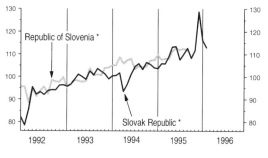

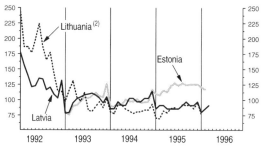

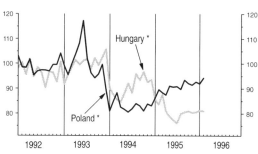

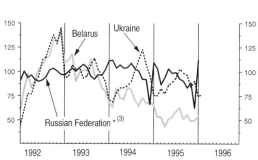

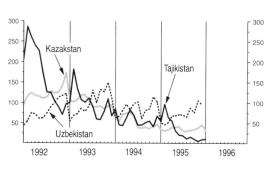

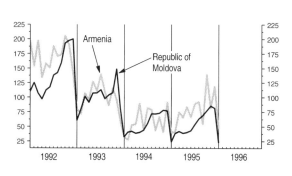

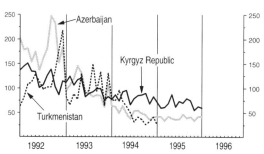

* Series adjusted for seasonal variations.

(1) The indices shown above are derived from volume indices as compiled by national sources, except for: Bulgaria, Poland and Slovak Republic, where value series have been deflated by the appropriate price index, by the OECD Secretariat.

(2) From July 1993, all outlets with five or more employees are surveyed. Prior to this only outlets with 20 or more employees were covered.

(3) New series including estimates of sales by non registered enterprises and private persons in informal markets.

* Après correction des variations saisonnières.

(1) Les indices ci-dessus sont dérivés des indices en volume publiés dans les sources nationales, à l'exception de : la Bulgarie, la Pologne et la République slovaque, pour lesquels les séries en valeur ont été corrigées de l'incidence des prix à l'aide de l'indice des prix approprié, par le Secrétariat de l'OCDE.

(2) A partir de juillet 1993, tous les points de vente d'au moins 5 employés sont inclus. Auparavant, seuls les points de vente employant 20 personnes ou plus étaient couverts par l'enquête.

(3) Nouvelle série comprenant les ventes effectuées par les entreprises non inscrites au registre du commerce et par les personnes privées sur les marchés informels.

UNEMPLOYMENT RATES
TAUX DE CHÔMAGE

(Per cent / Pourcentage)

	1993	1994	1995	1995 Sep	Oct	Nov	Dec	1996 Jan	Feb	Mar	
Central and Eastern Europe											**Europe Centrale et Orientale**
Bulgaria	16.3										Bulgarie
Estonia	2.1	1.8	1.8								Estonie
Hungary[1]	12.8	10.4	10.6	10.3	10.0	10.2	10.4	11.3	11.6	11.6	Hongrie[1]
Latvia	4.7	6.3	6.3	6.0	6.0	6.3	6.6	6.6	6.8	7.0	Lettonie
Lithuania[2]	4.2	3.6	6.1	6.3	6.7	7.1	7.3	7.9	8.2		Lituanie[2]
Poland	14.9	16.4	15.2	15.0	14.7	14.7	14.9	15.4	15.4	15.4	Pologne
Republic of Slovenia	14.4	14.5	14.0	14.2	14.4	14.4	14.5	14.4	14.2		République de Slovénie
Romania	9.2	11.0	9.9	9.2	9.0	8.8	8.9	9.3	9.4	9.2	Roumanie
Slovak Republic	12.9	14.6	13.8	13.2	12.8	12.8	13.1	13.7	13.7		République slovaque
New Independent States											**Nouveaux États Indépendants**
Armenia	5.2	6.4	6.6	7.4	7.7	8.0	8.1	8.3	8.6		Arménie
Azerbaijan	0.5	0.8	1.0	1.1	1.1	1.1	1.1	1.1	1.1		Azerbaïdjan
Belarus	1.1	1.9	2.4	2.5	2.6	2.6	2.7	3.0	3.3		Bélarus
Kazakstan	0.5	0.8	1.5	1.6	1.7	1.9	2.1	2.4	2.9		Kazakstan
Kyrgyz Republic	0.2	0.4	1.9	2.4	2.6	2.7	2.9	3.1	3.8		République kirghize
Republic of Moldova	0.6	0.9	1.4	1.4	1.5	1.5	1.4	1.5	1.6		République de Moldova
Russian Federation	1.0	1.7	2.8	2.9	2.9	3.0	3.2	3.3	3.5		Fédération de Russie
Tajikistan	0.7	1.5	1.8	1.9	1.6	1.8	2.0	2.1	2.2		Tadjikistan
Uzbekistan	0.2	0.2	0.3	0.3	0.3	0.3	0.3	0.3	0.4		Ouzbékistan

Note: Registered unemployed persons as a percentage of the labour force.

Note : Nombre de chômeurs inscrits en pourcentage de la population active.

(1) From May 1995, excluding jobseekers temporarily unable to work.
(2) Includes unemployed who have left a job of their own accord.

(1) A partir de mai 1995, sont exclues les personnes à la recherche d'un emploi mais temporairement non disponibles.
(2) Y compris les chômeurs ayant volontairement quitté leur emploi.

UNEMPLOYMENT RATES * – JOB VACANCIES
TAUX DE CHÔMAGE * – OFFRES D'EMPLOI

Hungary (1)

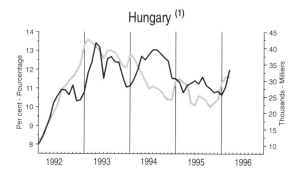

Latvia

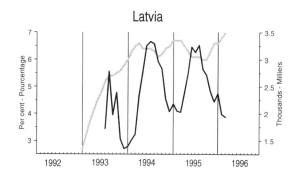

Lithuania (2)

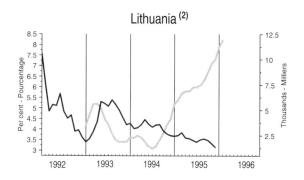

Poland

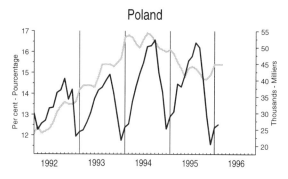

Republic of Slovenia

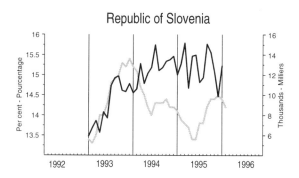

Romania

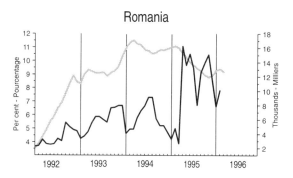

Slovak Republic

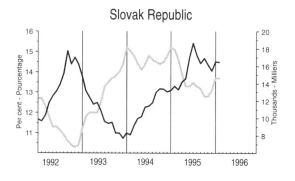

Unemployment rate
Left scale

Job vacancies
Right scale

* Registered unemployed persons as a percentage of the labour force.

(1) From May 1995, excluding job seekers temporarily unable to work.

(2) Includes unemployed who have left a job of their own accord.

* Nombre de chômeurs inscrits en pourcentage de la population active.

(1) À partir de mai 1995, sont exclues les personnes à la recherche d'un emploi mais temporairement non disponibles.

(2) Y compris les chômeurs ayant volontairement quitté leur emploi.

CONSUMER PRICE INDICES
INDICES DES PRIX A LA CONSOMMATION

(Rates of change / Taux de variation)

	1-year rate of change Variation sur 1 an			12-month rate of change Variation sur 12 mois							
				1995				1996			
	1993	1994	1995	Sep	Oct	Nov	Dec	Jan	Feb	Mar	
Central and Eastern Europe											**Europe Centrale et Orientale**
Bulgaria	72.8	96.0	62.1	46.0	40.0	36.0	32.9	30.9			Bulgarie
Estonia	89.8	47.7	29.0	25.9	28.4	28.2	28.8	28.8	29.4	28.3	Estonie
Hungary	22.5	18.9	28.3	28.8	29.0	28.6	28.3	28.9	28.3	25.7	Hongrie
Latvia	109.1	35.7	25.1	23.9	24.2	24.3	23.5	23.6	21.9	20.5	Lettonie
Lithuania	410.2	72.2	39.7	35.7	36.3	37.2	35.7	32.4	30.4		Lituanie
Poland	36.9	33.2	28.1	24.4	23.0	22.4	22.0	21.1	20.4		Pologne
Republic of Slovenia	32.9	21.0	13.5	10.7	9.4	8.9	9.0	8.3	8.3		République de Slovénie
Romania	256.1	136.8	32.3	25.3	24.3	25.8	27.8	26.7	27.3		Roumanie
Slovak Republic	23.2	13.5	9.9	8.8	7.9	7.5	7.2	6.4	6.2		République slovaque
New Independent States											**Nouveaux États Indépendants**
Armenia[1]	1822.9	4962.3	176.0	135.5	120.3	97.3	32.0	31.6	35.1		Arménie[1]
Azerbaijan[1]	980.9		411.8	424.4	271.0	128.1	48.7	14.9	18.8		Azerbaïdjan[1]
Belarus[1]	1576.8	2221.0	709.3	616.4	489.3	334.9	244.2	161.1	103.1		Bélarus[1]
Kazakstan[1]	1410.3	1877.4	176.2	114.7	86.1	70.1	60.0	52.9	46.9		Kazakstan[1]
Kyrgyz Republic[2]	1291.0	278.1	51.6	38.0	32.9	32.1	31.9	27.6	24.0		République kirghize[2]
Republic of Moldova[3]	1183.7	486.8	30.0	22.6	20.9	23.8	23.8	24.5	24.8		République de Moldova[3]
Russian Federation	874.3	307.5	197.4	214.4	186.2	161.0	131.4	104.5	89.4		Fédération de Russie
Tajikistan[1]	1484.5		443.1	770.1	1180.6	1451.6	2382.2				Tadjikistan[1]
Turkmenistan[1]	1774.7	2714.0									Turkménistan[1]
Ukraine[4]	4518.8		376.7	530.3	460.9	245.7	181.7	154.2	131.2		Ukraine[4]
Uzbekistan[2]	938.1	1550.0		206.3							Ouzbékistan[2]

(1) Laspeyres index from January 1993. New methodology introduced from 1994. Rates of change are calculated from the new series from 1994.
(2) Paasche index for the entire period. New methodology introduced from 1994. Rates of change are calculated from the new series from 1994.
(3) Laspeyres index from January 1993. New methodology introduced from 1993. Rates of change are calculated from the new series from 1993.
(4) Paasche index up to December 1993; modified Laspeyres index from January 1994. New indices are consumer price indices whereas the preceding ones were retail price indices.

(1) Indice de Laspeyres à partir de janvier 1993. Nouvelle méthodologie introduite depuis janvier 1994. Les taux de variation sont calculés à partir des nouvelles séries depuis 1994.
(2) Indice de Paasche pour toute la période. Nouvelle méthodologie introduite depuis janvier 1994. Les taux de variation sont calculés à partir des nouvelles séries depuis 1994.
(3) Indice de Laspeyres à partir de janvier 1993. Nouvelle méthodologie introduite depuis 1993. Les taux de variation sont calculés à partir des nouvelles séries depuis 1993.
(4) Indice de Paasche jusqu'en décembre 1993 ; indice de Laspeyres modifié à partir de janvier 1994. Les nouveaux indices sont des indices de prix à la consommation alors que les précédents étaient des indices de prix de détail.

CONSUMER PRICES – PRIX A LA CONSOMMATION

Index 1994 = 100 – Indice 1994 = 100

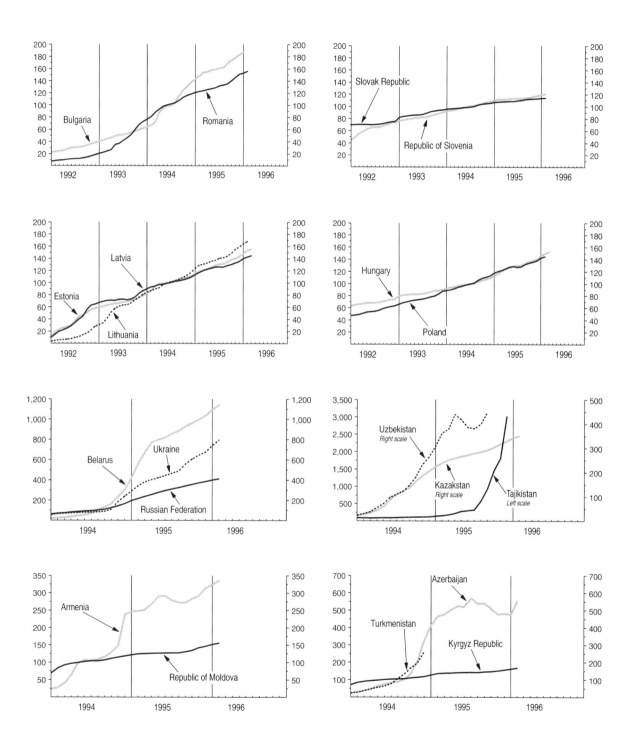

EXPORT/IMPORT RATIOS
TAUX DE COUVERTURE (EXPORTATIONS/IMPORTATIONS)

(Per cent / Pourcentage)

	1993	1994	1995	1994 Q3	1994 Q4	1995 Q1	1995 Q2	1995 Q3	1995 Q4	1996 Q1	
Central and Eastern Europe											**Europe Centrale et Orientale**
Bulgaria	74	96	101	89	79	97	99	112	97		Bulgarie
Estonia	90	79	73	81	76	76	72	76	68		Estonie
Hungary	71	73	84	75	75	73	76	92	92		Hongrie
Latvia	106	80	75	87	77	77	79	74	69		Lettonie
Lithuania	89	86		119	84	78	102	94			Lituanie
Poland	76	80		83	75	84	77	81			Pologne
Republic of Slovenia	94	93	88	95	90	95	82	90	85		République de Slovénie
Romania	74	86	79	99	75	73	86	74	83		Roumanie
Slovak Republic	86	101	101	101	102	101	99	105	98		République slovaque
New Independent States[1]											**Nouveaux États Indépendants**[1]
Armenia	34	55	37	56	55	26	43	48	34		Arménie
Azerbaijan	146	82	82	97	104	63	90	105	73		Azerbaïdjan
Belarus	97	82	91	90	93	87	89	99	88		Bélarus
Kazakstan	304	92	133	104	133	106	163	157	109		Kazakstan
Kyrgyz Republic	100	107	80	177	94	85	76	127	57		République kirghize
Republic of Moldova	97	86	90	97	80	86	97	75	103		République de Moldova
Russian Federation	165	170	167	192	163	179	176	164	152		Fédération de Russie
Tajikistan	70	75	102	49	120						Tadjikistan
Turkmenistan	209	256	241	233	131	612	268	208	139		Turkménistan
Ukraine	128	96	102	94	111	88	103	110	104		Ukraine
Uzbekistan	75	123	107	69	161	96	132	118	96		Ouzbékistan

Note: The ratios have been calculated by dividing the current value of total exports by the current value of total imports.

Note : Les ratios sont obtenus en divisant la valeur totale courante des exportations par celle des importations.

(1) Until end 1993, trade with countries of the Former Soviet Union other than Estonia, Latvia and Lithuania, is excluded. For Ukraine, trade with all FSU countries is excluded. From 1994 data for all countries refer to total trade.

(1) Jusqu'à la fin de 1993, le commerce avec les pays de l'ex-Union soviétique, autres que l'Estonie, la Lettonie et la Lituanie, est exclu. Pour l'Ukraine, le commerce avec tous les pays de l'ex-Union soviétique est exclu Depuis 1994, les données pour tous les pays se réfèrent au commerce total.

NET TRADE – SOLDE COMMERCIAL

Million U.S. dollars – Millions de dollars É.-U.

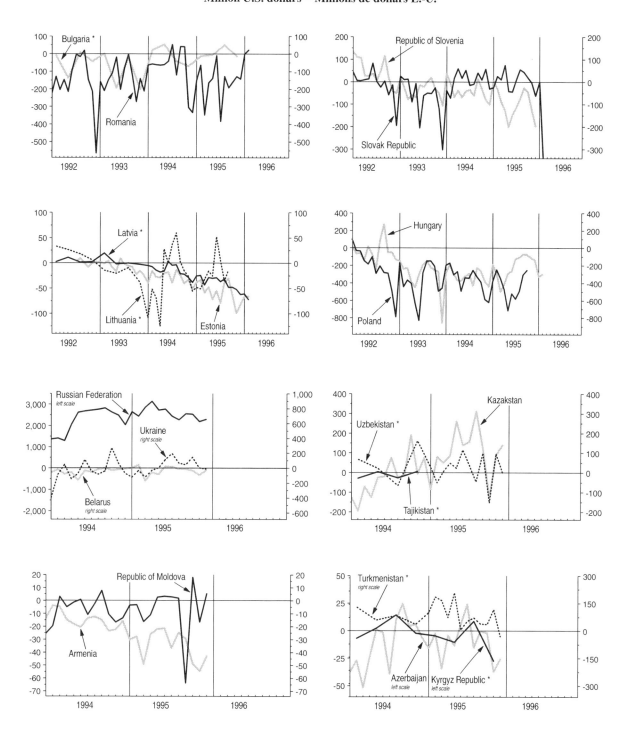

* Quarterly observations are shown in the midmonth of the quarter.

* Les observations trimestrielles sont affectées au deuxième mois du trimestre.

CENTRAL AND EASTERN EUROPE

INDICATORS BY COUNTRY

—

EUROPE CENTRALE ET ORIENTALE

INDICATEURS PAR PAYS

BULGARIA

		1993	1994	1995	1994 Q1	Q2	Q3	Q4	1995 Q1	Q2	Q3	Q4	1996 Q1
NATIONAL PRODUCT													
Gross domestic product	billion levs	298.9	543.5										
	billion levs PP	197.9	303.1										
INDUSTRIAL PRODUCTION													
Total	1990=100	60.8	63.2		58.8	57.2	57.6	62.3	59.1	59.9	60.5		
Total[1] *sa*	1990=100				58.0	58.7	60.2	59.1	58.3	61.3	63.0		
Manufacturing	1991=100	66.7			69.3	61.3	88.8		69.2	63.3	94.4		
Mining	1991=100	108.7			108.7	108.4	107.9		110.3	134.7	84.3		
Electricity and gas	1991=100	87.5			88.3	61.2	73.5		92.6	65.9	83.4		
Commodity output													
Coal	thousand tonnes	30183	29782	31901	8157	5279	7603	8743	7972	6909	7380	9640	
Crude steel	thousand tonnes	1941	2491	2725	486	659	661	685	665	717	703	640	581
Cement	thousand tonnes	2006	1910	2070	383	544	528	455	354	511	711	494	249
BUSINESS SURVEYS - MANUFACT.													
Business situation													
Tendency	balance				-22	-20	-11	-4	4	4	12	16	9
Order books / Demand													
Total: level	balance				-59	-53	-46	-39	-34	-34	-29	-22	-25
Export: level	balance				-57	-54	-48	-34	-33	-33	-27	-22	-29
Production													
Tendency	balance				-26	-18	-13	1	2	-2	4	6	-6
Future tendency	balance				20	15	13	21	36	32	32	35	33
Rate of capacity utilisation	%				57	59	58	60	60	60	61	63	63
Stocks													
Finished goods: level	balance				22	18	9	-1	-4	10	10	-4	-7
CONSTRUCTION													
Dwellings													
Completed	units	10931	7542	6024	829	1901	1546	3266	731	860	1090	3343	
DOMESTIC TRADE													
Retail sales: value	billion levs	124.73	250.12	410.71	33.32	47.58	61.43	107.79	74.24	80.71	99.82	155.93	108.16
LABOUR													
Employment													
Total	thousands	3076											
Total[2]	thousands	2294	2051	1902	2086	2069	2053	1995	1913	1908	1916	1886	
Industry[2]	thousands	894	815	760	831	821	812	796	768	762	761	749	
Unemployment													
Total registered	thousands	600.8	537.0	434.6	623.8	549.9	498.3	476.0	488.7	430.5	407.7	411.6	
Unemployment	% of labour force	16.3											
Job vacancies	units	8401	10997	15694	8431	10393	13392	11773	12965	15233	19333	15242	
WAGES													
Monthly earnings[2]													
Total	levs	3145	4823	7460	3822	4432	4903	5669	6182	7135	7717	8237	
Industry	levs	3404	5239		4205	4898	5402	6145	6956	8043	8777	9216	
PRICES													
Wholesale prices													
Total	SPPY=100	126.9	175.0	152.7	132.2	166.8	185.1	200.3	197.6	153.5	146.3	137.6	130.9
Consumer prices													
Total	PP=100												
Food	PP=100												
Beverages and tobacco	PP=100												
Clothing	PP=100												
Fuel and electricity	PP=100												
Services	PP=100												
DOMESTIC FINANCE													
Money supply (M1)	billion levs	48.3	75.1	107.9	50.1	55.0	63.7	75.1	70.9	76.1	89.8	107.9	
Quasi-money	billion levs	181.6	334.0	463.4	241.7	254.7	303.0	334.0	368.3	410.8	440.3	463.4	
Money supply (M2)[3]	billion levs	234.1	418.0	583.7	301.3	315.6	376.0	418.0	447.8	497.9	542.9	583.7	
Personal deposits	billion levs	132.9	243.9	378.7	164.2	180.2	206.6	243.9	278.5	327.4	349.9	378.7	

Footnotes appear at the end of the table.

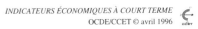

| 1995 | | | | | | | | | 1996 | | | | | |
Apr	May	Jun	Jul	Aug	Sep	Oct	Nov	Dec	Jan	Feb	Mar			
												PRODUIT NATIONAL		
												Produit intérieur brut		*milliards de levs*
														milliards de levs PP
												PRODUCTION INDUSTRIELLE		
60.1	61.2	58.2	53.4	63.8	62.9	63.5	63.3	55.6	49.3	57.7	59.3	Total		*1990=100*
60.5	60.6	61.3	62.6	62.4	60.1	62.1	60.4	50.9	60.4	54.6	53.0	Total[1]	cvs	*1990=100*
												Industries manufacturières		*1991=100*
												Industries extractives		*1991=100*
												Électricité et gaz		*1991=100*
												Quantités produites		
2379	1997	2533	2568	2419	2393	3131	3268	3241	3391	3200	3102	Charbon		*milliers de tonnes*
244	240	233	245	230	228	218	247	175	198	177	206	Acier brut		*milliers de tonnes*
155	171	185	224	259	228	225	167	102	87	53	109	Ciment		*milliers de tonnes*
												ENQUÊTES DE CONJONCTURE - IND. MANUF.		
												État des affaires		
3	5	5	7	14	15	14	20	15	11	9	8	Tendance		*solde*
												Carnets de commandes / Demande		
-31	-37	-35	-34	-28	-25	-25	-19	-23	-20	-27	-27	Total : niveau		*solde*
-32	-35	-33	-28	-29	-25	-26	-18	-22	-27	-31	-29	À l'exportation : niveau		*solde*
												Production		
-3	-1	-2	-6	7	12	17	5	-5	1	-12	-6	Tendance		*solde*
41	33	21	25	35	37	32	39	35	28	36	36	Perspectives		*solde*
												Taux d'utilisation des capacités		*%*
												Stocks		
10	13	7	13	11	7	-1	-7	-5	-7	-8	-5	Produits finis : niveau		*solde*
												CONSTRUCTION		
												Logements		
250	220	390	300	380	410	450	630	2263	200	250		Achevés		*unités*
												COMMERCE INTÉRIEUR		
26.34	26.48	27.90	30.03	32.38	37.41	42.80	50.76	62.38	35.86	35.83	36.48	Ventes de détail : valeur		*milliards de levs*
												MAIN-D'OEUVRE		
												Emploi		
												Total		*milliers*
1901	1907	1914	1918	1918	1913	1904	1888	1865				Total[2]		*milliers*
762	762	762	762	762	759	754	749	744				Industrie[2]		*milliers*
												Chômage		
456.7	426.4	408.5	415.4	407.0	400.7	398.5	412.5	423.8				Chômeurs inscrits : total		*milliers*
												Chômage		*% de main-d'oeuvre*
14500	14900	16300	17300	20500	20200	16800	14989	13938				Offres d'emploi		*unités*
												SALAIRES		
												Gains mensuels[2]		
6690	6898	7812	7336	7288	8527	7811	7960	8952				Total		*levs*
7534	7678	8917	8074	8120	10138	8589	8923	10144				Industrie		*levs*
												PRIX		
												Prix de gros		
162.0	151.0	147.0	148.0	143.9	147.2	137.1	137.9	138.9	136.4	132.0	126.7	Total		*PCAP=100*
												Prix à la consommation		
101.0	101.9	100.5	101.5	100.5	104.8	102.5	102.6	102.6	102.3	101.9	101.7	Total		*PP=100*
99.8	101.4	98.0	99.9	99.3	104.6	103.4	103.3	103.4	103.1	101.1	101.2	Alimentation		*PP=100*
103.9	101.1	103.0	111.9	102.9	102.2	100.7	102.8	101.3	101.0	100.2	101.3	Boissons et tabac		*PP=100*
103.5	104.2	103.2	101.2	101.9	104.6	104.8	103.7	103.0	100.8	101.0	101.6	Habillement		*PP=100*
99.8	101.3	103.4	101.2	100.0	110.0	100.1	100.0	101.0	100.3	100.3	104.3	Combustibles et électricité		*PP=100*
101.4	101.0	102.1	101.7	100.9	109.7	100.8	101.2	101.5	103.5	107.0	101.5	Services		*PP=100*
												FINANCES INTERNES		
74.9	79.2	76.1	82.9	86.7	89.8	92.1	91.3	107.9	93.4	95.8		Disponibilités monétaires (M1)		*milliards de levs*
373.8	390.9	410.8	420.5	430.4	440.3	443.5	448.3	463.4	470.3	474.2		Quasi-monnaie		*milliards de levs*
456.8	479.8	497.9	515.3	529.6	542.9	548.0	552.7	583.7	563.7	570.0		Disponibilités monétaires (M2)[3]		*milliards de levs*
284.1	..	327.4	336.6	342.8	349.9	354.9	362.1	378.7				Dépôts personnels		*milliards de levs*

Les notes se trouvent en fin de tableau.

BULGARIA *(continued)*

		1993	1994	1995	1994 Q1	Q2	Q3	Q4	1995 Q1	Q2	Q3	Q4	1996 Q1
FOREIGN FINANCE													
US$ exchange rate end period	*levs/US$*	32.71	66.02	70.70	64.94	53.66	61.20	66.02	66.16	66.06	68.02	70.70	
DM exchange rate end period	*levs/DM*	18.99	42.45	49.35	38.71	33.98	39.54	42.45	47.14	47.43	47.87	49.35	
ECU exchange rate end period	*levs/ECU*	36.66	80.53	90.47	74.53	64.95	75.49	80.53	86.33	87.32	88.55	90.47	
Official reserves including gold	*billion levs*	77.6	208.6	254.8	149.1	164.3	180.3	208.6	221.1	251.2	265.4	254.8	
Gross foreign debt													
Total	*billion levs*	417.5	340.2	265.2	850.2	744.7	872.9	340.2	361.2	332.6	288.4	265.2	
FOREIGN TRADE													
Imports	*billion levs*	139.8	234.1	339.4	50.8	48.6	68.2	66.4	79.4	87.6	85.4	87.0	
Exports	*billion levs*	102.9	225.5	343.3	55.1	57.3	60.4	52.6	76.9	86.6	95.6	84.2	
Net trade	*billion levs*	-37.0	-8.7	3.9	4.3	8.7	-7.7	-13.9	-2.5	-1.0	10.2	-2.8	

For notes concerning these series, refer to *Short-term Economic Indicators: Transition Economies, Sources and Definitions* (April 1996) and the *Methodological Notes* at the end of this publication.

(1) This series has been estimated by the OECD Secretariat.

(2) Public and co-operative sectors only.

(3) Prior to 1996, M2 refers to M1 plus quasi-money as well as import and restricted deposits. From January 1996 it includes M1 plus quasi-money only.

1995									1996				
Apr	May	Jun	Jul	Aug	Sep	Oct	Nov	Dec	Jan	Feb	Mar		
												FINANCES EXTÉRIEURES	
65.24	65.95	66.06	66.22	67.98	68.02	68.64	69.81	70.70	73.88	76.07		Taux de change du $É-U fin période	*levs/$É-U*
47.43	47.54	47.43	47.80	45.97	47.87	48.72	48.61	49.35	49.71			Taux de change du DM fin pér.	*levs/DM*
86.86	87.46	87.32	88.80	86.12	88.55	89.32	89.76	90.47	91.04			Taux de change de l'ECU fin pér.	*levs/ECU*
224.6	229.3	251.2	251.6	261.8	265.4	263.6	262.4	254.8	240.9	239.1		Réserves officielles or inclus	*milliards de levs*
												Dette extérieure brute	
358.9	343.4	332.6	327.8	289.5	288.4	288.8	267.0	265.2	269.8	283.9		Total	*milliards de levs*
												COMMERCE EXTÉRIEUR	
												Importations	*milliards de levs*
												Exportations	*milliards de levs*
												Solde commercial	*milliards de levs*

Pour les notes sur ces séries, veuillez consulter *Indicateurs économiques à court terme : Economies en transition, Sources et définitions* (avril 1996) et les *Notes méthodologiques* à la fin de cette publication.

(1) Cette série a été estimée par le Secrétariat de l'OCDE.

(2) Secteur public et coopératif uniquement.

(3) Avant 1996, M2 couvre M1 plus quasi-monnaie ainsi que les dépôts à l'importation et les dépôts réglementés. Depuis janvier 1996, M2 couvre M1 plus quasi-monnaie uniquement.

ESTONIA

		1993	1994	1995	1994 Q1	1994 Q2	1994 Q3	1994 Q4	1995 Q1	1995 Q2	1995 Q3	1995 Q4	1996 Q1
NATIONAL PRODUCT													
Gross domestic product	billion kroons	22.1	30.1										
	billion kroons 1993	22.1	21.5										
INDUSTRIAL PRODUCTION													
Total[1]	1993=100	100.0	97.8	102.4	103.2	96.0	88.6	103.5	98.4	100.5	100.7	109.9	102.7
Commodity output													
Oil shale	thousand tonnes	14888	14800	13309	4276	3080	3459	3985	3830	2841	2781	3857	4095
Cement	thousand tonnes	355	402	418	86	115	122	79	59	129	128	102	53
Cotton fabrics	million m²	55.5	73.6	89.6	17.1	20.8	14.3	21.4	19.9	22.3	20.8	26.7	30.9
Mineral fertiliser	thousand tonnes	14.0	37.8	56.5	1.4	15.5	5.5	15.4	17.6	11.2	8.4	19.3	14.0
BUSINESS SURVEYS - MANUFACT.													
Order books / Demand													
Total: tendency	balance				24	19	5	21	2	3	11	17	-30
Export: tendency	balance				26	6	1	19	14	-3	1	9	-17
Production													
Tendency	balance				-1	20	-4	20	-3	13	7	3	-35
Future tendency	balance				51	12	21	10	63	16	10	5	52
Rate of capacity utilisation	%				54	59	59	56	55	57	59	59	53
Stocks													
Finished goods: level	balance				1	23	22	9	10	18	13	12	16
CONSTRUCTION													
Dwellings													
Started	units	1174	759	846	125	336	132	166	216	261	174	195	
Started: public sector	units	463	307	398	26	204	35	42	105	101	112	80	
Completed	units	2431	1953	1149	750	409	281	513	199	271	107	572	
Completed: public sector	units	1945	1436	677	624	287	195	330	85	151	30	411	
DOMESTIC TRADE													
Retail sales: value	million kroons	7700	8896	12332	1976	2209	2245	2466	2730	3024	3136	3442	
Retail sales: volume	1993=100	100.0	97.5	120.6	91.0	97.0	98.2	103.6	111.0	121.3	124.9	125.3	
LABOUR													
Employment													
Total	thousands	669.9	661.7	651.9	671.4	664.6	656.7	654.0	654.8	652.0	651.0	649.6	
Unemployment													
Beneficiaries	thousands	18.2	15.7	15.2	18.3	18.7	13.8	12.2	16.0	16.3	13.7	14.7	18.4
Unemployment	% of labour force	2.1	1.8	1.8	2.2	2.0	1.5	1.5	2.0	1.9	1.6	1.8	2.3
Time worked													
Working days per period	units	256	255	255	63	62	66	64	64	63	65	63	64
WAGES													
Monthly earnings													
Total	kroons	1066.0	1734.0		1410.0	1741.0	1723.3	2096.2	2086.0	2395.0	2363.0	2697.0	
Industry	kroons	1108.5	1898.0		1535.0	1875.0	1956.4	2274.8	2253.0	2582.0	2584.0	2860.0	
Manufacturing	kroons	1035.9	1784.0		1429.1	1790.0	1828.0	2108.9	2138.0	2450.0	2498.0	2665.0	
PRICES													
Producer prices													
Industry	1993=100	100.0	136.3	169.8	123.4	132.1	139.7	148.7	165.1	166.7	168.5	178.7	189.3
Manufacturing	1993=100	100.0	135.7	160.7	123.8	133.8	138.4	144.4	156.0	158.0	160.0	168.7	181.1
Mining	1993=100	100.0	142.4	189.9	121.6	124.3	153.8	166.3	183.4	185.1	186.9	204.1	206.0
Electricity and gas	1993=100	100.0	133.0	221.5	115.7	115.7	134.0	170.5	217.1	217.1	217.1	234.7	237.2
Consumer prices													
Total	1993=100	100.0	147.7	190.5	130.1	145.6	153.5	161.6	174.4	185.2	195.0	207.6	224.6
Food	1993=100	100.0	133.4	154.5	127.1	135.7	133.8	137.1	150.2	153.1	152.5	162.1	178.5
Alcohol and tobacco	1993=100	100.0	119.4	145.0	111.3	120.0	121.9	124.3	132.9	145.6	145.0	156.4	209.7
Clothing and footwear	1993=100	100.0	129.0	154.9	118.5	124.4	130.8	142.1	147.8	152.0	156.1	163.7	168.5
Housing and municipal services	1993=100	100.0	188.4	283.7	142.8	179.4	209.3	222.1	240.4	269.1	302.4	323.0	335.8
Fuel and electricity	1993=100	100.0	136.9	174.1	129.2	130.6	138.0	149.9	164.2	165.4	174.2	192.5	197.5
Total goods	1993=100	100.0	131.0	154.5	124.0	130.9	131.9	137.2	147.8	152.6	154.1	163.5	179.1
Services	1993=100	100.0	182.0	264.5	142.6	175.8	198.0	211.6	228.7	252.1	278.9	298.0	318.1
DOMESTIC FINANCE													
Money supply (M1)	million kroons	5227	6318	8201	5212	5378	5741	6318	6330	7066	7623	8201	8348
Quasi-money	million kroons	852	1609	2140	1053	1163	1275	1609	1784	1866	1927	2140	2525
Personal deposits	million kroons	1040	1401	2251	1172	1199	1268	1401	1477	1703	1929	2251	2607

Footnotes appear at the end of the table.

1995									1996					
Apr	May	Jun	Jul	Aug	Sep	Oct	Nov	Dec	Jan	Feb	Mar			
												PRODUIT NATIONAL		
												Produit intérieur brut	*mrd couronnes*	
													mrd couronnes 1993	
												PRODUCTION INDUSTRIELLE		
94.5	104.8	102.1	88.5	106.2	107.4	113.0	113.2	103.5	103.2	99.4	105.6	Total[1]	*1993=100*	
												Quantités produites		
975	988	878	872	914	995	1281	1369	1207	1395	1362	1338	Huile de schiste	*milliers de tonnes*	
43	42	44	39	45	44	36	35	31	21	15	17	Ciment	*milliers de tonnes*	
6.5	7.5	8.3	3.7	9.6	7.4	10.0	9.3	7.4	9.0	10.8	11.1	Tissus de coton	*millions de m²*	
4.2	4.0	3.0	0.1	3.8	4.5	4.5	7.1	7.7	6.3	3.6	4.1	Engrais minéral	*milliers de tonnes*	
												ENQUÊTES DE CONJONCTURE - IND. MANUF.		
												Carnets de commandes / Demande		
												Total : tendance	*solde*	
												À l'exportation : tendance	*solde*	
												Production		
												Tendance	*solde*	
												Perspectives	*solde*	
												Taux d'utilisation des capacités	*%*	
												Stocks		
												Produits finis : niveau	*solde*	
												CONSTRUCTION		
												Logements		
												Mis en chantier	*unités*	
												Mis en chantier : sect. public	*unités*	
												Achevés	*unités*	
												Achevés : secteur public	*unités*	
												COMMERCE INTÉRIEUR		
944	1021	1059	1021	1061	1054	1081	1106	1255	1148	1156		Ventes de détail : valeur	*mln couronnes*	
113.2	123.1	127.5	123.1	127.5	124.2	125.3	125.3	125.3	120.9	117.3		Ventes de détail : volume	*1993=100*	
												MAIN-D'OEUVRE		
												Emploi		
												Total	*milliers*	
												Chômage		
16.8	16.7	15.5	14.4	13.4	13.2	13.6	14.9	15.6	17.1	18.6	19.5	Allocataires	*milliers*	
												Chômage	*% de main-d'oeuvre*	
												Temps travaillé		
20	22	21	21	23	21	22	22	19	22	21	21	Jours ouvrables	*unités*	
												SALAIRES		
												Gains mensuels		
												Total	*couronnes*	
												Industrie	*couronnes*	
												Industries manufacturières	*couronnes*	
												PRIX		
												Prix à la production		
167.1	166.9	166.2	166.2	168.4	170.8	175.6	177.3	183.3	187.4	189.0	191.4	Industrie	*1993=100*	
158.5	158.1	157.3	157.3	159.9	162.7	164.8	166.9	174.3	179.3	181.2	182.9	Industries manufacturières	*1993=100*	
184.8	184.8	185.8	186.1	186.5	188.2	203.8	204.8	203.6	205.7	206.5	205.9	Industries extractives	*1993=100*	
217.1	217.1	217.1	217.1	217.1	217.1	234.7	234.7	234.7	234.7	234.7	242.1	Électricité et gaz	*1993=100*	
												Prix à la consommation		
180.6	185.4	189.6	192.9	194.1	198.1	204.3	207.1	211.3	218.6	225.9	229.4	Total	*1993=100*	
154.9	152.7	151.8	151.1	151.8	154.7	158.3	162.5	165.6	172.1	180.2	183.2	Alimentation	*1993=100*	
145.4	145.8	145.5	144.5	144.4	146.0	147.2	148.1	174.0	204.0	212.2	213.0	Alcool et tabac	*1993=100*	
151.0	152.0	152.9	154.1	155.7	158.5	162.0	164.0	165.1	167.2	168.2	170.2	Habillement et chaussures	*1993=100*	
248.9	273.6	284.9	300.0	301.1	306.0	322.3	323.2	323.6	326.5	338.7	342.3	Logement et services municipaux	*1993=100*	
165.1	165.4	165.7	172.5	174.3	175.7	192.4	192.5	192.5	195.1	195.5	202.0	Combustibles et électricité	*1993=100*	
153.0	152.4	152.3	152.4	153.6	156.4	159.3	162.9	168.2	174.6	180.2	182.6	Biens : total	*1993=100*	
237.3	253.0	266.1	276.0	277.1	283.7	296.5	297.8	299.8	309.0	319.7	325.5	Services	*1993=100*	
												FINANCES INTERNES		
6428	6800	7066	7294	7493	7623	7562	7719	8201	8232	8253	8348	Disponibilités monétaires (M1)	*mln couronnes*	
1635	1785	1866	1900	1955	1927	1967	2029	2140	2365	2486	2525	Quasi-monnaie	*mln couronnes*	
1540	1602	1703	1823	1872	1929	2011	2125	2251	2389	2505	2607	Dépôts personnels	*mln couronnes*	

Les notes se trouvent en fin de tableau.

ESTONIA *(continued)*

		1993	1994	1995	1994 Q1	Q2	Q3	Q4	1995 Q1	Q2	Q3	Q4	1996 Q1
FOREIGN FINANCE													
US$ exchange rate per. ave.	*kroon/US$*	13.22	12.98	11.46	13.79	13.30	12.49	12.35	11.84	11.17	11.46	11.39	11.75
ECU exchange rate per. ave.	*kroon/ECU*	15.47	15.35	14.82	15.49	15.42	15.26	15.24	14.95	14.73	14.90	14.70	14.76
Official reserves excluding gold[2]	*million kroons*	5237.2	4709.5	5894.7	4502.7	4438.4	4398.7	4709.5	4578.6	5099.3	5520.8	5894.7	5841.4
Gross foreign debt													
Total	*million kroons*	1540.6	2200.7	3078.3	1865.4	1916.9	2049.8	2200.7	2478.9	2668.9	2562.4	3078.3	
FOREIGN TRADE													
Imports													
Total	*million kroons*	11848	21243	29110	4721	5035	5079	6408	6348	7046	6957	8759	
from non-FSU countries	*million kroons*	8622	16075	22577	3399	3778	3953	4944	4858	5373	5424	6922	
from FSU countries	*million kroons*	3226	5168	6533	1322	1257	1126	1463	1490	1673	1533	1837	
Exports													
Total	*million kroons*	10642	16724	21177	3593	4145	4121	4865	4821	5108	5280	5969	
to non-FSU countries	*million kroons*	6105	9280	13286	1837	2354	2339	2751	2973	3383	3309	3622	
to FSU countries	*million kroons*	4537	7444	7891	1756	1791	1783	2114	1848	1725	1971	2347	
Net trade													
Total	*million kroons*	-1206	-4519	-7933	-1128	-890	-958	-1543	-1527	-1938	-1677	-2790	
with non-FSU countries	*million kroons*	-2517	-6794	-9291	-1562	-1424	-1615	-2193	-1885	-1990	-2115	-3301	
with FSU countries	*million kroons*	1311	2275	1358	434	534	657	651	358	52	438	510	

For notes concerning these series, refer to *Short-term Economic Indicators: Transition Economies, Sources and Definitions* (April 1996) and the *Methodological Notes* at the end of this publication.

(1) This series has been estimated by the OECD Secretariat.

(2) Prior to January 1994, includes gold.

1995									1996					
Apr	May	Jun	Jul	Aug	Sep	Oct	Nov	Dec	Jan	Feb	Mar			
												FINANCES EXTÉRIEURES		
11.03	11.27	11.21	11.11	11.56	11.70	11.32	11.33	11.52	11.69	11.73	11.82	Taux de change du $É-U moy. pér.	*couronne/$É-U*	
14.67	14.74	14.78	14.81	14.97	14.93	14.70	14.69	14.71	14.76	14.70	14.83	Taux de change de l'ECU moy. pér.	*couronne/ECU*	
4669.3	4876.0	5099.3	5335.1	5467.9	5520.8	5466.2	5463.9	5894.7	5874.8	5930.6	5841.4	Réserves officielles or exclu[2]	*mln couronnes*	
												Dette extérieure brute		
												Total	*mln couronnes*	
												COMMERCE EXTÉRIEUR		
												Importations		
2076	2512	2457	2187	2362	2409	2850	3153	2757	2506	2539		Total	*mln couronnes*	
1540	1943	1889	1667	1846	1911	2293	2477	2152	1962	1986		depuis autres que ex-URSS	*mln couronnes*	
536	569	568	520	515	498	556	676	605	544	553		depuis ex-URSS	*mln couronnes*	
												Exportations		
1553	1709	1845	1311	1912	2057	2125	2025	1819	1740	1762		Total	*mln couronnes*	
1014	1119	1250	774	1272	1263	1294	1241	1087	1101	1037		vers autres que ex-URSS	*mln couronnes*	
540	590	595	537	640	794	832	784	732	640	726		vers ex-URSS	*mln couronnes*	
												Solde commercial		
-523	-803	-612	-876	-450	-352	-724	-1128	-938	-766	-777		Total	*mln couronnes*	
-527	-825	-639	-893	-575	-648	-1000	-1236	-1065	-862	-950		avec autres que ex-URSS	*mln couronnes*	
4	21	27	17	125	296	275	108	127	96	173		avec ex-URSS	*mln couronnes*	

Pour les notes sur ces séries, veuillez consulter *Indicateurs économiques à court terme : Economies en transition, Sources et définitions* (avril 1996) et les *Notes méthodologiques* à la fin de cette publication.

(1) Cette série a été estimée par le Secrétariat de l'OCDE.

(2) Avant janvier 1994, or inclus.

HUNGARY

					1994				1995				1996
		1993	1994	1995	Q1	Q2	Q3	Q4	Q1	Q2	Q3	Q4	Q1
NATIONAL PRODUCT[1]													
Gross domestic product	billion forints	3548.3	4364.8	5500.0									
	billion forints 1991	2407.9	2478.8	2516.0									
INDUSTRIAL PRODUCTION													
Total	1990=100	103.9	113.9	119.5	109.8	109.3	110.4	125.9	120.1	117.0	114.8	126.1	
sa	1990=100				81.8	82.2	87.1	85.1	88.2	88.5	89.9	86.6	
Manufacturing	1990=100	103.3	112.8	119.0	105.3	108.4	111.5	126.2	116.7	117.0	115.8	126.5	
sa	1990=100				79.2	78.9	84.3	83.8	86.7	86.1	87.2	84.8	
Mining	1990=100	98.6	82.8	70.3	103.6	62.6	75.4	89.5	73.1	60.1	65.6	82.2	
sa	1990=100				68.1	53.0	62.2	57.9	48.4	51.9	54.2	52.9	
Electricity and gas	1990=100	81.8	83.1	84.7	98.2	75.4	63.7	95.2	100.4	75.5	67.3	95.5	
sa	1990=100				85.0	83.4	82.3	81.4	86.1	83.3	87.3	82.9	
Commodity output													
Coal	thousand tonnes	14122	13451	14469	3614	3221	2914	3702	3896	3424	3249	3900	
Crude steel	thousand tonnes	1753	1937	1865	489	503	460	485	444	465	461	495	
Cement	thousand tonnes	2534	2815	2873	402	906	884	623	449	933	911	580	
BUSINESS SURVEYS - MANUFACT.													
Business situation													
Tendency	balance				0	-1	4	22	8	12	33	40	15
Order books / Demand													
Total: level	balance				-14	2	7	3	6	7	13	17	-5
Export: level[2]	balance				-13	11	-2	12	18	14	14	16	-4
Production													
Tendency	balance				-3	24	16	37	9	28	24	22	-2
Future tendency	balance				37	34	23	33	38	30	31	22	50
Rate of capacity utilisation	%				72	75	75	76	76	76	78	79	77
Stocks													
Finished goods: level	balance				5	4	-5	-8	3	18	4	8	17
SALES													
Sales volume													
Total	1985=100	68.9	75.6	78.8	69.9	73.6	75.1	83.7	76.7	77.9	77.1	83.4	
sa	1985=100				73.8	74.4	78.0	76.4	79.5	78.6	79.6	77.8	
Export goods	1985=100	68.7	83.1	99.3	71.6	78.7	83.7	98.2	93.7	95.1	96.4	112.2	
sa	1985=100				85.3	79.2	89.5	82.8	108.0	96.3	100.0	97.8	
Domestic trade	1985=100	70.6	75.0	74.1	70.4	72.8	75.8	81.2	72.7	73.1	74.3	76.2	
sa	1985=100				73.4	74.0	77.6	75.3	75.1	74.6	75.3	72.0	
CONSTRUCTION													
Dwellings													
Started	thousands	88.4	90.1	98.1									
Completed[3]	thousands	20.9	20.9	24.7	..	6.8	4.9	9.3	3.1	4.5	5.6	11.6	
DOMESTIC TRADE													
Retail sales: value	billion forints	1745	2046	2396	406	470	537	633	494	556	620	726	
Retail sales: volume	1990=100	100.0	91.0	80.8	77.1	87.2	95.2	104.5	73.5	77.3	81.8	90.7	
sa	1990=100				87.7	88.2	92.5	92.8	85.5	79.0	78.7	80.5	
FOREIGN INVESTMENT[4]													
New joint ventures	units	4286	4431		1042	2073	3062	4431	901	1865	2775		
New joint venture capital	billion forints	65.8	42.2		9.4	23.5	34.2	42.2	6.0	12.1	20.9		
LABOUR													
Employment													
Total	thousands	2836	2899	2744	2931	2908	2893	2862	2805	2775	2725	2675	
Industry	thousands	882	880	833	899	886	876	859	857	845	828	803	
Manufacturing	thousands	756	761	721	778	766	758	742	742	732	717	693	
Unemployment													
Total registered[5]	thousands	671.8	568.4	507.7	627.5	571.1	551.1	523.9	545.5	500.3	498.3	486.5	558.9
Beneficiaries	thousands	404.9	228.9	182.8	309.4	231.0	187.3	188.1	205.1	172.6	165.6	187.9	209.0
Unemployment[5]	% of labour force	12.8	10.4	10.6	12.2	11.4	11.0	10.5	11.4	10.5	10.5	10.2	11.5
Job vacancies	thousands	34.38	35.49	28.68	30.75	37.36	39.15	34.68	28.85	29.34	29.59	26.94	29.05
Time worked													
Hours worked: manufacturing	monthly averages	144.3	146.6	147.1	148.3	148.4	144.7	145.1	152.3	148.1	143.4	144.5	
Working days per period	units	260	260	253	64	65	66	65	64	62	65	62	

Footnotes appear at the end of the table.

	1995									1996				
	Apr	May	Jun	Jul	Aug	Sep	Oct	Nov	Dec	Jan	Feb	Mar		
PRODUIT NATIONAL[1]														
Produit intérieur brut														mrd forints
														mrd forints 1991
PRODUCTION INDUSTRIELLE														
Total	104.9	118.8	127.3	107.2	116.8	120.3	121.8	131.9	124.6					1990=100
	84.1	95.6	85.8	90.0	91.0	88.7	90.4	87.0	82.4				cvs	1990=100
Industries manufacturières	99.5	121.2	130.3	106.5	116.4	124.5	125.1	131.0	123.5					1990=100
	80.8	94.2	83.3	87.5	86.5	89.1	85.1	80.0					cvs	1990=100
Industries extractives	57.0	61.1	62.2	70.7	63.9	62.3	71.6	105.7	69.3					1990=100
	51.8	51.5	52.4	51.4	58.1	52.9	58.2	55.4	45.2				cvs	1990=100
Électricité et gaz	89.4	66.4	70.8	64.4	70.3	67.3	76.9	96.1	113.4					1990=100
	80.9	86.8	82.3	89.3	84.5	88.3	79.5	86.0	83.3				cvs	1990=100
Quantités produites														
Charbon	1296	1076	1052	990	1106	1153	1204	1342	1354	1461	1488			milliers de tonnes
Acier brut	127	170	168	165	143	153	173	162	160					milliers de tonnes
Ciment	303	338	292	287	303	321	305	199	76	51	82			milliers de tonnes
ENQUÊTES DE CONJONCTURE - IND. MANUF.														
État des affaires														
Tendance														solde
Carnets de commandes / Demande														
Total : niveau														solde
À l'exportation : niveau[2]														solde
Production														
Tendance														solde
Perspectives														solde
Taux d'utilisation des capacités														%
Stocks														
Produits finis : niveau														solde
VENTES														
Ventes en volume														
Total	70.1	78.2	85.4	72.7	78.5	80.2	82.8	85.5	82.0					1985=100
	74.8	83.9	77.0	79.4	81.1	78.3	81.0	78.2	74.2				cvs	1985=100
Biens d'exportation	86.2	105.7	93.4	91.1	95.0	103.0	111.0	115.6	110.1					1985=100
	90.1	105.0	93.7	96.0	101.6	102.4	105.5	104.7	83.1				cvs	1985=100
Commerce intérieur	66.8	70.8	81.7	74.4	74.8	73.8	75.2	75.2	78.3					1985=100
	71.4	79.4	72.9	74.7	78.1	73.1	74.6	71.5	69.8				cvs	1985=100
CONSTRUCTION														
Logements														
Mis en chantier														milliers
Achevés[3]														milliers
COMMERCE INTÉRIEUR														
Ventes de détail : valeur	182	184	190	194	210	216	226	231	269	184	186			mrd forints
Ventes de détail : volume	77.6	76.7	77.5	77.9	83.7	83.9	86.0	86.7	99.4	65.4	65.3			1990=100
	80.9	78.7	77.5	76.0	79.8	80.5	80.9	80.3	80.4	81.1	80.9		cvs	1990=100
INVESTISSEMENTS ÉTRANGERS[4]														
Coentreprises nouvelles														unités
Capitaux de coentreprises nvlles														mrd forints
MAIN-D'OEUVRE														
Emploi														
Total														milliers
Industrie	849	845	841	837	833	818	810	805	793	781	786			milliers
Industries manufacturières	735	731	728	725	721	707	700	696	684	674	679			milliers
Chômage														
Chômeurs inscrits : total[5]	531.9	486.4	482.7	504.3	499.3	491.4	479.1	484.6	495.9	517.8	530.6	628.4		milliers
Allocataires	181.4	172.3	164.1	166.0	167.4	163.3	177.1	187.7	198.9	210.0	211.7	205.4		milliers
Chômage[5]	11.2	10.2	10.1	10.6	10.5	10.3	10.0	10.2	10.4	11.3	11.6	11.6		% de main-d'oeuvre
Offres d'emploi	28.70	29.25	30.07	29.09	31.15	28.54	27.62	26.43	26.76	25.69	28.12	33.33		milliers
Temps travaillé														
Heures effectuées: ind. manufac.														moy. mensuelles
Jours ouvrables	19	22	21	21	23	21	21	22	19					unités

Les notes se trouvent en fin de tableau.

		1993	1994	1995	1994 Q1	Q2	Q3	Q4	1995 Q1	Q2	Q3	Q4	1996 Q1
WAGES													
Monthly earnings													
Total	forints	27178	33289	38900	28580	32142	33018	39543	34066	37399	38739	45564	
Manufacturing	forints	21751	26162	31454	22649	25644	26526	29989	27522	30695	31732	36138	
PRICES													
Producer prices													
Industry	1990=100	168.5	189.1	243.1	180.1	184.9	191.5	199.7	220.7	239.3	249.9	262.4	
Consumer prices													
Total	1990=100	203.3	241.7	310.1	227.2	235.3	244.9	259.5	282.9	306.7	317.1	333.8	360.8
Food	1990=100	188.3	232.6	304.2	213.3	223.8	234.7	258.4	286.8	306.1	303.8	320.2	342.0
Beverages and tobacco	1990=100	177.7	207.0	248.4	194.2	198.6	210.8	224.6	235.4	242.1	251.1	265.0	297.0
Clothing	1990=100	189.5	220.0	264.6	205.4	217.2	220.5	236.7	243.3	258.5	266.3	290.3	304.1
Durable goods	1990=100	167.4	187.1	232.4	179.3	183.0	189.2	197.1	206.2	227.6	242.7	252.9	265.8
Other goods	1990=100	221.9	264.2	336.8	249.7	256.6	268.8	281.8	303.3	327.4	347.9	368.5	396.3
Fuel and electricity	1990=100	311.6	347.6	521.8	342.0	342.4	347.1	358.9	429.0	530.3	546.6	581.4	616.8
Services	1990=100	222.0	266.9	336.7	253.0	263.1	272.5	279.0	306.6	331.6	348.3	360.3	399.3
DOMESTIC FINANCE													
Money supply (M2)	billion forints	1759	1993	2607	1731	1816	1872	1993	1981	2043	2175	2607	
Personal deposits	billion forints	695.5	866.5	1091.0	704.3	732.1	777.5	866.5	899.0	931.0	969.3	1091.0	
INTEREST RATES													
Discount rate	% p.a. end period	22.0	25.0	28.0	22.0	25.0	25.0	25.0	28.0	28.0	28.0	28.0	
Call money	% p.a. period ave.	15.4	25.6		20.8	24.1	27.9	29.6	33.1	33.9			
Short-term rate	% p.a. period ave.	17.2	26.9	32.0	23.5	24.5	29.5	30.3	32.4	33.4	32.4	30.1	
FOREIGN FINANCE													
US$ exchange rate end period	forint/US$	100.70	110.69	139.47	102.40	102.09	107.88	110.69	119.72	125.84	132.50	139.47	146.72
US$ exchange rate per. ave.	forint/US$	91.91	105.12	125.72	102.69	102.86	105.55	109.40	113.24	123.21	130.21	136.21	144.12
DM exchange rate per. ave.	forint/DM	55.57	64.99	87.88	59.57	61.92	67.59	70.87	76.71	88.21	90.95	95.64	98.15
ECU exchange rate per. ave.	forint/ECU	107.4	124.7	162.7	115.4	119.4	129.0	135.1	143.2	162.4	169.4	175.7	181.1
Official reserves excluding gold	million US$	6691	6727	11968	6488	5983	6793	6727	6743	7523	8782	11968	
Gross foreign debt													
Total	million US$	24566	28526	31655	25543	26561	27559	28526	31684	33034	32490	31655	
FOREIGN TRADE													
Imports	billion forints	1162.5	1537.0	1936.4	311.4	360.6	396.5	468.6	420.1	497.2	475.3	543.8	
Exports	billion forints	819.9	1128.7	1622.0	232.5	250.5	296.5	349.1	308.2	378.4	435.8	499.7	
Net trade	billion forints	-342.6	-408.3	-314.4	-78.8	-110.0	-100.0	-119.5	-112.0	-118.8	-39.5	-44.1	
Indices													
Import prices	1985=100	241.7	279.1	369.0	254.4	257.7	275.0	318.2	321.6	352.8	365.5	419.1	
Export prices	1985=100	226.3	262.7	357.9	241.5	241.9	263.0	308.9	305.7	326.8	360.3	415.8	
Imports: volume	1985=100	119.4	136.7	131.3	120.2	134.7	144.5	150.0	131.4	135.7	130.3	133.4	
Exports: volume	1985=100	86.7	101.1	109.6	86.7	99.5	106.2	113.1	93.8	111.2	113.9	121.8	
GROSS CAPITAL FORMATION													
Total	billion forints	638.3	842.7	1070.1	105.6	187.5	211.8	337.8	141.3	239.9	245.6	443.3	
Total: volume[4]	1989=100	80.0	93.0	93.3	50.5	84.6	93.0	144.0	55.7	82.1	89.5	145.9	
Total: volume[4] sa	1989=100				88.4	98.0	92.0	92.9	96.6	95.1	90.1	93.9	
Machinery and equipment	billion forints	257.6	334.5	439.9	44.1	78.0	83.2	129.2	64.2	109.3	102.8	163.6	
Construction	billion forints	323.6	432.4	541.1	52.1	92.5	111.4	176.4	65.2	109.6	124.9	241.4	
Other goods and services	billion forints	53.2	52.9		6.2	11.5	12.2	23.1	8.3	14.6	12.5		

For notes concerning these series, refer to *Short-term Economic Indicators: Transition Economies, Sources and Definitions* (April 1996) and the *Methodological Notes* at the end of this publication.

(1) Preliminary estimate for 1995.

(2) Export orders refer to those made by western countries only.

(3) Dwellings completed in the first quarter 1994 are included in second quarter 1994 figures.

(4) Cumulative from the beginning of the year.

(5) From May 1995, excluding jobseekers temporarily unable to work. In May 1995, persons in this category numbered 27 288.

	1995 Apr	May	Jun	Jul	Aug	Sep	Oct	Nov	Dec	1996 Jan	Feb	Mar	
SALAIRES Gains mensuels													
Total	36554	39957	41246	40706	40894	39850	41295	47033	52209	41912	42462		*forints*
Industries manufacturières													*forints*
PRIX Prix à la production													
Industrie	235.1	240.0	242.9	246.1	249.3	254.3	259.4	263.0	264.7	270.7	275.6		*1990=100*
Prix à la consommation													
Total	300.6	308.0	311.6	314.3	315.4	321.6	329.0	334.2	338.2	353.1	361.3	368.1	*1990=100*
Alimentation	301.4	309.0	307.9	304.7	299.7	307.1	315.9	320.3	324.5	336.1	342.0	347.9	*1990=100*
Boissons et tabac	239.1	242.4	244.7	247.7	250.0	255.5	262.1	265.3	267.7	292.6	297.9	300.5	*1990=100*
Habillement	255.2	260.0	260.3	263.9	263.4	271.5	283.5	291.2	296.2	299.5	302.1	310.7	*1990=100*
Biens durables	220.4	227.7	234.8	238.8	242.6	246.8	250.4	252.3	255.9	262.6	266.0	268.9	*1990=100*
Autres biens	319.7	328.1	334.5	342.1	347.0	354.6	362.9	368.8	373.9	390.4	396.8	401.7	*1990=100*
Combustibles et électricité	513.1	535.5	542.4	543.4	545.0	551.3	564.5	586.5	593.2	603.9	618.2	628.2	*1990=100*
Services	325.3	331.5	338.0	343.6	348.4	352.9	357.0	360.6	363.4	384.1	401.1	412.8	*1990=100*
FINANCES INTERNES													
Disponibilités monétaires (M2)	1978	2014	2043	2085	2125	2175	2179	2238	2607	2358			*mrd forints*
Dépôts personnels	901.0	911.0	931.0	940.9	954.7	969.3	959.2	1000.8	1091.0	1085.2			*mrd forints*
TAUX D'INTÉRÊT													
Taux d'escompte	28.0	28.0	28.0	28.0	28.0	28.0	28.0	28.0	28.0	28.0	27.0		*% p.a. fin période*
Taux de l'argent au jour le jour	34.0	34.0	33.6	31.8	29.2								*% p.a. moy. période*
Taux à court terme	33.4	33.9	32.8	32.6	32.7	31.8	30.3	29.8	30.1	29.1			*% p.a. moy. période*
FINANCES EXTÉRIEURES													
Taux de change du $É-U fin période	121.10	123.52	125.84	126.22	132.77	132.50	134.61	137.58	139.47	145.31	144.62	146.72	*forint/$É-U*
Taux de change du $É-U moy. pér.	120.24	123.87	125.53	126.38	130.56	133.68	133.88	135.75	138.99	141.92	144.40	146.04	*forint/$É-U*
Taux de change du DM moy. pér.	87.10	87.92	89.60	90.98	90.41	91.45	94.58	95.86	96.49	97.12	98.49	98.83	*forint/DM*
Taux de change de l'ECU moy. pér.	159.8	162.0	165.5	168.5	169.2	170.7	173.8	176.0	177.4	179.2	181.0	183.2	*forint/ECU*
Réserves officielles or exclu	6433	6654	7523	8242	8040	8782	9378	8928	11968				*millions de $É-U*
Dette extérieure brute													
Total	31784	32269	33034	33219	31661	32490	32666	31648	31655				*millions de $É-U*
COMMERCE EXTÉRIEUR													
Importations	161.3	168.8	167.0	155.1	151.4	168.7	177.0	186.6	180.1	162.6	178.0		*mrd forints*
Exportations	111.6	132.9	133.9	139.3	137.5	159.0	167.0	171.6	161.1	116.6	134.5		*mrd forints*
Solde commercial	-49.7	-35.9	-33.1	-15.8	-13.9	-9.8	-10.0	-15.0	-19.1	-46.1	-43.5		*mrd forints*
Indices													
Prix à l'importation													*1985=100*
Prix à l'exportation													*1985=100*
Importations : volume													*1985=100*
Exportations : volume													*1985=100*
FORMATION BRUTE DE CAPITAL													
Total													*mrd forints*
Total: volume[4]													*1989=100*
Total: volume[4]												*cvs*	*1989=100*
Machines et équipements													*mrd forints*
Construction													*mrd forints*
Autres biens et services													*mrd forints*

Pour les notes sur ces séries, veuillez consulter *Indicateurs économiques à court terme : Economies en transition, Sources et définitions* (avril 1996) et les *Notes méthodologiques* à la fin de cette publication.

(1) Estimation préliminaire pour 1995.

(2) Les carnets de commandes à l'exportation se réfèrent aux commandes des pays de l'ouest.

(3) Les données du deuxième trimestre 1994 comprennent les logements achevés lors du premier trimestre 1994.

(4) Cumul depuis le début de l'année.

(5) A partir de mai 1995, sont exclues les personnes à la recherche d'un emploi mais temporairement non disponibles. En mai 1995, cette catégorie comprenait 27 288 personnes.

LATVIA

		1993	1994	1995	1994 Q1	Q2	Q3	Q4	1995 Q1	Q2	Q3	Q4	1996 Q1
NATIONAL PRODUCT													
Gross domestic product	million lats	1467	2043	2361									
	million lats 1993	1467	1477										
INDUSTRIAL PRODUCTION													
Total	1990=100	39.5	35.8	33.4	35.4	34.8	34.4	38.6	32.5	31.3	33.2	36.8	31.9
Total[1] *sa*	1990=100				37.3	35.8	35.5	34.7	34.4	32.3	34.2	33.0	33.9
Commodity output													
Cement	thousand tonnes	114	244	205	17	80	86	61	44	65	61	35	12
Textiles	thousand m²	15386	11217	6617	4020	2157	2487	2553	1591	1843	1573	1610	2050
Electricity	mln kilowatt hours	3923	4438	3941	1105	2126	403	804	1541	1397	294	709	730
Telephone sets	thousands	310	118	62	57	16	25	20	26	9	11	17	19
BUSINESS SURVEYS - MANUFACT.													
Business situation													
Tendency	balance				-16	-37	-22	-25	-12	-23	-20	-17	-11
Order books / Demand													
Total: level	balance				-53	-65	-55	-64	-66	-54	-64	-56	-63
Export: level	balance				-38	-43	-44	-44	-53	-35	-48	-46	-45
Production													
Tendency	balance				8	-4	2	2	4	0	2	-1	5
Future tendency	balance				15	6	20	18	22	17	15	5	15
Rate of capacity utilisation	%				43	48	50	51	49	51	50	51	52
Stocks													
Finished goods: level	balance				20	28	27	25	12	14	5	-8	2
CONSTRUCTION													
Dwellings													
Completed: total	units	3754	3369	1568	881	655	484	1349	412	263	201	692	
Completed: public sector	units	1624	1059		273	311	196	279	57				
DOMESTIC TRADE													
Retail sales: value	million lats	425.3	643.6	725.3	141.0	154.0	165.6	183.0	170.1	171.6	188.4	195.2	189.0
Retail sales: volume	1993=100	100.0	97.6	90.0	89.5	95.2	99.0	106.6	89.5	85.7	91.4	93.3	85.7
LABOUR													
Employment													
Total	thousands	1265	1205	1189	1215	1209	1201	1196	1193	1191	1189	1183	1175
Industry	thousands	320	265	250	280	279	252	251	251	250	250	248	247
Unemployment													
Total registered	number	62460	83790	81054	84103	86119	83269	81667	85983	80683	77565	79983	86099
Beneficiaries	number	44261	37542	37105	38853	34452	34631	42232	40452	34778	37626	35561	35457
Non-beneficiaries	number	18200	46248	43949	45249	51667	48638	39435	45531	45905	39939	44422	50642
Unemployment	% of labour force	4.7	6.3	6.3	6.3	6.5	6.3	6.4	6.7	6.3	6.1	6.3	6.8
Job vacancies[2]	number	1352	2466	2597	1507	2784	3194	2378	2082	2785	3073	2449	2098
WAGES													
Monthly earnings													
Total	lats	47.2	72.4	89.5	61.4	71.8	75.8	80.5	82.3	89.5	90.3	95.3	
Industry	lats	48.9	79.8	102.9	60.4	78.3	82.6	94.8	94.2	101.2	105.1	111.5	107.1
PRICES													
Producer prices													
Manufacturing	DEC 90=100	19126	22902	26032	22133	22777	23092	23604	25067	25514	26120	27428	28586
Consumer prices													
Total	JUN 92=100	256	348	435	322	341	355	373	406	432	441	462	495
Food	JUN 92=100	253	330	368	334	337	324	325	362	371	363	377	407
Catering	JUN 92=100	358	632	827	534	602	677	717	774	801	850	885	913
Alcohol and tobacco	JUN 92=100	195	228	297	210	209	225	267	281	290	298	317	330
Clothing	JUN 92=100	172	235	308	211	226	239	262	279	298	316	340	357
Fuel and electricity	JUN 92=100	378	379	486	354	364	390	408	411	477	508	546	585
Housing	JUN 92=100	264	504	786	331	521	554	611	676	769	850	850	988
Total goods	JUN 92=100	219	292	352	279	289	294	306	337	351	352	369	392
Services	JUN 92=100	615	868	1189	715	826	934	996	1050	1169	1243	1293	1413
DOMESTIC FINANCE													
Money supply (M2)	million lats	336.9	491.2	357.9	351.9	401.7	430.9	491.2	495.6	446.1	444.9	357.9	342.7
INTEREST RATES													
Official discount rate	% p.a. end period	27.0	25.0	24.0	27.0	27.0	27.0	25.0	25.0	26.5	26.5	24.0	

Footnotes appear at the end of the table.

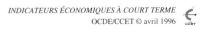

1995 Apr	May	Jun	Jul	Aug	Sep	Oct	Nov	Dec	1996 Jan	Feb	Mar			
												PRODUIT NATIONAL		
												Produit intérieur brut		millions de lats
														millions de lats 1993
												PRODUCTION INDUSTRIELLE		
31.3	30.8	31.7	33.7	32.5	33.4	34.3	37.4	38.8	31.1	32.1	32.4	Total		1990=100
33.0	33.0	31.0	35.0	34.3	33.3	33.0	33.5	32.6	35.7	34.6	31.4	Total[1]	cvs	1990=100
												Quantités produites		
18	26	21	25	18	18	16	14	5	5	2	5	Ciment		milliers de tonnes
751	539	553	276	647	650	770	440	400	560	640	850	Textiles		milliers de m^2
637	507	253	127	85	82	199	255	255	254	232	244	Électricité		mln kw-heures
5	3	1	5	2	4	3	7	7	4	6	9	Appareils téléphoniques		milliers
												ENQUÊTES DE CONJONCTURE - IND. MANUF.		
												État des affaires		
												Tendance		solde
												Carnets de commandes / Demande		
												Total : niveau		solde
												Exportations : niveau		solde
												Production		
												Tendance		solde
												Perspectives		solde
												Taux d'utilisation des capacités		%
												Stocks		
												Produits finis : niveau		solde
												CONSTRUCTION		
												Logements		
												Achevés : total		unités
												Achevés : secteur public		unités
												COMMERCE INTÉRIEUR		
56.5	57.3	57.8	62.4	62.6	63.4	63.1	62.7	69.4	58.9	63.4	66.7	Ventes de détail : valeur		millions de lats
85.7	85.7	85.7	85.7	91.4	97.1	91.4	91.4	97.1	80.0	85.7	91.4	Ventes de détail : volume		1993=100
												MAIN-D'OEUVRE		
												Emploi		
												Total		milliers
												Industrie		milliers
												Chômage		
83542	80634	77874	78499	77637	76559	76790	79929	83231	83760	86342	88195	Chômeurs inscrits : total		nombre
35578	34328	34429	37606	38433	36838	36048	35878	34758	35217	35206	35947	Allocataires		nombre
47964	46306	43445	40893	39204	39721	40742	44051	48473	48543	51136	52248	Non allocataires		nombre
6.5	6.3	6.1	6.1	6.1	6.0	6.0	6.3	6.6	6.6	6.8	7.0	Chômage		% de main-d'oeuvre
2379	2742	3234	3132	3266	2821	2713	2414	2220	2370	1988	1936	Offres d'emploi[2]		nombre
												SALAIRES		
												Gains mensuels		
												Total		lats
												Industrie		lats
												PRIX		
												Prix à la production		
25609	25506	25427	25743	26036	26580	26825	27560	27899	28314	28586	28858	Industries manufacturières		DÉC 90=100
												Prix à la consommation		
425	432	438	440	438	446	453	462	470	487	496	503	Total		JUN 92=100
375	368	370	366	360	363	369	378	386	397	407	416	Alimentation		JUN 92=100
796	796	811	838	853	860	873	887	894	903	911	925	Restauration		JUN 92=100
288	290	291	291	298	303	308	317	327	328	331	331	Alcool et tabac		JUN 92=100
294	298	301	308	314	326	333	340	347	351	356	362	Habillement		JUN 92=100
444	481	506	506	508	511	516	558	565	584	585	587	Combustibles et électricité		JUN 92=100
716	787	804	846	848	856	878	828	844	975	992	997	Logement		JUN 92=100
350	350	354	352	349	355	361	369	376	385	392	400	Biens : total		JUN 92=100
1122	1177	1207	1231	1238	1260	1276	1294	1310	1396	1417	1426	Services		JUN 92=100
												FINANCES INTERNES		
496.3	453.4	446.1	441.1	440.8	444.9	441.2	444.3	357.9	342.4	345.1	342.7	Disponibilités monétaires (M2)		millions de lats
												TAUX D'INTÉRÊT		
25.0	25.0	26.5	26.5	26.5	26.5	26.5	25.0	24.0				Taux d'escompte officiel		% p.a. fin période

Les notes se trouvent en fin de tableau.

LATVIA *(continued)*

		1993	1994	1995	1994 Q1	Q2	Q3	Q4	1995 Q1	Q2	Q3	Q4	1996 Q1
FOREIGN FINANCE													
US$ exchange rate end period	*lats/US$*	0.60	0.55	0.54	0.57	0.55	0.55	0.55	0.52	0.51	0.53	0.54	0.55
US$ exchange rate per. ave.	*lats/US$*		0.56	0.53	0.58	0.56	0.55	0.55	0.54	0.51	0.53	0.54	0.55
DM exchange rate per. ave.	*lats/DM*		0.35	0.37	0.34	0.34	0.35	0.35	0.36	0.37	0.37	0.38	0.37
ECU exchange rate per. ave.	*lats/ECU*		0.66	0.68	0.65	0.66	0.67	0.67	0.68	0.67	0.69	0.69	0.69
Official reserves excluding gold	*million lats*	265.54	329.44	266.13	260.90	259.50	280.51	329.44	254.39	207.71	239.36	266.13	281.30
FOREIGN TRADE													
Imports[3]													
Total	*million lats*	639.3	694.6	923.4	157.3	173.3	162.6	201.4	210.2	208.4	228.5	276.2	
from countries other than NIS	*million lats*	217.2	365.2	662.8	63.6	90.8	92.7	118.1	145.0	156.3	166.4	195.0	
from NIS	*million lats*	422.1	329.4	260.6	93.7	82.5	69.8	83.3	65.2	52.1	62.1	81.2	
Exports													
Total	*million lats*	675.6	553.4	688.4	120.9	135.5	142.1	154.9	162.2	165.5	169.0	191.7	
to countries other than NIS	*million lats*	312.1	272.0	424.9	55.5	69.4	68.8	78.3	98.6	107.8	106.5	111.9	
to NIS	*million lats*	363.5	281.4	263.6	65.4	66.0	73.3	76.7	63.6	57.7	62.5	79.8	
Net trade													
Total	*million lats*	36.4	-141.2	-235.0	-36.4	-37.9	-20.4	-46.5	-48.0	-42.9	-59.5	-84.5	
with countries other than NIS	*million lats*	94.9	-93.2	-238.0	-8.1	-21.4	-23.9	-39.8	-46.4	-48.5	-59.9	-83.1	
with NIS	*million lats*	-58.6	-48.0	3.0	-28.3	-16.5	3.5	-6.7	-1.6	5.6	0.4	-1.4	

For notes concerning these series, refer to *Short-term Economic Indicators: Transition Economies, Sources and Definitions* (April 1996) and the *Methodological Notes* at the end of this publication.

(1) This series has been estimated by the OECD Secretariat.

(2) Annual 1993 figure refers to the end of the period; subsequent years and all quarterly data refer to period averages.

(3) From 1996, imports are valued CIF.

1995									1996					
Apr	May	Jun	Jul	Aug	Sep	Oct	Nov	Dec	Jan	Feb	Mar			
												FINANCES EXTÉRIEURES		
0.51	0.51	0.51	0.52	0.54	0.53	0.53	0.54	0.54	0.55	0.54	0.55	Taux de change du $É-U fin période		*lats/$É-U*
0.51	0.51	0.51	0.51	0.53	0.54	0.53	0.54	0.54	0.54	0.55	0.55	Taux de change du $É-U moy. pér.		*lats/$É-U*
0.37	0.37	0.37	0.37	0.37	0.37	0.38	0.38	0.37	0.37	0.37	0.37	Taux de change du DM moy. pér.		*lats/DM*
0.67	0.67	0.67	0.68	0.69	0.69	0.69	0.69	0.69	0.69	0.68	0.69	Taux de change de l'ECU moy. pér.		*lats/ECU*
252.13	217.70	207.71	209.37	251.28	239.36	250.17	253.17	266.13	244.25	250.86	281.30	Réserves officielles or exclu		*millions de lats*
												COMMERCE EXTÉRIEUR		
												Importations[3]		
66.6	70.1	70.2	69.6	75.5	82.6	88.0	91.6	96.1	86.8	92.3		Total		*millions de lats*
48.3	52.8	54.5	52.7	53.5	59.8	62.9	64.5	67.4	63.4	67.0		depuis autres que les NEI		*millions de lats*
18.3	17.3	15.7	16.9	22.0	22.7	25.1	27.1	28.7	23.4	25.2		depuis les NEI		*millions de lats*
												Exportations		
52.0	54.7	55.4	50.8	58.9	56.8	62.4	63.7	62.9	53.7	53.0		Total		*millions de lats*
34.5	37.0	34.6	32.5	36.8	36.2	38.9	37.7	33.8	31.1	29.8		vers autres que les NEI		*millions de lats*
17.6	17.7	20.8	18.4	22.1	20.6	23.5	26.1	29.0	22.5	23.1		vers les NEI		*millions de lats*
												Solde commercial		
-14.6	-15.4	-14.9	-18.7	-16.7	-25.8	-25.6	-27.9	-33.3	-33.1	-39.3		Total		*millions de lats*
-13.8	-15.7	-19.9	-20.2	-16.7	-23.6	-24.0	-26.8	-33.6	-32.2	-37.2		avec autres que les NEI		*millions de lats*
-0.7	0.3	5.1	1.5	0.1	-2.1	-1.5	-1.1	0.3	-0.9	-2.1		avec les NEI		*millions de lats*

Pour les notes sur ces séries, veuillez consulter *Indicateurs économiques à court terme : Economies en transition, Sources et définitions* (avril 1996) et les *Notes méthodologiques* à la fin de cette publication.

(1) Cette série a été estimée par le Secrétariat de l'OCDE.

(2) Le chiffre annuel pour 1993 se rapporte à la fin de la période; les données annuelles ultérieures ainsi que les données trimestrielles se rapportent à la moyenne de la période.

(3) Depuis 1996, les importations sont évaluées caf.

LITHUANIA

		1993	1994	1995	1994 Q1	Q2	Q3	Q4	1995 Q1	Q2	Q3	Q4	1996 Q1
NATIONAL PRODUCT													
Gross domestic product	billion litas	11.1	17.0										
Gross domestic product[1]	billion litas 1993	11.1	11.2										
INDUSTRIAL PRODUCTION													
Manufacturing	DEC 90=100	59.0	41.4	41.8	44.0	39.8	40.6	41.4	35.9	41.6	45.0	44.4	
Commodity output													
Cement	thousand tonnes	727	735	649	113	262	194	166	72	199	203	175	
Textiles	million m²	95.9	75.6	76.3	22.4	18.8	15.1	19.3	19.5	19.1	17.0	20.7	
Mineral fertiliser	thousand tonnes	225.1	272.9	389.0	94.1	39.2	48.2	91.4	96.5	88.5	79.0	125.0	
Electricity	mln kilowatt hours	14105	9961	13871	3655	725	2029	3552	3488	2626	3151	4606	
Refrigerators	thousands	207.1	181.5	192.6	52.8	34.7	48.6	45.4	44.9	46.8	58.4	42.5	
BUSINESS SURVEYS - MANUFACT.													
Business situation													
Tendency	balance				-48	-52	-41	-45	-27	-18	-21	-19	
Order books / Demand													
Total: level	balance				-48	-70	-43	-35	-30	-24	-18	-20	
Export: level	balance				-38	-60	-52	-43	-33	-33	-34	-32	
Production													
Tendency	balance				-21	-25	-11	-5	-11	2	8	-4	
Future tendency	balance				-4	-18	-11	-5	21	10	6	-9	
Rate of capacity utilisation	%				49	49	51	49	44	44	44	45	
Stocks													
Finished goods: level	balance				23	30	16	6	-1	7	4	12	
CONSTRUCTION													
Dwellings													
Completed	thousands	8.8	6.8		1.4	1.7	1.7	2.0	1.0	1.1	1.1		
Completed: enterprises	thousands	7.0	3.3		0.6	0.8	1.0	0.9	0.3	0.4	0.6		
DOMESTIC TRADE													
Retail sales: value[2]	million litas								1830.7	2102.9	2443.5	2676.1	
Retail sales: volume	JUL 93=100	120.4	101.4	102.2	100.6	104.1	96.3	104.6	89.4	101.7	107.8	109.7	
LABOUR													
Employment													
Total	thousands	1778	1675		1670	1690	1686	1654	1631	1642	1653		
Industry	thousands	457.0	377.5		391.8	386.5	375.9	355.8	355.8	348.9	340.9		
Manufacturing	thousands	419.6	335.5		355.7	345.4	330.5	310.4	311.6	301.7	293.7		
Unemployment													
Total[3]	thousands	81.1	65.7	109.0	67.7	62.9	59.6	72.6	99.5	106.6	107.0	123.0	
Total registered	number	30399	28730	48378	29228	26681	27268	31744	39073	46481	51993	55964	
Beneficiaries	number	20864	18174	34132	17862	15764	17762	21306	27188	33841	36853	38644	
Non-beneficiaries	number	9535	10557	14246	11366	10917	9506	10438	11885	12640	15140	17320	
Unemployment[3]	% of labour force	4.2	3.6	6.1	3.6	3.4	3.3	4.2	5.4	5.9	6.1	7.0	
Registered unemployment	% of labour force	1.6	1.6	2.7	1.6	1.4	1.5	1.8	2.2	2.5	3.0	3.2	
Job vacancies	number	4335	3326	2116	3382	3749	3470	2702	2567	2169	2037	1692	
Time worked													
Working days per period	units	256	255	254	63	64	65	63	64	64	64	62	
WAGES													
Monthly earnings													
Total	litas	166.1	325.0	500.6	292.6	310.0	330.7	376.7	384.2	437.6	460.8	524.1	
Total: public sector	litas	189.7	371.0	516.0	326.2	345.6	368.0	418.5	435.8	497.5	529.1	601.8	
Manufacturing	litas	206.0	347.0	554.1	326.6	376.0	400.6	447.1	470.9	529.4	581.3	634.7	
Manufacturing: public sector	litas	204.3	376.1	566.5	326.5	380.1	403.7	462.3	476.7	542.2	600.1	646.9	
PRICES													
Producer prices													
Manufacturing	DEC 90=100	19975	28913	37105	26153	28195	29101	32201	36862	35110	36397	40050	
Consumer prices													
Total	MAY 92=100	858	1478	2064	1290	1419	1533	1670	1888	1994	2096	2278	
Food	MAY 92=100	932	1487	2085	1344	1455	1517	1633	1927	2009	2095	2311	
Catering	MAY 92=100	902	1805	2477	1438	1628	1965	2191	2339	2450	2528	2592	
Alcohol and tobacco	MAY 92=100	654	957	1244	817	905	1026	1079	1129	1194	1282	1372	
Clothing and footwear	MAY 92=100	665	1259	1663	1105	1221	1297	1411	1520	1612	1690	1831	
Fuel and electricity	MAY 92=100	5521	14871	24858	11239	12397	15818	20029	21367	23691	25820	28553	
Housing	MAY 92=100	1359	3064	4957	2292	2667	3339	3956	4270	4736	5187	5635	
Total goods	MAY 92=100	849	1427		1266	1383	1471	1586					
Services	MAY 92=100	933	1961		1513	1755	2116	2462					

Footnotes appear at the end of the table.

1995									1996				
Apr	May	Jun	Jul	Aug	Sep	Oct	Nov	Dec	Jan	Feb	Mar		
												PRODUIT NATIONAL	
												Produit intérieur brut	*milliards de litas*
												Produit intérieur brut[1]	*milliards de litas 1993*
												PRODUCTION INDUSTRIELLE	
39.2	42.3	43.4	41.8	47.8	45.5	45.4	45.1	42.8	40.1	36.6		Industries manufacturières	*DÉC 90=100*
												Quantités produites	
69	65	65	59	67	77	70	57	48	35	27		Ciment	*milliers de tonnes*
6.4	7.0	5.7	5.3	5.8	5.9	7.6	7.1	6.0	5.6	5.4		Textiles	*millions de m²*
37.9	26.4	24.2	24.3	20.3	34.4	39.5	40.3	45.2	48.9	41.9		Engrais minéral	*milliers de tonnes*
833	916	877	900	1151	1100	1173	1533	1900	1964	1898		Électricité	*mln kw-heures*
11.3	19.8	15.8	18.5	22.8	17.0	18.4	15.2	8.9	5.7	11.4		Réfrigérateurs	*milliers*
												ENQUÊTES DE CONJONCTURE - IND. MANUF.	
												État des affaires	
												Tendance	*solde*
												Carnets de commandes / Demande	
-19	-31	-23	-18	-23	-13	-21	-18	-20	-37	-38		Total : niveau	*solde*
-34	-33	-31	-37	-33	-33	-34	-29	-32	-39	-31		Exportations : niveau	*solde*
												Production	
-5	4	7	12	3	10	1	-2	-12	-12	-1		Tendance	*solde*
22	0	7	15	3	0	-6	-16	-4	14	27		Perspectives	*solde*
												Taux d'utilisation des capacités	*%*
												Stocks	
14	2	4	0	0	12	13	11	12	13	19		Produits finis : niveau	*solde*
												CONSTRUCTION	
												Logements	
												Achevés	*milliers*
												Achevés : entreprises	*milliers*
												COMMERCE INTÉRIEUR	
660.5	709.9	732.5	787.2	829.6	826.7	857.6	837.1	981.4	810.9			Ventes de détail : valeur[2]	*millions de litas*
95.6	104.0	105.6	102.2	111.3	109.9	110.3	103.3	115.4	92.0			Ventes de détail: volume	*JUIL 93=100*
												MAIN-D'OEUVRE	
												Emploi	
												Total	*milliers*
												Industrie	*milliers*
												Industries manufacturières	*milliers*
												Chômage	
107.9	107.4	104.5	103.7	106.9	110.2	116.8	124.4	127.7	137.4	142.3		Total[3]	*milliers*
45183	47275	46985	49711	52419	53848	54637	55971	57284	58789	58951		Chômeurs inscrits : total	*nombre*
31974	34626	34924	34014	38112	38432	38651	38867	38414	40903	40519		Allocataires	*nombre*
13209	12649	12061	15697	14307	15416	15986	17104	18870	17886	18432		Non allocataires	*nombre*
5.8	5.8	6.0	6.0	6.1	6.3	6.7	7.1	7.3	7.9	8.2		Chômage[3]	*% de main-d'oeuvre*
2.4	2.5	2.7	2.9	3.0	3.1	3.1	3.2	3.3	3.4	3.4		Chômage enregistré	*% de main-d'oeuvre*
2269	2203	2036	1863	2085	2163	2023	1711	1343				Offres d'emploi	*nombre*
												Temps travaillé	
19	23	22	20	23	21	22	21	19				Jours ouvrables	*unités*
												SALAIRES	
												Gains mensuels	
474.0	498.6	513.9	530.0	536.4	527.6	570.4	572.5	653.3	637.0			Total	*litas*
480.9	499.3	512.4	528.2	534.8	524.4	568.1	570.4	666.8	666.6			Total: secteur public	*litas*
485.8	546.9	555.6	578.9	585.3	579.6	622.3	623.5	658.3	618.0			Industries manufacturières	*litas*
494.7	568.0	563.8	577.8	609.6	612.8	628.0	632.5	680.2	619.9			Industries manufact. : sect. public	*litas*
												PRIX	
												Prix à la production	
35627	34825	34877	35241	36331	37620	38737	40442	40970	41630	42056		Industries manufacturières	*DÉC 90=100*
												Prix à la consommation	
1958	2002	2021	2076	2085	2126	2195	2289	2350	2424	2482		Total	*MAI 92=100*
1998	2015	2014	2086	2075	2124	2220	2315	2398	2510	2593		Alimentation	*MAI 92=100*
2421	2442	2487	2516	2516	2553	2556	2602	2619	2654	2708		Restauration	*MAI 92=100*
1154	1209	1220	1265	1283	1299	1320	1386	1411	1429	1434		Alcool et tabac	*MAI 92=100*
1585	1616	1637	1650	1682	1738	1785	1841	1868	1901	1912		Habillement et chaussures	*MAI 92=100*
21551	23864	25659	25755	25829	25875	26113	29756	29790	29823	29952		Combustibles et électricité	*MAI 92=100*
4413	4761	5035	5091	5225	5247	5302	5784	5820	5846	5983		Logement	*MAI 92=100*
												Biens : total	*MAI 92=100*
												Services	*MAI 92=100*

Les notes se trouvent en fin de tableau.

LITHUANIA (continued)

		1993	1994	1995	1994 Q1	Q2	Q3	Q4	1995 Q1	Q2	Q3	Q4	1996 Q1
DOMESTIC FINANCE													
Money supply (M1)	*million litas*	1775	2474	3501	1847	1997	2251	2474	2434	2661	3122	3501	
Quasi-money	*million litas*	946	1899	2206	1240	1563	1913	1899	2059	2202	2317	2206	
Personal deposits	*million litas*	1121	1457		808	1111	1304	1457	1681	1819	1939		
INTEREST RATES													
Official discount rate	*% p.a. period ave.*	104.3	69.1	27.0	86.6	92.6	66.1	31.2	27.5	29.7	28.3	22.3	
FOREIGN FINANCE													
US$ exchange rate end period	*litas/US$*	3.90	4.00	4.00	4.00	4.00	4.00	4.00	4.00	4.00	4.00	4.00	
FOREIGN TRADE													
Imports													
Total	*million litas*	9798	9355		2562	2281	2127	2385	2366	2377	2817		
	million US$	2274.6	2353.4		654.9	570.3	531.8	596.4	591.6	594.3	704.3		
Exports													
Total	*million litas*	8707	8077		1668	1892	2521	1996	1841	2420	2642		
	million US$	2024.7	2028.8		426.2	473.0	630.4	499.2	460.3	605.2	660.6		
Net trade													
Total	*million litas*	-1091	-1278		-894	-389	394	-389	-525	43	-175		
	million US$	-249.9	-324.6		-228.7	-97.3	98.6	-97.2	-131.3	10.9	-43.7		

For notes concerning these series, refer to *Short-term Economic Indicators: Transition Economies, Sources and Definitions* (April 1996) and the *Methodological Notes* at the end of this publication.

(1) Constant price data estimated from the production side.

(2) From January 1995, retail trade data cover trade in market places and in all private enterprises.

(3) Includes unemployed who have left a job of their own accord.

1995									1996					
Apr	May	Jun	Jul	Aug	Sep	Oct	Nov	Dec	Jan	Feb	Mar			
												FINANCES INTERNES		
2422	2529	2661	2870	2967	3122	3223	3241	3501	3194			Disponibilités monétaires (M1)		*millions de litas*
2112	2116	2202	2295	2308	2317	2395	2411	2206	2081			Quasi-monnaie		*millions de litas*
1737	1774	1819	1874	1902	1939	1980	1971					Dépôts personnels		*millions de litas*
												TAUX D'INTÉRÊT		
30.0	29.7	29.3	33.0	31.0	21.0	25.0	20.0	22.0	28.0			Taux d'escompte officiel		*% p.a. moy. période*
												FINANCES EXTÉRIEURES		
4.00	4.00	4.00	4.00	4.00	4.00	4.00	4.00	4.00	4.00			Taux de change du $É-U fin période		*litas/$É-U*
												COMMERCE EXTÉRIEUR		
												Importations		
857	897	623	781	1062	974							Total		*millions de litas*
214.4	224.1	155.8	195.3	265.5	243.5									*millions de $É-U*
												Exportations		
794	794	832	804	920	918							Total		*millions de litas*
198.6	198.6	208.0	201.1	230.1	229.4									*millions de $É-U*
												Solde commercial		
-63	-103	209	23	-142	-56							Total		*millions de litas*
-15.8	-25.5	52.2	5.8	-35.4	-14.1									*millions de $É-U*

Pour les notes sur ces séries, veuillez consulter *Indicateurs économiques à court terme : Economies en transition, Sources et définitions* (avril 1996) et les *Notes méthodologiques* à la fin de cette publication.

(1) Les données à prix constants sont estimées du côté de la production.

(2) Depuis janvier 1995, la série couvre les ventes sur les marchés ainsi que dans toutes les entreprises privées.

(3) Y compris les chômeurs ayant volontairement quitté leur emploi.

POLAND

		1993	1994	1995	1994 Q1	Q2	Q3	Q4	1995 Q1	Q2	Q3	Q4	1996 Q1
NATIONAL PRODUCT													
Gross domestic product	'000 bln old zlotys	1557.8	2104.1										
	'000 bln old zlotys PP	1193.1	1638.8										
INDUSTRIAL PRODUCTION[1]													
Total	1990=100	97.0	108.8	120.0	99.1	103.9	111.2	114.1	113.1	114.1	117.9	123.6	
Total[2] sa	1990=100				99.4	106.4	111.8	110.5	113.7	116.6	118.5	119.7	
Manufacturing	1990=100	103.1	117.7	132.6	101.7	112.4	122.5	123.0	120.1	125.7	132.1	136.4	
Mining	1990=100	83.6	89.2	88.7	86.5	78.4	88.6	101.2	90.8	83.6	89.4	91.7	
Electricity and gas	1990=100	71.8	73.8	73.2	94.3	74.4	65.2	77.8	91.3	72.8	70.4	78.2	
Construction	1990=100	132.9	129.3	144.9	83.1	110.5	117.6	138.2	94.7	120.8	138.2	161.4	88.9
Commodity output													
Brown coal	thousand tonnes	68104	66770	63549	18427	14415	15372	18556	18472	14134	14337	16606	
Black coal	million tonnes	130.6	133.6	135.8	35.1	30.5	33.1	35.0	36.0	31.7	33.6	34.4	
Crude steel	thousand tonnes	9937	11055	11886	2672	2605	2932	2846	2927	2980	3018	2961	
Cement	thousand tonnes	12243	13908	13831	2059	4221	4416	3214	2552	3970	4542	2767	
Crude petroleum	thousand tonnes	235	287	293	71	70	75	71	75	75	67	75	
Natural gas	million m³	4928	4617	4820	1294	1038	1007	1278	1350	1067	1097	1307	
Plastics	thousand tonnes	674	652	715	167	186	157	142	193	195	160	167	
Passenger cars	thousands	333.0	338.0	363.8	72.2	93.8	77.1	94.7	92.6	95.7	85.6	89.9	
BUSINESS SURVEYS - MANUFACT.													
Business situation													
Tendency	balance				-21	-17	-8	-1	-5	0	5	4	
Order books / Demand													
Total: tendency	balance				-8	9	16	13	-3	9	8	-1	
Export: tendency	balance				2	5	6	6	0	1	3	0	
Production													
Tendency	balance				-4	10	15	4	0	14	8	1	
Future tendency	balance				30	29	27	3	34	25	27	13	
Rate of capacity utilisation	%				64	66	65	70	68	69	69	71	
Stocks													
Finished goods: level	balance				2	0	-9	-10	-4	-1	-4	-3	
CONSTRUCTION													
Dwellings													
Started: public sector	thousands	25.9	27.2	23.2	5.1	7.1	7.5	7.6	5.8	6.7	6.4	4.3	
Completed: total	thousands	94.4	76.1	58.4	16.6	15.0	14.3	30.1	10.9	13.2	11.5	25.4	10.8
Completed: public sector	thousands	61.0	40.6	29.0	10.9	8.0	7.9	13.8	5.7	6.1	6.4	11.5	
Under construction: total	thousands												
Under construction: publ. sector	thousands	54.8	46.2	41.5	51.5	51.2	51.4	46.2	45.7	46.4	46.6	41.5	
DOMESTIC TRADE													
Retail sales: value	'000 bln old zlotys	998.2	1128.1	1701.1	109.3	114.5	133.5	150.3	148.3	172.7	179.6	208.4	
Retail sales: volume[2]	1992=100	109.3	92.5	109.4	74.7	73.6	80.9	83.8	76.7	84.1	87.0	95.1	
Retail sales: volume[2] sa	1992=100				83.4	73.9	79.4	76.9	85.8	84.2	85.5	87.4	
LABOUR													
Employment													
Total	thousands	9163	9106	9353	8486	8485	8517	8587	8507	8562	8534	8591	
Industry	thousands	3353	3222	3249	3243	3236	3212	3239	3261	3271	3262	3286	
Manufacturing	thousands	2608	2549	2616	2555	2541	2541	2559	2601	2621	2615	2634	
Unemployment													
Total registered	thousands	2737	2919	2695	2950	2933	2954	2838	2820	2661	2689	2608	2727
Beneficiaries	thousands	1312	1349	1436	1429	1333	1250	1384	1456	1448	1341	1502	
Unemployment	% of labour force	14.9	16.4	15.2	16.0	16.6	16.7	16.1	15.8	15.1	15.2	14.8	15.4
Job vacancies	thousands	32.0	39.1	38.5	33.4	45.4	51.1	34.7	32.8	41.8	49.6	29.9	
WAGES													
Monthly earnings													
Total	thousand old zlotys	3263	4421		4062	4202	4432	4985					
Total[3]	zlotys			702.6					662.4	684.9	717.2	842.1	
Industry	thousand old zlotys	3467			4302	4634	4844						
Industry[3]	zlotys			796.1					704.5	771.1	791.9	917.0	
Manufacturing	thousand old zlotys	3177			3889	4294							
Manufacturing[3]	zlotys			697.7					612.6	688.8	713.9	775.7	

Footnotes appear at the end of the table.

1995									1996					
Apr	May	Jun	Jul	Aug	Sep	Oct	Nov	Dec	Jan	Feb	Mar			
												PRODUIT NATIONAL		
												Produit intérieur brut		'000 mrd anciens zlotys
														'000 mrd anciens zlotys PP
												PRODUCTION INDUSTRIELLE[1]		
105.4	114.2	114.4	108.5	117.5	119.0	122.6	121.8	117.1	117.7			Total		1990=100
110.6	115.0	114.8	117.6	117.4	118.7	116.3	117.0	114.9	117.8			Total[2]	cvs	1990=100
113.8	127.2	128.7	121.5	132.5	134.6	138.7	134.7	127.5	127.0			Industries manufacturières		1990=100
81.7	80.0	80.7	81.3	89.9	87.8	82.2	94.7	88.9	96.2			Industries extractives		1990=100
81.1	71.9	65.1	61.3	60.0	62.1	69.0	78.5	86.7	91.2			Électricité et gaz		1990=100
109.4	120.0	132.6	129.7	136.5	148.1	162.6	140.3	181.9	94.8	79.4	92.9	Construction		1990=100
												Quantités produites		
5035	4772	4327	4487	4816	5034	5012	5577	6017	6254	6143		Lignite		milliers de tonnes
10.3	10.4	11.1	11.0	11.4	11.2	12.1	12.0	10.4	12.3	11.1		Houille		millions de tonnes
935	976	1069	1003	1029	986	1059	984	918	960	923		Acier brut		milliers de tonnes
1075	1439	1456	1589	1517	1437	1391	964	413	330	357		Ciment		milliers de tonnes
22	26	27	17	25	25	22	29	24	26			Pétrole brut		milliers de tonnes
360	381	326	351	370	376	411	425	471	473	371		Gaz naturel		millions de m^3
63	70	63	67	53	40	64	57	47	60	57		Plastiques		milliers de tonnes
31.1	31.7	32.9	28.0	22.6	35.0	31.2	33.2	25.4	34.6	37.2		Voitures particulières		milliers
												ENQUÊTES DE CONJONCTURE - IND. MANUF.		
												État des affaires		
-2	0	2	4	7	5	3	4	4	0	-11		Tendance		solde
												Carnets de commandes / Demande		
7	12	8	2	10	12	5	-5	-2	-10	-9		Total : tendance		solde
1	1	2	-8	4	13	6	-2	-3	-8	-1		À l'exportation : tendance		solde
												Production		
7	16	20	-12	16	21	14	-3	-7	-6	-7		Tendance		solde
33	19	24	24	30	27	21	7	10	20	40		Perspectives		solde
70	69	68	69	69	70	71	71	71	69	67		Taux d'utilisation des capacités		%
												Stocks		
-3	1	-1	-3	-4	-6	-1	-2	-5	0	1		Produits finis : niveau		solde
												CONSTRUCTION		
												Logements		
2.0	2.6	2.1	2.4	2.5	1.5	1.5	1.6	1.2	1.1	1.8		Mis en chantier : sect. public		milliers
3.3	3.8	6.1	3.7	3.9	3.9	5.3	5.1	15.0	3.6	3.8	3.4	Achevés : total		milliers
1.8	2.0	2.3	2.4	2.2	1.8	3.3	2.7	5.5	1.9	2.0		Achevés : secteur public		milliers
												En cours de construction : total		milliers
45.8	46.6	46.4	46.5	47.1	46.6	45.4	44.5	41.5	40.7	39.5		En cours de constr.: sect. publ.		milliers
												COMMERCE INTÉRIEUR		
53.5	56.9	58.4	57.4	60.0	60.7	63.3	62.4	70.6	59.8	62.6		Ventes de détail : valeur		'000 mrd anciens zlotys
85.7	89.5	91.0	91.3	95.2	93.0	95.1	92.3	102.6	84.9	87.7		Ventes de détail : volume[2]		1992=100
87.4	91.0	90.7	90.9	89.8	93.4	92.1	91.5	92.7	92.0	94.3		Ventes de détail : volume[2]	cvs	1992=100
												MAIN-D'OEUVRE		
												Emploi		
												Total		milliers
3232	3231	3227	3222	3223	3227	3253	3247	3223	3202	3212		Industrie		milliers
2595	2600	2600	2596	2599	2602	2625	2619	2595	2579	2590		Industries manufacturières		milliers
												Chômage		
2690	2599	2694	2721	2690	2657	2596	2597	2629	2718	2734	2730	Chômeurs inscrits : total		milliers
1448	1419	1476	1286	1292	1444	1461	1494	1549	1609	1621		Allocataires		milliers
15.2	14.8	15.2	15.3	15.2	15.0	14.7	14.7	14.9	15.4	15.4	15.4	Chômage		% de main-d'oeuvre
38.0	41.5	45.9	47.3	51.5	50.0	40.4	28.9	20.5	25.6	26.5		Offres d'emploi		milliers
												SALAIRES		
												Gains mensuels		
												Total		milliers d'anciens zlotys
												Total[3]		zlotys
												Industrie		milliers d'anciens zlotys
769.1	778.4	765.9	771.9	792.8	811.0	824.3	927.9	999.0	889.5	888.7		Industrie[3]		zlotys
												Industries manufacturières		milliers d'anciens zlotys
677.4	689.5	699.4	698.2	710.0	733.6	748.6	774.8	803.7	760.5	777.7		Industries manufacturières[3]		zlotys

Les notes se trouvent en fin de tableau.

		1993	1994	1995	1994				1995				1996
					Q1	Q2	Q3	Q4	Q1	Q2	Q3	Q4	Q1
PRICES													
Producer prices													
Industry	*JAN 90=100*	295.4	384.3	484.0	351.5	367.6	391.8	426.1	457.6	474.7	491.8	511.9	
Manufacturing	*JAN 90=100*	287.3											
Consumer prices													
Total	*JAN 90=100*	532.3	709.2	908.3	640.1	682.6	726.1	787.8	851.8	901.0	915.6	964.8	
Food	*JAN 90=100*	387.5	521.9	664.1	473.1	502.9	531.8	579.9	634.6	675.7	651.7	694.5	
Catering	*JAN 90=100*	854.1	1165.5	1518.6	1051.0	1114.3	1199.0	1297.7	1404.0	1492.0	1556.3	1622.4	
Alcoholic beverages	*JAN 90=100*	473.0	617.1	795.4	550.3	585.1	633.1	699.9	719.7	768.4	814.3	879.2	
Goods less food	*JAN 90=100*	588.0	781.5	998.3	708.2	753.1	799.4	865.2	918.1	971.2	1023.6	1080.4	
Total goods	*JAN 90=100*	468.5	625.5	797.7	566.7	602.2	638.4	694.7	748.0	795.0	799.2	848.8	
Services	*JAN 90=100*	937.3	1242.3	1606.1	1108.2	1195.8	1282.2	1383.2	1511.4	1578.2	1644.8	1690.1	
DOMESTIC FINANCE													
Money supply (M1)	*'000 bln old zlotys*	196.5	274.5		204.1	214.5	229.8	274.5					
	billion zlotys			37.44					26.40	29.66	32.28	37.44	
Quasi-money	*'000 bln old zlotys*	362.8	498.5		384.8	415.9	458.4	498.5					
	billion zlotys			66.91					54.91	57.77	62.32	66.91	
Personal deposits	*'000 bln old zlotys*	317.0	430.1		333.9	357.5	386.7	430.1					
	billion zlotys			59.38					47.69	50.40	54.56	59.38	
INTEREST RATES													
Official discount rate	*% p.a. end period*	35.0	33.0	29.0	35.0	33.0	33.0	33.0	35.0	31.0	29.0	29.0	
FOREIGN FINANCE													
US$ exchange rate end period	*old zloty/US$*	21344	24372		22119	22450	23216	24372					
	zloty/US$			2.4680					2.4020	2.3420	2.4330	2.4680	
US$ exchange rate per. ave.	*old zloty/US$*	18136	22721		21836	22498	22846	23706					
	zloty/US$			2.4245					2.4238	2.3771	2.4222	2.4748	
Official reserves excluding gold	*million US$*	4092	5842	14774	4906	5010	5855	5842	7385	10539	12798	14774	
Gross foreign debt													
Total	*'000 bln old zlotys*	1008.1			1066.0	1049.9	1102.1						
Convertible currencies	*million US$*	47246	42174		48192	46765	47470	42174	44139	44557	44244		
FOREIGN TRADE													
Imports	*'000 bln old zlotys*	340.2	486.3		94.5	117.7	124.8	149.3					
	billion zlotys								15.14	17.52	17.38		
Exports	*'000 bln old zlotys*	257.6	387.7		79.7	93.0	103.6	111.4					
	billion zlotys								12.78	13.45	14.05		
Net trade	*'000 bln old zlotys*	-82.6	-98.6		-14.8	-24.8	-21.2	-37.9					
	billion zlotys								-2.36	-4.07	-3.33		
Indices													
Import prices[4]	*SPPY=100*												
Export prices[4]	*SPPY=100*												
Imports: volume	*1985=100*	188.2	210.7		180.2	209.6	206.0	254.9	224.0	249.4	246.6		
Exports: volume	*1985=100*	126.7	151.9		128.5	151.3	154.4	171.7	155.9	174.6	186.5		
GROSS CAPITAL FORMATION													
Total	*'000 bln old zlotys*	146.76			28.76	40.37							
Machinery and equipment	*'000 bln old zlotys*	65.61			13.57	22.23							
Construction and assembly works	*'000 bln old zlotys*	63.47			9.50	13.83							
Other goods and services	*'000 bln old zlotys*	17.68			5.69	4.30							

The zloty was redenominated on the 1st January 1995 with the new zloty equal to 10 000 old zlotys.

For notes concerning these series, refer to *Short-term Economic Indicators: Transition Economies, Sources and Definitions* (April 1996) and the *Methodological Notes* at the end of this publication.

(1) Totals derived from monthly and quarterly data may differ from each other and from annual totals due to different coverage of surveys.

(2) This series has been estimated by the OECD Secretariat.

(3) From 1995 on, wage data refer to gross wages.

(4) Monthly import and export price indices are calculated cumulatively from the beginning of the year.

	1995									1996				
	Apr	May	Jun	Jul	Aug	Sep	Oct	Nov	Dec	Jan	Feb	Mar		
PRIX														
Prix à la production														
Industrie	471.1	474.8	478.2	483.9	490.2	501.5	506.0	513.6	516.1	522.8			*JAN 90=100*	
Industries manufacturières													*JAN 90=100*	
Prix à la consommation														
Total	887.3	903.3	912.3	904.1	907.7	935.0	951.8	964.2	978.6	1011.9	1027.1		*JAN 90=100*	
Alimentation	666.1	678.8	682.2	649.5	640.4	665.3	682.0	694.2	707.4	723.7	736.7		*JAN 90=100*	
Restauration	1456.8	1496.1	1523.0	1538.2	1545.9	1584.6	1605.2	1622.8	1639.1	1673.5	1751.8		*JAN 90=100*	
Boissons alcoolisées	763.8	768.4	773.0	778.5	807.3	857.3	861.6	864.2	911.7	941.8	945.6		*JAN 90=100*	
Biens sauf alimentation	953.9	972.0	987.6	1002.4	1020.4	1048.0	1066.8	1080.7	1093.7	1117.7	1130.0		*JAN 90=100*	
Biens : total	783.0	797.0	805.0	788.9	790.5	818.2	835.3	847.9	863.1	883.0	895.3		*JAN 90=100*	
Services	1556.3	1581.2	1597.0	1629.0	1640.4	1665.0	1680.0	1690.1	1700.2	1807.3	1839.8		*JAN 90=100*	
FINANCES INTERNES														
Disponibilités monétaires (M1)	27.86	29.08	29.66	31.13	32.21	32.28	33.64	34.81	37.44	36.21	37.23		*'000 mrd anciens zlotys* / *milliards de zlotys*	
Quasi-monnaie	56.38	56.38	57.77	59.40	61.31	62.32	63.82	64.87	66.91	69.27	70.86		*'000 mrd anciens zlotys* / *milliards de zlotys*	
Dépôts personnels	49.08	49.25	50.40	52.04	53.76	54.56	55.95	57.62	59.38	62.09	64.01		*'000 mrd anciens zlotys* / *milliards de zlotys*	
TAUX D'INTÉRÊT														
Taux d'escompte officiel	35.0	31.0	31.0	31.0	31.0	29.0	29.0	29.0	29.0				*% p.a. fin période*	
FINANCES EXTÉRIEURES														
Taux de change du $É-U fin période	2.3971	2.3220	2.3420	2.3685	2.4720	2.4330	2.4525	2.5100	2.4680				*ancien zloty/$É-U* / *zloty/$É-U*	
Taux de change du $É-U moy. pér.	2.3942	2.3926	2.3446	2.3652	2.4399	2.4616	2.4429	2.4718	2.5098	2.5110	2.5442		*ancien zloty/$É-U* / *zloty/$É-U*	
Réserves officielles or exclu	8879	9846	10539	10776	11553	12798	13287	14032	14774				*millions de $É-U*	
Dette extérieure brute														
Total													*'000 mrd anciens zlotys*	
Monnaies convertibles	44965	44722	44557	45057	43779	44244	44279	43878					*millions de $É-U*	
COMMERCE EXTÉRIEUR														
Importations	5.33	6.11	6.08	5.86	5.56	5.96	6.95						*'000 mrd anciens zlotys* / *milliards de zlotys*	
Exportations	4.19	4.40	4.86	4.49	4.36	5.20	6.33						*'000 mrd anciens zlotys* / *milliards de zlotys*	
Solde commercial	-1.14	-1.71	-1.22	-1.38	-1.20	-0.75	-0.62						*'000 mrd anciens zlotys* / *milliards de zlotys*	
Indices														
Prix à l'importation[4]	127.0	127.0	126.6	125.1	123.9	122.7	122.7						*PCAP=100*	
Prix à l'exportation[4]	129.8	129.5	128.4	126.0	123.7	122.3	122.2						*PCAP=100*	
Importations : volume	198.0	286.1	267.9	243.5	239.3	257.4	307.2						*1985=100*	
Exportations : volume	166.8	165.9	190.3	175.0	176.5	209.8	224.9						*1985=100*	
FORMATION BRUTE DE CAPITAL														
Total													*'000 mrd anciens zlotys*	
Machines et équipements													*'000 mrd anciens zlotys*	
Construction et assemblage													*'000 mrd anciens zlotys*	
Autres biens et services													*'000 mrd anciens zlotys*	

Une nouvelle dénomination du zloty a été introduite le 1er janvier 1995, le nouveau zloty équivalant à 10 000 anciens zlotys.

Pour les notes sur ces séries, veuillez consulter *Indicateurs économiques à court terme : Economies en transition, Sources et définitions* (avril 1996) et les *Notes méthodologiques* à la fin de cette publication.

1) Les totaux dérivés des données mensuelles et trimestrielles peuvent être différents entre eux, et avec les chiffres annuels à cause de couvertures différentes des enquêtes.

2) Cette série a été estimée par le Secrétariat de l'OCDE.

3) Depuis 1995, les données concernant les salaires correspondent aux gains mensuels bruts.

4) Les indices des prix mensuels à l'importation et à l'exportation sont calculés par cumul depuis le début de l'année.

REPUBLIC OF SLOVENIA

			1993	1994	1995	1994 Q1	Q2	Q3	Q4	1995 Q1	Q2	Q3	Q4	1996 Q1
NATIONAL PRODUCT[1]														
Gross domestic product		billion tolars	1435.1	1844.7	2198.5									
Gross domestic product[2]		billion tolars 1992	1037.0	1087.6	1125.9									
INDUSTRIAL PRODUCTION														
Total		1990=100	73.9	78.7	80.3	75.6	81.1	77.2	80.8	82.9	82.4	76.2	79.5	
Total[3]	sa	1990=100				76.5	79.6	79.6	79.4	83.0	81.4	79.1	77.8	
Manufacturing		1990=100	72.4	77.2	79.3	74.7	79.1	76.6	78.5	81.3	82.6	75.4	77.7	
Mining		1990=100	79.1	75.0	75.7	75.5	75.1	68.2	81.4	78.5	79.1	70.8	74.3	
Electricity		1990=100	93.5	100.8	100.6	99.8	105.9	85.8	111.7	107.6	89.1	98.9	106.6	
Commodity output														
Coal		thousand tonnes	5121	4853	4883	1299	1351	883	1320	1387	1269	1052	1175	
Crude steel		thousand tonnes	355	425	407	94	119	101	111	119	106	101	81	
Cement		thousand tonnes	707	898	990	113	268	274	243	144	307	293	246	
Crude petroleum		tonnes	1925	1716	1858	460	374	397	485	469	460	460	469	
Natural gas		thousand m^3	13392	12595	18220	3369	1431	2507	5288	6091	4377	3664	4088	
Textiles		million m^2	76	84	94	20	23	20	21	25	25	20	24	
Electricity		mln kilowatt hours	11603	12499	12551	3095	3283	2659	3462	3338	2765	3142	3306	
Refrigerators		thousands	665	799	865	188	200	183	228	221	228	201	215	
CONSTRUCTION														
Dwellings														
Started: enterprises		units	..	671	..	176	142	187	166	..	253	42	71	
Completed		units	7925	5522										
Completed: enterprises		units	768	589	615	104	85	118	282	25	93	227	270	
Time worked														
Person hours worked		1990=100	53.9	53.8	54.3	51.5	55.0	55.4	53.5	52.0	55.5	56.0	53.8	
DOMESTIC TRADE														
Retail sales: value		billion tolars	483.61	608.66		128.05	155.00	155.95	169.66	152.09	179.79	183.40		
Retail sales: volume		1992=100	105.1	111.4		100.2	116.1	112.5	116.9	102.0	120.0	120.9		
Retail sales: volume[3]	sa	1992=100				111.7	112.5	109.5	111.8	114.0	116.3	117.7		
LABOUR														
Employment														
Total		thousands	764.8	752.2	750.2	755.0	754.7	750.0	749.2	750.3	752.4	749.6	748.6	
Total: enterprises		thousands	626.2	605.3	593.8	608.5	607.7	602.9	602.2	599.6	596.6	591.1	588.1	
Unemployment														
Total registered		thousands	129.09	127.06	121.48	133.28	125.37	125.21	124.36	121.37	117.29	121.25	126.02	
Beneficiaries		thousands	35.57	37.46	29.02	42.45	38.98	36.06	32.34	30.96	28.58	28.08	28.46	
Unemployment		% of labour force	14.4	14.5	14.0	15.0	14.2	14.3	14.3	13.9	13.5	13.9	14.4	
Job vacancies		units	9067	12572	12769	11313	12015	13383	13578	13432	12849	12681	12112	
WAGES														
Monthly earnings														
Total[4]		thousand tolars	75.43	94.62	112.00	86.62	90.95	95.91	105.05	107.78	110.14	112.04	118.11	
PRICES														
Producer prices														
Manufacturing		1992=100	118.6	137.1	153.3	129.3	133.9	139.6	145.5	149.7	152.8	154.0	156.8	159.8
Consumer prices														
Total		1992=100	132.9	160.8	182.4	150.0	157.7	163.8	171.5	178.7	181.1	182.7	187.1	
Food		1992=100	125.7	154.7	178.9	141.7	151.2	158.6	167.1	178.6	181.0	177.4	178.7	
Clothing and footwear		1992=100	147.2	168.3	185.5	160.2	167.0	169.6	176.4	180.4	184.8	186.6	190.2	
Alcohol and tobacco		1992=100	126.2	170.0	197.7	153.9	166.4	176.3	183.2	190.5	195.9	199.7	204.8	
Fuel and electricity		1992=100	134.4	163.1	181.9	159.1	154.7	157.6	180.9	183.1	172.8	177.5	194.1	
Housing		1992=100	161.9	214.7	260.1	202.8	210.0	217.6	228.3	240.0	249.4	265.5	285.3	
Total goods		1992=100	129.9	155.8	174.9	145.5	152.9	158.7	166.1	173.1	174.3	174.3	177.8	
Services		1992=100	150.1	184.5	224.3	155.9	185.8	193.3	202.8	212.1	219.7	228.5	237.0	
Retail prices														
Total		1992=100	132.3	158.5	178.5	148.5	155.3	161.2	169.0	174.3	176.2	179.3	184.2	
Total goods		1992=100	129.6	154.0	171.3	144.4	150.8	156.6	164.1	168.5	169.4	171.4	175.7	
DOMESTIC FINANCE														
Money supply (M1)		billion tolars	115.60	170.24	203.90	115.14	129.86	135.32	170.24	157.52	183.74	182.15	203.90	
Quasi-money		billion tolars	397.27	562.44	728.32	442.47	485.24	517.75	562.44	616.80	649.09	689.74	728.32	
Personal deposits		billion tolars	246.63	371.18	498.17	277.37	304.95	325.15	371.18	408.82	445.53	456.96	498.17	
INTEREST RATES														
Official discount rate		% p.a. end period	18	16	10	16	16	16	16	16	10	10	10	
Call money		% p.a. period ave.	39.2	29.1	12.2	29.8	28.3	27.6	30.7	18.6	8.2	8.6	13.3	

Footnotes appear at the end of the table.

 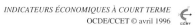

RÉPUBLIQUE DE SLOVÉNIE

1995									1996						
Apr	May	Jun	Jul	Aug	Sep	Oct	Nov	Dec	Jan	Feb	Mar				
												PRODUIT NATIONAL[1]			
												Produit intérieur brut			*milliards de tolars*
												Produit intérieur brut[2]			*milliards de tolars 1992*
												PRODUCTION INDUSTRIELLE			
74.6	84.1	88.5	78.1	68.2	82.5	81.3	85.7	71.5	76.6	75.9		Total			*1990=100*
79.3	80.9	84.0	82.4	74.6	80.3	77.1	80.2	76.0	80.3	76.5		Total[3]	*cvs*		*1990=100*
74.5	85.6	87.6	77.2	67.5	81.6	80.2	83.8	69.2	75.1	75.4		Industries manufacturières			*1990=100*
64.0	77.5	95.9	72.7	60.9	78.9	83.5	88.0	51.6	64.6	65.7		Industries extractives			*1990=100*
93.8	73.8	99.8	100.8	91.4	104.4	104.3	105.1	110.4	107.4	99.7		Électricité			*1990=100*
												Quantités produites			
319	398	552	380	273	399	426	480	269	364	372		Charbon			*milliers de tonnes*
37	37	32	25	40	36	37	29	15	36	31		Acier brut			*milliers de tonnes*
111	113	83	89	102	102	100	72	74	39	39		Ciment			*milliers de tonnes*
145	151	164	105	152	203	162	159	148	147	120		Pétrole brut			*tonnes*
1568	1479	1330	506	1446	1712	1537	1320	1231	1197	610		Gaz naturel			*milliers de m³*
8	8	9	7	5	8	9	8	7	9	9		Textiles			*millions de m²*
970	763	1032	1116	946	1080	1079	1086	1141	1118	1037		Électricité			*mln kw-heures*
62	81	85	54	60	87	82	76	57	76	67		Réfrigérateurs			*milliers*
												CONSTRUCTION			
												Logements			
												Mis en chantier : entreprises			*unités*
												Achevés			*unités*
												Achevés : entreprises			*unités*
												Temps travaillé			
52.6	56.8	56.9	55.5	56.3	56.3	56.8	56.4	48.0				Heures travaillées			*1990=100*
												COMMERCE INTÉRIEUR			
56.36	60.15	63.28	60.83	60.21	62.36							Ventes de détail : valeur			*milliards de tolars*
113.4	120.6	125.9	120.9	119.5	122.5							Ventes de détail : volume			*1992=100*
113.4	117.1	118.4	117.6	118.2	117.2							Ventes de détail : volume[3]	*cvs*		*1992=100*
												MAIN-D'OEUVRE			
												Emploi			
752.7	751.9	752.7	750.9	749.4	748.6	749.8	749.5	746.4	746.1			Total			*milliers*
598.2	596.2	595.5	592.8	591.0	589.3	589.3	588.8	586.3	586.0			Total : entreprises			*milliers*
												Chômage			
119.15	116.35	116.38	120.11	120.22	123.42	125.69	125.61	126.76	125.65	123.69		Chômeurs inscrits : total			*milliers*
29.44	28.53	27.76	28.00	28.35	27.90	28.50	28.59	28.31	29.96			Allocataires			*milliers*
13.7	13.4	13.4	13.8	13.8	14.2	14.4	14.4	14.5	14.4	14.2		Chômage			*% de main-d'oeuvre*
10691	13870	13987	11244	11728	15072	14217	12270	9848	12911			Offres d'emploi			*unités*
												SALAIRES			
												Gains mensuels			
108.53	111.31	110.58	111.12	112.90	112.11	115.13	119.17	120.04	119.71			Total[4]			*milliers de tolars*
												PRIX			
												Prix à la production			
152.1	152.9	153.3	153.3	153.9	154.8	155.7	156.9	157.9	158.3	160.1	161.0	Industries manufacturières			*1992=100*
												Prix à la consommation			
179.5	181.4	182.3	182.5	181.9	183.8	184.7	187.3	189.2	191.8	194.1		Total			*1992=100*
178.4	182.8	181.9	180.1	176.0	176.2	175.5	178.4	182.3	186.3	190.0		Alimentation			*1992=100*
184.3	184.6	185.5	185.9	186.4	187.5	189.1	190.4	191.1	191.3	191.9		Habillement et chaussures			*1992=100*
193.7	195.0	198.9	199.3	199.1	200.8	203.8	204.9	205.8	206.8	208.1		Alcool et tabac			*1992=100*
172.1	172.1	174.2	174.2	174.2	184.0	186.6	198.7	197.1	197.5	197.7		Combustibles et électricité			*1992=100*
249.6	249.2	249.4	255.4	265.4	275.6	279.6	285.6	290.5	300.7	314.0		Logement			*1992=100*
172.9	174.7	175.2	174.7	173.4	174.9	175.4	178.2	179.9	182.1	184.2		Biens : total			*1992=100*
218.1	219.5	221.6	224.7	228.4	232.3	234.6	236.9	239.6	244.2	247.7		Services			*1992=100*
												Prix de détail			
175.2	176.1	177.4	177.9	178.8	181.2	182.2	184.6	185.8	187.7	189.3		Total			*1992=100*
168.5	169.2	170.5	170.7	170.9	172.7	173.7	176.2	177.1	178.3	179.8		Biens : total			*1992=100*
												FINANCES INTERNES			
171.37	172.47	183.74	185.49	179.37	182.15	180.88	181.74	203.90	186.28			Disponibilités monétaires (M1)			*milliards de tolars*
625.14	636.97	649.09	662.35	678.91	689.74	696.48	708.67	728.32	759.40			Quasi-monnaie			*milliards de tolars*
417.25	431.39	445.53	452.30	454.88	456.96	466.17	476.53	498.17	511.88			Dépôts personnels			*milliards de tolars*
												TAUX D'INTÉRÊT			
10	10	10	10	10	10	10	10	10	10	10		Taux d'escompte officiel			*% p.a. fin période*
11.0	6.4	7.3	7.7	8.9	9.3	11.5	12.4	15.9	12.5	14.7		Taux de l'argent au jour le jour			*% p.a. moy. période*

Les notes se trouvent en fin de tableau.

REPUBLIC OF SLOVENIA *(continued)*

		1993	1994	1995	1994				1995				1996
					Q1	Q2	Q3	Q4	Q1	Q2	Q3	Q4	Q1
FOREIGN FINANCE													
US$ exchange rate end period	*tolar/US$*	131.84	126.46	125.99	131.81	126.02	124.37	126.46	112.42	113.65	117.89	125.99	
DM exchange rate end period	*tolar/DM*	76.37	81.65	87.89	78.52	79.56	80.30	81.65	81.61	81.37	83.09	87.89	
ECU exchange rate end period	*tolar/ECU*	147.80	155.13	161.45	151.27	152.26	153.54	155.13	148.74	149.98	153.71	161.45	
Official reserves excluding gold	*million US$*	788	1495	1802	774	1026	1354	1495	1577	1737	1710	1802	
Gross foreign debt													
Total	*million US$*	1873	2258	2956	1924	2003	2023	2258	2480	2557	2685	2956	
FOREIGN TRADE													
Imports	*million US$*	6499	7304	9451	1536	1843	1790	2135	2174	2630	2207	2441	
Exports	*million US$*	6082	6828	8286	1500	1695	1708	1925	2059	2155	1991	2080	
Net trade	*million US$*	-417	-476	-1165	-36	-148	-81	-210	-114	-475	-216	-361	

For notes concerning these series, refer to *Short-term Economic Indicators: Transition Economies, Sources and Definitions* (April 1996) and the *Methodological Notes* at the end of this publication.

(1) Preliminary estimate for 1995.

(2) Constant price data estimated from the production side.

(3) This series has been estimated by the OECD Secretariat.

(4) Gross monthly earnings.

1995									1996					
Apr	May	Jun	Jul	Aug	Sep	Oct	Nov	Dec	Jan	Feb	Mar			
112.47	112.75	113.65	112.85	120.71	117.89	119.73	124.14	125.99	132.69	131.39		**FINANCES EXTÉRIEURES**		
												Taux de change du $É-U fin période	*tolar/$É-U*	
81.43	81.31	81.37	81.44	81.75	83.09	84.96	86.40	87.89	89.38	90.22		Taux de change du DM fin pér.	*tolar/DM*	
149.41	149.67	149.98	151.31	153.29	153.71	155.75	159.71	161.45	163.70	166.81		Taux de change de l'ECU fin pér.	*tolar/ECU*	
1643	1731	1737	1707	1594	1710	1688	1687	1802	1695			Réserves officielles or exclu	*millions de $É-U*	
												Dette extérieure brute		
2465	2485	2557	2641	2528	2685	2708	2695	2956	2916			Total	*millions de $É-U*	
												COMMERCE EXTÉRIEUR		
779	908	943	843	603	761	782	851	808				Importations	*millions de $É-U*	
652	708	795	728	528	735	740	728	612				Exportations	*millions de $É-U*	
-127	-200	-147	-115	-75	-26	-42	-123	-196				Solde commercial	*millions de $É-U*	

Pour les notes sur ces séries, veuillez consulter *Indicateurs économiques à court terme : Economies en transition, Sources et définitions* (avril 1996) et les *Notes méthodologiques* à la fin de cette publication.

(1) Estimation préliminaire pour 1995.

(2) Les données à prix constants sont estimées du côté de la production.

(3) Cette série a été estimée par le Secrétariat de l'OCDE.

(4) Gains mensuels bruts.

ROMANIA

					1994				1995				1996
		1993	1994	1995	Q1	Q2	Q3	Q4	Q1	Q2	Q3	Q4	Q1
NATIONAL PRODUCT[1]													
Gross domestic product	billion lei	20036	49795	72249									
	billion lei PP	6121	20817	53207									
INDUSTRIAL PRODUCTION													
Total[2]	1990=100	58.0	59.8	65.4	55.7	60.6	60.8	61.9	61.5	65.6	66.4	68.2	
Manufacturing	1990=100	54.0	56.0	62.8	50.8	57.3	58.2	57.9	57.5	63.5	64.5	65.8	
Mining	1990=100	82.0	83.4	82.9	81.8	87.2	81.2	83.3	81.2	84.4	85.3	80.6	
Electricity and gas	1990=100	76.7	76.7	79.2	83.8	66.8	69.2	86.8	90.5	69.1	66.9	90.3	
Construction	1985=100	53.1	68.5	77.1	42.1	59.9	70.1	72.1	43.6	66.5	76.4	97.6	
Commodity output													
Coal	thousand tonnes	39696	40533	41128	10362	10796	9875	9501	10095	10673	10844	9517	
Crude steel	thousand tonnes	5446	5793	6555	1335	1582	1534	1342	1625	1712	1731	1488	
Cement	thousand tonnes	6837	6676	7562	1283	1979	1844	1570	1351	2340	2280	1591	
Crude petroleum	thousand tonnes	6673	6693	6712	1639	1685	1699	1670	1651	1681	1703	1679	
Natural gas	million m³	21309	19590	19012	5497	4439	4324	5331	5329	4410	4110	5164	
BUSINESS SURVEYS - MANUFACT.													
Business situation													
Tendency	balance				29	12	10	18	14	22	22	25	25
Order books / Demand													
Total: level	balance				-32	-45	-43	-28	-27	-23	-23	-12	-10
Production													
Tendency	balance				13	2	-2	3	19	22	20	21	23
Future tendency	balance				6	18	10	16	22	38	27	31	32
Current capacity	balance				29	31	39	32	35	35	29	28	27
Stocks													
Finished goods: level	balance				16	21	26	13	9	11	4	1	0
CONSTRUCTION													
Dwellings[3]													
Started	units	4048	1887	4794	392	429	550	516	431	1663	299	2401	
Completed	units	10851	12088	9300	1006	2155	2880	6047	1606	1447	2145	4102	
Under construction	thousands	61.5	40.3	33.2	58.4	52.6	46.1	40.3	37.1	38.8	35.6	33.2	
DOMESTIC TRADE													
Retail sales: value	billion lei	5127	12160	15729	2308	2640	3478	3734	3119	3608	4109	4893	
Retail sales: volume	PP=100												
FOREIGN INVESTMENT													
Foreign investors	thousands		35.03	46.34	30.00	32.79	36.56	40.78	44.04	45.51	47.15	48.67	
Foreign capital	million US$		902.3	1410.7	776.1	844.3	940.7	1048.1	1301.9	1353.2	1438.3	1549.4	
LABOUR													
Employment[4]													
Total	thousands	6672	6133	5884	6206	6253	6127	5946	5862	5952	5939	5784	
Industry	thousands	3017	2793	2640	2880	2833	2747	2710	2675	2659	2630	2597	
Manufacturing	thousands	2590	2371	2230	2457	2409	2325	2291	2264	2247	2219	2188	
Unemployment													
Total registered	thousands	1047.3	1229.7	1111.3	1265.7	1243.6	1193.1	1216.6	1236.4	1150.1	1061.8	997.0	
Beneficiaries	thousands	548.9	551.7	406.8	618.0	581.1	506.5	501.2	522.0	446.5	356.4	302.3	
Non-beneficiaries	thousands	498.4	678.1	704.5	647.7	662.6	686.7	715.4	714.4	703.6	705.4	694.7	
Unemployment	% of labour force	9.2	11.0	9.9	11.3	11.1	10.6	10.8	11.0	10.2	9.4	8.9	
Job vacancies	units	6060	6149	10833	4471	7127	8123	4874	3571	15014	11277	13467	
WAGES													
Monthly earnings													
Total	thousand lei	59.72	141.95	215.63	106.93	127.93	150.01	175.59	175.82	201.27	226.14	259.28	
Industry	thousand lei	62.39	147.00	221.79	109.82	134.81	158.06	175.24	173.82	207.06	237.27	269.00	
Manufacturing	thousand lei	56.48	131.95	205.92	99.90	122.71	144.40	160.58	160.23	192.10	221.14	250.21	
PRICES													
Producer prices													
Industry	1992=100	244.00	637.40	861.10	504.73	633.38	682.27	729.17	763.91	825.57	895.60	959.30	
Consumer prices													
Total	OCT 90=100	3033	7181	9498	5896	6991	7523	8315	8789	9133	9595	10475	
Food	OCT 90=100	3397	8025	10581	6565	7914	8318	9302	9960	10224	10616	11523	
Goods less food	OCT 90=100	2964	6901	8945	5756	6660	7273	7913	8241	8613	9059	9867	
Services	OCT 90=100	2293	5751	8207	4539	5475	6155	6835	7211	7718	8441	9457	

Footnotes appear at the end of the table.

1995									1996					
Apr	May	Jun	Jul	Aug	Sep	Oct	Nov	Dec	Jan	Feb	Mar			
												PRODUIT NATIONAL[1]		
												Produit intérieur brut	*milliards de lei*	
													milliards de lei PP	
												PRODUCTION INDUSTRIELLE		
62.8	66.9	67.0	64.1	67.3	67.6	71.3	72.2	61.1	61.8	62.7		Total[2]	*1990=100*	
59.9	64.8	65.7	62.2	65.4	65.9	69.8	69.7	57.8	58.5	59.9		Industries manufacturières	*1990=100*	
81.7	87.5	83.9	83.4	87.3	85.3	84.4	84.8	72.6	74.6	75.1		Industries extractives	*1990=100*	
76.9	66.6	63.9	64.2	67.8	68.8	79.3	95.0	96.5	94.9	90.3		Électricité et gaz	*1990=100*	
												Construction	*1985=100*	
												Quantités produites		
3415	3723	3535	3551	3667	3625	3449	3395	2673	2690	2897		Charbon	*milliers de tonnes*	
554	564	594	584	586	562	586	479	423	380	273		Acier brut	*milliers de tonnes*	
762	790	788	788	757	736	669	585	337	144	77		Ciment	*milliers de tonnes*	
552	573	555	569	578	556	576	541	562	555	517		Pétrole brut	*milliers de tonnes*	
1562	1483	1365	1306	1350	1454	1581	1781	1801	1822	1715		Gaz naturel	*millions de m³*	
												ENQUÊTES DE CONJONCTURE - IND. MANUF.		
												État des affaires		
												Tendance	*solde*	
												Carnets de commandes / Demande		
												Total : niveau	*solde*	
												Production		
												Tendance	*solde*	
												Perspectives	*solde*	
												Capacité actuelle	*solde*	
												Stocks		
												Produits finis : niveau	*solde*	
												CONSTRUCTION		
												Logements[3]		
												Mis en chantier	*unités*	
220	414	813	850	462	833	489	748	2865				Achevés	*unités*	
												En cours de construction	*milliers*	
												COMMERCE INTÉRIEUR		
1120	1236	1252	1275	1439	1395	1569	1642	1682	1511	1447		Ventes de détail : valeur	*milliards de lei*	
94	109	100	99	111	95	109	100	99	89	94		Ventes de détail : volume	*PP=100*	
												INVESTISSEMENTS ÉTRANGERS		
45.00	45.50	46.02	46.63	47.14	47.67	48.30	48.64	49.06	49.38	49.75		Investisseurs étrangers	*milliers*	
1350.0	1339.2	1370.5	1399.0	1436.7	1479.1	1521.2	1543.2	1583.8	1619.3	1677.4		Capitaux étrangers	*millions de $É-U*	
												MAIN-D'OEUVRE		
												Emploi[4]		
5925	5965	5967	5993	5930	5893	5862	5783	5707	5648	5638		Total	*milliers*	
2662	2662	2653	2644	2629	2618	2613	2601	2577	2567	2560		Industrie	*milliers*	
2249	2249	2242	2232	2218	2208	2204	2192	2168	2160	2153		Industries manufacturières	*milliers*	
												Chômage		
1183.7	1151.8	1114.7	1085.5	1061.8	1038.0	1007.1	985.5	998.4	1042.2	1055.3		Chômeurs inscrits : total	*milliers*	
472.3	447.6	419.8	397.2	354.3	317.8	293.7	296.1	317.1	368.8	400.5		Allocataires	*milliers*	
711.4	704.3	695.0	688.3	707.5	720.2	713.4	689.4	681.3	673.4	654.8		Non allocataires	*milliers*	
10.5	10.3	9.9	9.7	9.4	9.2	9.0	8.8	8.9	9.3	9.4		Chômage	*% de main-d'oeuvre*	
16264	13600	15178	13187	8034	12611	13885	15075	11442	7842	10064		Offres d'emploi	*unités*	
												SALAIRES		
												Gains mensuels		
199.03	199.70	205.08	218.54	230.34	229.54	242.61	252.22	283.00	256.56	248.88		Total	*milliers de lei*	
204.15	205.65	211.38	225.77	243.50	242.54	254.51	263.64	288.85	258.03	257.49		Industrie	*milliers de lei*	
185.79	192.03	198.47	211.05	225.59	226.78	238.43	248.75	263.46	242.08	241.39		Industries manufacturières	*milliers de lei*	
												PRIX		
												Prix à la production		
801.90	822.30	852.50	880.50	894.60	911.70	933.90	959.80	984.20	1009.40			Industrie	*1992=100*	
												Prix à la consommation		
9028	9125	9245	9483	9575	9727	10074	10484	10868	11000	11207		Total	*OCT 90=100*	
10169	10245	10258	10574	10575	10701	11072	11488	12009	12138	12370		Alimentation	*OCT 90=100*	
8502	8587	8751	8919	9056	9200	9507	9905	10190	10345	10529		Biens sauf alimentation	*OCT 90=100*	
7488	7680	7986	8201	8434	8688	9069	9512	9792	9874	10084		Services	*OCT 90=100*	

Les notes se trouvent en fin de tableau.

ROMANIA (continued)

		1993	1994	1995	1994 Q1	Q2	Q3	Q4	1995 Q1	Q2	Q3	Q4	1996 Q1
DOMESTIC FINANCE													
Money supply (M1)	*billion lei*	2231	4541	7071	2133	2670	3321	4541	4069	4639	5490	7071	
Quasi-money	*billion lei*	2241	6108	11138	3098	3621	4725	6108	7122	8114	9056	11138	
Personal deposits	*billion lei*	646	2727	5143	742	1196	1775	2727	3278	3739	4185	5143	
INTEREST RATES													
Official discount rate	*% p.a. period ave.*	70	66	40	70	70	66	58	49	40	37	33	
FOREIGN FINANCE													
US$ exchange rate end period	*leu/US$*	1276	1767	2578	1650	1677	1756	1767	1847	1975	2128	2578	
US$ exchange rate per. ave.	*leu/US$*	760	1654	2033	1490	1665	1700	1761	1802	1911	2047	2373	
DM exchange rate end period	*leu/DM*	748	1122	1799	983	1064	1135	1122	1340	1423	1492	1799	
ECU exchange rate end period	*leu/ECU*	1446	2134	3299	1895	2035	2170	2134	2441	2619	2762	3299	
Official reserves excluding gold	*million US$*	994	2030	1649	956	1506	1720	2030	1843	1751	1562	1649	
FOREIGN TRADE													
Imports	*billion lei*	5087	11919	19574	2123	2734	2893	4169	3775	4238	5462	6099	
Exports	*billion lei*	3776	10273	15511	1851	2456	2852	3114	2754	3647	4033	5077	
Net trade	*billion lei*	-1311	-1646	-4063	-272	-278	-42	-1055	-1021	-591	-1429	-1022	
GROSS CAPITAL FORMATION[3]													
Total	*billion lei*	1958.5			478.1	934.7	1184.0						
Equipment	*billion lei*	879.8			151.4	285.5	306.6						

For notes concerning these series, refer to *Short-term Economic Indicators: Transition Economies, Sources and Definitions* (April 1996) and the *Methodological Notes* at the end of this publication.

(1) Preliminary estimate for 1995.

(2) A change in the weights used in the calculation of this series was introduced during 1995. There is therefore a break in the series between 1992 and 1993 meaning that the seasonally adjusted series cannot be calculated at this stage.

(3) Public sector only.

(4) Monthly series refer to the end of the month; quarterly series are an average of corresponding months.

	1995									1996					
	Apr	May	Jun	Jul	Aug	Sep	Oct	Nov	Dec	Jan	Feb	Mar			
													FINANCES INTERNES		
	4242	4355	4639	4991	5253	5490	5901	6252	7071	6565			Disponibilités monétaires (M1)		*milliards de lei*
	7263	7683	8114	8362	8826	9056	9365	10402	11138	11593			Quasi-monnaie		*milliards de lei*
	3386	3556	3739	3932	4114	4185	4241	4427	5143	5525			Dépôts personnels		*milliards de lei*
													TAUX D'INTÉRÊT		
	40	40	40	40	35	35	33	33	35	35			Taux d'escompte officiel		*% p.a. moy. période*
													FINANCES EXTÉRIEURES		
	1879	1936	1975	2018	2069	2128	2225	2547	2578	2640	2858		Taux de change du $É-U fin période		*leu/$É-U*
	1865	1911	1956	1994	2046	2100	2166	2395	2558	2599	2774		Taux de change du $É-U moy. pér.		*leu/$É-U*
	1364	1395	1423	1455	1409	1492	1592	1779	1799	1777	1966		Taux de change du DM fin pér.		*leu/DM*
	2502	2571	2619	2700	2637	2762	2916	3291	3299	3245	3630		Taux de change de l'ECU fin pér.		*leu/ECU*
	1764	1686	1751	1657	1562	1562	1481	1553	1649	1497	1455		Réserves officielles or exclu		*millions de $É-U*
													COMMERCE EXTÉRIEUR		
	1480	1428	1329	1944	1613	1905	1876	1974	2250	1038	1249		Importations		*milliards de lei*
	1175	1162	1310	1180	1352	1501	1527	1665	1885	1035	1309		Exportations		*milliards de lei*
	-305	-266	-20	-765	-261	-404	-349	-309	-365	-3	60		Solde commercial		*milliards de lei*
													FORMATION BRUTE DE CAPITAL[3]		
													Total		*milliards de lei*
													Équipements		*milliards de lei*

Pour les notes sur ces séries, veuillez consulter *Indicateurs économiques à court terme : Economies en transition, Sources et définitions* (avril 1996) et les *Notes méthodologiques* à la fin de cette publication.

(1) Estimation préliminaire pour 1995.

(2) Un changement des poids utilisés dans le calcul de cette série a été introduit pendant l'année 1995. La rupture de série résultante entre 1992 et 1993 fait en sorte que le calcul de la série corrigée des variations saisonnières n'est plus possible.

(3) Secteur public uniquement.

(4) Fin de période pour les séries mensuelles ; moyenne mensuelle pour les séries trimestrielles.

SLOVAK REPUBLIC

					1994				1995				1996
		1993	1994	1995	Q1	Q2	Q3	Q4	Q1	Q2	Q3	Q4	Q1
NATIONAL PRODUCT[1]													
Gross domestic product	bln slk koruny	369.9	441.3	518.0									
	bln slk koruny 1993	369.9	388.0										
INDUSTRIAL PRODUCTION													
Total	1990=100	70.3	73.6	79.7	70.4	73.9	71.4	78.8	74.4	80.9	78.2	85.5	
Total[2]　　　　sa	1990=100	70.6	74.4	75.1	74.4	74.9	81.1	81.7	81.4				
Commodity output													
Brown coal	thousand tonnes	3488			919	791							
Crude steel	thousand tonnes	3924	3973	3893	1024	1006	969	974	1057	967	1062	807	
Cement	thousand tonnes	2656	2879	2982	385	940	923	631	437	980	943	622	
Crude petroleum	thousand tonnes	67	67	74	16	17	17	17	19	18	19	19	
Natural gas	million m³	263.6	287.8	348.8	77.3	54.3	61.4	94.7	111.2	76.0	65.6	96.0	
Passenger cars	units	5084	8339	22307	1991	1846	1633	2869	3201	5499	5438	8169	
BUSINESS SURVEYS - MANUFACT.[3]													
Business situation													
Tendency	balance				-2	5	-2	-1	-1	15	-1	-6	6
Order books / Demand													
Total: tendency[4]	balance				-2	13	-6	20	-9	11	-5	-14	-18
Export: tendency	balance				28	4	-3	17	5	6	-5	-12	-14
Production													
Tendency	balance				14	1	-2	39	12	7	-13	-6	26
Future tendency	balance				34	15	35	44	67	20	43	26	57
Rate of capacity utilisation	%				77	78	76	77	74	75	74	76	78
Stocks													
Finished goods: level	balance				37	34	37	33	20	22	25	25	34
CONSTRUCTION													
Dwellings[5]													
Started	units	4387											
Completed	units	14146	6709			2971		3738					
DOMESTIC TRADE													
Retail sales: value	bln slk koruny	202.1	233.8	279.7	49.7	54.5	62.2	67.5	57.4	69.7	72.1	80.5	
Retail sales: volume[2]	1993=100	100.0	102.0	111.1	90.0	97.3	107.9	112.6	93.3	112.3	114.0	124.8	
Retail sales: volume[2]　sa	1993=100				100.8	97.0	104.5	105.3	105.1	111.8	110.1	116.3	
LABOUR													
Employment													
Total	thousands	2012	1977	2020	1950	1979	2002	1976	1987	2027	2043	2023	
Industry	thousands	611	597	621	590	593	603	600	611	618	625	629	
Unemployment													
Total	thousands	327.7	366.3	348.2	375.2	358.4	366.8	364.8	381.2	344.0	339.3	328.4	
Beneficiaries	thousands	113.9	89.6	76.8	109.2	80.5	85.1	83.5	81.1	61.1	79.5	85.5	
Non-beneficiaries	thousands	213.8	276.7	271.4	266.0	277.9	281.8	281.3	300.1	282.9	259.9	242.8	
Unemployment	% of labour force	12.9	14.6	13.8	15.0	14.3	14.6	14.6	15.0	13.5	13.4	12.9	
Job vacancies	units	10617	11077	15563	8518	10471	12046	13272	13402	15257	17413	16179	
Private enterprises													
Entrepreneurs registered	thousands	288	280		279	278	281	283	288	286	278		
Time worked													
Working days per period	units	256	251	249	63	63	62	63	64	62	61	62	
WAGES													
Monthly earnings													
Total	slk koruny	5379	6294	7195	5593	6138	6315	7124	6374	7014	7170	8204	
PRICES													
Producer prices													
Industry	1990=100	208.4	229.3	249.9	219.5	221.4	240.7	235.6	244.5	249.0	252.1	254.1	
Consumer prices													
Total	1990=100	218.2	247.8	272.3	238.9	242.5	249.8	259.8	266.3	269.1	274.2	279.4	
Food	1990=100	191.0	222.0	248.6	209.3	212.1	224.7	242.1	245.7	243.4	248.5	256.6	
Catering	1990=100	224.2	253.6	283.1	244.1	247.8	254.5	268.0	277.1	279.8	285.7	289.7	
Goods less food	1990=100	235.2	265.2	287.9	258.2	262.6	267.4	272.6	280.4	286.2	290.2	294.8	
Services	1990=100	218.2	241.8	263.7	235.8	239.2	242.7	249.4	256.1	260.1	268.5	270.1	

Footnotes appear at the end of the table.

1995 Apr	May	Jun	Jul	Aug	Sep	Oct	Nov	Dec	1996 Jan	Feb	Mar			
												PRODUIT NATIONAL[1]		
												Produit intérieur brut		*mrd couronnes slk*
														mrd cour. slk 1993
												PRODUCTION INDUSTRIELLE		
75.9	83.6	83.3	72.4	80.0	82.2	87.6	89.1	79.7	81.1	80.0		Total		*1990=100*
78.8	82.8	81.6	81.2	82.3	81.7	84.1	82.0	78.2	82.9	84.2		Total[2]	*cvs*	*1990=100*
												Quantités produites		
360	326	281	380	354	328	300	304	203	285			Lignite		*milliers de tonnes*
336	346	298	334	301	308	283	196	143	46			Acier brut		*milliers de tonnes*
												Ciment		*milliers de tonnes*
6	5	7	6	6	6	7	7	5	5			Pétrole brut		*milliers de tonnes*
25.4	27.2	23.5	22.3	23.3	20.0	32.6	32.8	30.6	22.2			Gaz naturel		*millions de m³*
1552	1694	2253	1211	2103	2124	2477	2958	2734	2793			Voitures particulières		*unités*
												ENQUÊTES DE CONJONCTURE - IND. MANUF.[3]		
												État des affaires		
19	14	13	-2	-2	2	-3	-7	-8	6	8	3	Tendance		*solde*
												Carnets de commandes / Demande		
17	11	4	-8	-8	2	-4	-12	-26	-21	-15	-19	Total : tendance[4]		*solde*
5	10	2	-12	-4	1	-6	-13	-16	-17	-11	-14	Exportations : tendance		*solde*
												Production		
-35	66	-9	-63	14	11	26	3	-46	28	13	38	Tendance		*solde*
77	-18	2	39	22	68	34	13	32	50	56	64	Perspectives		*solde*
74	75	75	72	75	76	76	76	76	78	78	79	Taux d'utilisation des capacités		*%*
												Stocks		
8	24	33	31	18	27	29	23	22	39	46	17	Produits finis : niveau		*solde*
												CONSTRUCTION		
												Logements[5]		
												Mis en chantier		*unités*
												Achevés		*unités*
												COMMERCE INTÉRIEUR		
22.4	23.4	23.9	23.5	24.3	24.3	24.4	24.5	31.6	21.1	22.2		Ventes de détail : valeur		*mrd couronnes slk*
108.4	113.1	115.4	112.3	115.5	114.1	113.8	114.1	146.6	97.4	102.2		Ventes de détail : volume[2]		*1993=100*
108.8	113.2	113.4	107.6	110.0	112.7	108.3	111.7	128.8	116.2	113.0		Ventes de détail : volume[2]	*cvs*	*1993=100*
												MAIN-D'OEUVRE		
												Emploi		
												Total		*milliers*
618	618	619	623	625	628	631	630	626	621	620		Industrie		*milliers*
												Chômage		
354.1	338.9	339.1	343.1	338.8	336.1	325.5	326.3	333.3	352.6	352.1		Total		*milliers*
64.0	57.9	61.4	75.6	78.4	84.4	82.5	84.2	89.9	99.2	95.2		Allocataires		*milliers*
290.1	281.0	277.7	267.5	260.4	251.7	243.0	242.1	243.4	253.4	256.9		Non allocataires		*milliers*
13.9	13.3	13.3	13.5	13.3	13.2	12.8	12.8	13.1	13.7	13.7		Chômage		*% de main-d'oeuvre*
14194	14584	16993	18638	17273	16328	16902	16162	15473	16512	16480		Offres d'emploi		*unités*
												Entreprises privées		
287	286	284	279	277	277	276						Entrepreneurs inscrits		*milliers*
												Temps travaillé		
18	22	22	20	22	19	22	21	19	22	21		Jours ouvrables		*unités*
												SALAIRES		
												Gains mensuels		
												Total		*couronnes slk*
												PRIX		
												Prix à la production		
248.0	249.1	249.8	250.6	252.0	253.7	254.8	253.8	253.6	253.0	256.7		Industrie		*1990=100*
												Prix à la consommation		
268.4	269.3	269.5	272.2	273.4	277.1	278.5	279.5	280.2	282.2	282.9		Total		*1990=100*
244.2	244.7	241.3	244.0	246.4	255.1	256.2	256.5	257.0	256.2	254.9		Alimentation		*1990=100*
278.7	279.7	281.0	284.4	285.4	287.4	288.7	289.8	290.6	291.2	293.3		Restauration		*1990=100*
284.5	286.0	288.1	289.0	290.0	291.6	293.4	294.9	296.0	300.1	301.5		Biens sauf alimentation		*1990=100*
259.5	259.9	261.0	267.9	268.3	269.2	269.8	270.0	270.4	272.5	274.3		Services		*1990=100*

Les notes se trouvent en fin de tableau.

SLOVAK REPUBLIC (continued)

		1993	1994	1995	1994 Q1	Q2	Q3	Q4	1995 Q1	Q2	Q3	Q4	1996 Q1
DOMESTIC FINANCE													
Money supply (M1)	bln slk koruny	116.3	128.9	148.4	100.3	105.9	115.2	128.9	114.6	121.2	130.7	148.4	
Quasi-money	bln slk koruny	136.9	171.5	208.7	141.0	147.1	150.9	171.5	177.4	182.1	187.4	208.7	
Personal deposits	bln slk koruny	113.4	129.5	163.1	112.1	113.2	114.7	129.5	133.9	139.0	143.4	163.1	
INTEREST RATES													
Official discount rate	% p.a. end period	12.0	12.0	9.8	12.0	12.0	12.0	12.0	12.0	11.0	11.0	9.8	
FOREIGN FINANCE													
US$ exchange rate end period	slk koruny/US$	33.20	31.28	29.57	32.64	31.58	31.22	31.28	28.99	29.35	29.54	29.57	
US$ exchange rate per. ave.	slk koruny/US$	30.77	32.05	29.74	33.18	32.47	31.40	31.14	30.33	29.32	29.74	29.55	
FOREIGN TRADE[6]													
Imports	bln slk koruny	195.0	211.8	252.3	50.5	50.0	51.8	59.6	59.2	65.8	60.0	67.3	
Exports	bln slk koruny	167.7	214.4	254.1	47.3	54.2	52.3	60.6	59.5	65.4	63.1	66.0	
Net trade	bln slk koruny	-27.3	2.6	1.8	-3.1	4.1	0.5	1.1	0.3	-0.4	3.2	-1.3	
GROSS CAPITAL FORMATION													
Total	bln slk koruny	115.91	124.76	149.67	20.39	26.62	29.36	48.39	24.12	32.64	34.73	58.18	
Machinery and equipment	bln slk koruny	55.31	54.81	73.15	9.26	11.88	12.58	21.09	11.75	15.64	17.13	28.63	
Construction	bln slk koruny	52.26	54.98	68.11	8.70	11.59	13.30	21.40	10.95	15.32	15.81	26.02	
Other capital formation	bln slk koruny	6.28	11.66	5.17	1.94	2.59	2.81	4.33	0.92	1.11	1.19	1.95	

For notes concerning these series, refer to *Short-term Economic Indicators: Transition Economies, Sources and Definitions* (April 1996) and the *Methodological Notes* at the end of this publication.

(1) Preliminary estimate for 1995.

(2) This series has been estimated by the OECD Secretariat.

(3) Prior to January 1995, total Industry; afterward, manufacturing sector only.

(4) Prior to January 1995, refers to domestic demand only.

(5) First quarter figures are included in the second quarter and third quarter figures are included in the fourth quarter.

(6) Includes trade with the Czech Republic.

OECD
OCDE
SHORT-TERM ECONOMIC INDICATORS
OECD/CCET © April 1996

68

INDICATEURS ÉCONOMIQUES À COURT TERME
OCDE/CCET © avril 1996

1995									1996					
Apr	May	Jun	Jul	Aug	Sep	Oct	Nov	Dec	Jan	Feb	Mar			
												FINANCES INTERNES		
119.2	119.6	121.2	123.9	126.8	130.7	130.0	134.1	148.4	137.4			Disponibilités monétaires (M1)	*mrd couronnes slk*	
177.5	179.1	182.1	184.2	188.4	187.4	189.7	191.9	208.7	212.4			Quasi-monnaie	*mrd couronnes slk*	
135.5	137.1	139.0	140.7	142.0	143.4	145.5	148.1	163.1	167.1			Dépôts personnels	*mrd couronnes slk*	
												TAUX D'INTÉRÊT		
11.0	11.0	11.0	11.0	11.0	11.0	9.8	9.8	9.8	8.8	8.8		Taux d'escompte officiel	*% p.a. fin période*	
												FINANCES EXTÉRIEURES		
28.96	29.27	29.35	29.19	30.34	29.54	29.44	29.71	29.57	30.20	29.86		Taux de change du $É-U fin période	*couronne slk/$É-U*	
29.04	29.50	29.43	29.25	29.86	30.13	29.49	29.45	29.71	29.90	29.99		Taux de change du $É-U moy. pér.	*couronne slk/$É-U*	
												COMMERCE EXTÉRIEUR[6]		
19.2	23.1	23.5	19.3	19.7	20.9	22.7	23.3	21.4	21.3	29.9		Importations	*mrd couronnes slk*	
21.3	21.9	22.2	19.5	21.3	22.3	23.3	23.2	19.5	21.3	19.4		Exportations	*mrd couronnes slk*	
2.1	-1.2	-1.3	0.2	1.6	1.3	0.6	-0.1	-1.8	0.0	-10.5		Solde commercial	*mrd couronnes slk*	
												FORMATION BRUTE DE CAPITAL		
												Total	*mrd couronnes slk*	
												Machines et équipements	*mrd couronnes slk*	
												Construction	*mrd couronnes slk*	
												Autre formation de capital	*mrd couronnes slk*	

Pour les notes sur ces séries, veuillez consulter *Indicateurs économiques à court terme : Economies en transition, Sources et définitions* (avril 1996) et les *Notes méthodologiques* à la fin de cette publication.

(1) Estimation préliminaire pour 1995.

(2) Cette série a été estimée par le Secrétariat de l'OCDE.

(3) Avant janvier 1995, secteur de l'industrie; ensuite, secteur manufacturier seulement.

(4) Avant janvier 1995, se réfère uniquement à la demande intérieure.

(5) Les données du deuxième trimestre comprennent les données du premier trimestre; celles du quatrième trimestre comprennent les données du troisième trimestre.

(6) Inclut les échanges avec la République tchèque.

NEW INDEPENDENT STATES

INDICATORS BY COUNTRY

—

NOUVEAUX ÉTATS INDÉPENDANTS

INDICATEURS PAR PAYS

ARMENIA

					1994				1995				1996
		1993	1994	1995	Q1	Q2	Q3	Q4	Q1	Q2	Q3	Q4	Q1
INDUSTRIAL PRODUCTION													
Total[1]	*1990=100*	42.9	45.9	47.0									
Manufacturing	*1990=100*	42.6											
Mining	*1990=100*	22.1											
Commodity output													
Cement	*thousand tonnes*	198	128	228	4	47	43	34	16	92	96	25	
Electricity	*bln kilowatt hours*	6.3	5.7	5.6	1.4	1.5	1.4	1.4	1.4	1.3	1.4	1.5	
Metal cutting machines	*units*	1600	742	432	107	227	269	139	46	129	153	104	
CONSTRUCTION													
Dwellings													
Completed: total	*thousands*	4.3	4.4	3.3	0.0	0.8	0.8	2.8	0.1	0.8	0.9	1.5	
Completed: area	*thousand m²*	370	262	285	3	67	68	124	12	70	74	129	
DOMESTIC TRADE													
Retail sales: value	*million roubles*	94767											
	million dram		13273	44005	726	2718	3809	5718	7674	9996	10490	15846	
Retail sales value: total[2]	*million dram*			220025					30697	39984	70117	79227	
Retail sales: volume	*1990=100*	11.9	7.5	9.5	4.4	6.7	7.5	9.4	5.9	7.7	8.7	13.5	
LABOUR													
Employment													
Total	*thousands*	1543	1500	1465	1500	1510	1490	1500	1480	1490	1470	1420	
Industry	*thousands*	362	340	330	340	355	335	329	325	335	330	330	
Manufacturing	*thousands*	263	248	240									
Unemployment													
Total registered	*thousands*	86.9	105.4	105.5	106.4	111.3	110.4	93.6	84.1	95.3	113.8	128.6	
Beneficiaries	*thousands*	38.7	21.9	42.3	29.1	23.3	16.6	18.6	33.1	46.0	47.5	42.4	
Non-beneficiaries	*thousands*	48.2	83.5	63.2	77.3	88.0	93.8	75.1	51.0	49.3	66.4	86.2	
Unemployment	*% of labour force*	5.2	6.4	6.6	6.5	6.8	6.7	5.7	5.3	6.0	7.1	7.9	
WAGES													
Monthly earnings													
Total	*roubles*	12169											
	dram		1738	6500	354	1065	2067	3466	4691	6160	7151	7998	
Industry	*roubles*	14330											
	dram		2963	8705	640	2119	3707	5387	6669	8225	9426	10500	
Manufacturing	*roubles*	13600											
	dram		2900	8600									
PRICES													
Consumer prices[3]													
Total	*PP=100*	1922.9	5062.3	276.0									
Food	*PP=100*	1216.3	4325.5	290.5									
Goods less food	*PP=100*	961.4	6675.5	174.5									
Total goods	*PP=100*	1112.0	4676.5	262.1									
Services	*PP=100*	2400.5	11677.3	411.2									
DOMESTIC FINANCE													
Personal deposits	*million roubles*	30268											
	million dram		546.4	1086.5	205.2	331.4	432.7	546.4	651.4	822.6	953.9	1086.5	
FOREIGN FINANCE													
US$ exchange rate end period	*dram/US$*	75	406	402	228	309	349	406	406	408	406	402	
Rouble exchange rate end period	*dram/rouble*	0.059	0.107	0.084	0.130	0.160	0.145	0.107	0.080	0.087	0.088	0.084	
Rouble exchange rate per. ave.	*dram/rouble*		0.129	0.086	0.087	0.161	0.152	0.117	0.088	0.081	0.090	0.086	
FOREIGN TRADE													
Imports													
Total	*million US$*		393.8	661.1	52.0	111.5	92.9	137.4	144.0	120.8	175.5	220.8	
from countries other than NIS	*million US$*	86.3	188.3	334.0	24.8	53.1	44.5	65.9	65.1	65.3	91.7	111.9	
from NIS	*million US$*		205.5	327.1	27.2	58.4	48.4	71.5	78.9	55.5	83.8	108.9	
Exports													
Total	*million US$*		215.5	247.5	30.0	57.9	51.9	75.7	36.9	51.5	84.7	74.4	
to countries other than NIS	*million US$*	29.7	57.6	102.6	8.0	15.4	13.9	20.3	14.0	17.6	29.3	41.7	
to NIS	*million US$*		157.9	144.9	22.0	42.5	38.0	55.4	22.9	33.9	55.4	32.7	
Net trade													
Total	*million US$*		-178.3	-413.6	-22.0	-53.6	-41.0	-61.7	-107.1	-69.3	-90.8	-146.4	
with countries other than NIS	*million US$*	-56.6	-130.7	-231.4	-16.8	-37.7	-30.6	-45.6	-51.1	-47.7	-62.4	-70.2	
with NIS	*million US$*		-47.6	-182.2	-5.2	-15.9	-10.4	-16.1	-56.0	-21.6	-28.4	-76.2	

Footnotes appear at the end of the table.

ARMÉNIE

1995									1996				
Apr	May	Jun	Jul	Aug	Sep	Oct	Nov	Dec	Jan	Feb	Mar		
												PRODUCTION INDUSTRIELLE	
												Total[1]	*1990=100*
												Industries manufacturières	*1990=100*
												Industries extractives	*1990=100*
												Quantités produites	
27	25	40	40	31	25	10	11	4	3			Ciment	*milliers de tonnes*
0.5	0.4	0.4	0.5	0.4	0.5	0.4	0.4	0.7	0.7	0.6		Électricité	*mrd kw-heures*
52	31	46	46	61	46	43	24	37				Machines à usiner les métaux	*unités*
												CONSTRUCTION	
												Logements	
												Achevés : total	*milliers*
												Achevés : surface	*milliers de m²*
												COMMERCE INTÉRIEUR	
2903	2992	3913	3667	3417	3348	6229	4847	4701	3612			Ventes de détail : valeur	*millions de roubles*
													millions de dram
11976	11076	15631	15034	22651	26907	31018	24703	23506	13507			Ventes de détail en valeur : total[2]	*millions de dram*
7.4	9.4	7.5	10.0	10.4	6.1	15.6	9.2	13.3	5.5			Ventes de détail : volume	*1990=100*
												MAIN-D'OEUVRE	
												Emploi	
												Total	*milliers*
												Industrie	*milliers*
												Industries manufacturières	*milliers*
												Chômage	
90.8	92.7	102.5	108.6	113.4	119.5	124.6	129.6	131.6	133.3	137.4		Chômeurs inscrits : total	*milliers*
39.2	50.9	47.9	48.8	48.1	45.5	43.3	42.4	41.6	39.2	41.4		Allocataires	*milliers*
51.6	41.8	54.6	59.8	65.3	74.0	81.3	87.2	90.0	94.1	96.0		Non allocataires	*milliers*
5.7	5.8	6.4	6.8	7.0	7.4	7.7	8.0	8.1	8.3	8.6		Chômage	*% de main-d'oeuvre*
												SALAIRES	
												Gains mensuels	
												Total	*roubles*
													dram
												Industrie	*roubles*
													dram
												Industries manufacturières	*roubles*
													dram
												PRIX	
												Prix à la consommation[3]	
107.1	107.8	100.6	95.4	97.9	99.9	104.1	102.7	107.6	103.6	103.4		Total	*PP=100*
107.8	109.0	99.7	93.5	96.4	99.0	102.5	103.1	107.9	105.5	104.8		Alimentation	*PP=100*
101.3	101.7	100.4	99.8	100.7	101.1	103.0	102.3	101.0	98.7	100.4		Biens sauf alimentation	*PP=100*
105.9	107.3	99.7	94.6	97.5	99.6	102.8	103.1	106.3	103.9	103.7		Biens : total	*PP=100*
118.7	112.0	108.2	101.9	101.1	102.4	112.7	100.4	115.7	101.8	101.2		Services	*PP=100*
												FINANCES INTERNES	
												Dépôts personnels	*millions de roubles*
718.3	800.0	822.6	920.9	905.4	953.9	1025.3	1024.2	1086.5					*millions de dram*
												FINANCES EXTÉRIEURES	
408	409	408	409	408	406	401	403	402	402	403		Taux de change du $É-U fin période	*dram/$É-U*
0.079	0.080	0.087	0.090	0.092	0.088	0.086	0.088	0.084	0.083	0.081		Taux de change du rouble fin pér.	*dram/rouble*
0.079	0.080	0.084	0.089	0.092	0.090	0.087	0.087	0.085	0.084	0.082		Taux de change du rouble moy. pér.	*dram/rouble*
												COMMERCE EXTÉRIEUR	
												Importations	
38.5	38.3	44.0	65.0	53.9	56.6	73.6	76.7	70.5				Total	*millions de $É-U*
22.4	18.0	24.9	34.0	24.6	33.1	37.3	35.5	39.1				depuis autres que les NEI	*millions de $É-U*
16.1	20.3	19.1	31.0	29.3	23.5	36.3	41.2	31.4				depuis les NEI	*millions de $É-U*
												Exportations	
12.5	16.4	22.6	28.4	29.2	27.1	24.8	22.0	27.6				Total	*millions de $É-U*
4.1	4.5	9.0	13.0	8.3	8.0	13.9	13.2	14.6				vers autres que les NEI	*millions de $É-U*
8.4	11.9	13.6	15.4	20.9	19.1	10.9	8.8	13.0				vers les NEI	*millions de $É-U*
												Solde commercial	
-26.0	-21.9	-21.4	-36.6	-24.7	-29.5	-48.8	-54.7	-42.9				Total	*millions de $É-U*
-18.3	-13.5	-15.9	-21.0	-16.3	-25.1	-23.4	-22.3	-24.5				avec autres que les NEI	*millions de $É-U*
-7.7	-8.4	-5.5	-15.6	-8.4	-4.4	-25.4	-32.4	-18.4				avec les NEI	*millions de $É-U*

Les notes se trouvent en fin de tableau.

ARMENIA *(continued)*

		1993	1994	1995	1994				1995				1996
					Q1	Q2	Q3	Q4	Q1	Q2	Q3	Q4	Q1
GROSS CAPITAL FORMATION													
Total	*million roubles*	72290											
	million dram		16791	32829	108	3094	4275	9314	2746	5692	11396	12995	
Total: volume	*1990=100*	4.0	3.0										
Construction and installation	*million roubles*	53820											
	million dram		11285	29193	74	2192	2681	6339	2348	4947	10204	11694	

A new currency, the dram, was introduced on the 22nd November 1993.

For notes concerning these series, refer to *Short-term Economic Indicators: Transition Economies, Sources and Definitions* (April 1996) and the *Methodological Notes* at the end of this publication.

(1) The sub-annual indices previously published are currently being assessed by the OECD Secretariat: for further information see the industrial production subject table in the "Recent trends" section.

(2) Total retail sales including estimates of sales by non registered enterprises and private persons in informal markets.

(3) Laspeyres index from January 1993; new consumer price index from January 1994.

1995									1996					
Apr	May	Jun	Jul	Aug	Sep	Oct	Nov	Dec	Jan	Feb	Mar			

FORMATION BRUTE DE CAPITAL
Total — *millions de roubles* / *millions de dram*
Total : volume — *1990=100*
Construction et installation — *millions de roubles* / *millions de dram*

Une nouvelle monnaie, le dram, a été introduite le 22 novembre 1993.

Pour les notes sur ces séries, veuillez consulter *Indicateurs économiques à court terme : Economies en transition, Sources et définitions* (avril 1996) et les *Notes méthodologiques* à la fin de cette publication.

(1) Les indices mensuels et trimestriels précédemment publiés sont actuellement examinés par le Secrétariat de l'OCDE: pour plus de détails, voir le tableau sujet sur la production industrielle dans la partie "Tendances récentes".

(2) Ventes de détail totales, comprenant les ventes effectuées par les entreprises non inscrites au registre du commerce et par les personnes privées sur les marchés informels.

(3) Indice de Laspeyres à partir de janvier 1993; nouvel indice des prix à la consommation depuis janvier 1994.

AZERBAIJAN

		1993	1994	1995	1994 Q1	Q2	Q3	Q4	1995 Q1	Q2	Q3	Q4	1996 Q1
INDUSTRIAL PRODUCTION													
Total[1]	1990=100	74.4	57.5	45.2									
Manufacturing	1990=100	72.6	54.3										
Mining	1990=100	79.00	70.10										
Commodity output													
Crude steel	thousand tonnes	236.0	40.1	19.7	10.1	11.1	12.3	6.3	6.1	5.7	4.8	3.1	
Cement	thousand tonnes	622	467	192	132	138	80	65	20	52	70	50	
Electricity	bln kilowatt hours	19.0	17.5	17.0	5.1	4.1	3.6	4.7	5.1	3.9	3.3	4.7	
Mineral fertiliser	million tonnes	32.3	5.0	1.7	1.3	1.9	0.7	0.7	0.1	0.3	0.7	0.6	
Refrigerators	thousands	229.2	96.9	25.2	47.5	29.0	10.3	10.1	8.4	8.6	4.8	3.4	
CONSTRUCTION													
Dwellings													
Completed: total	thousands	15.9	9.3	4.6	1.5	2.2	1.9	3.7	0.6	0.8	1.5	1.7	
Completed: area	thousand m²	1430	779	437	126	189	173	292	54	86	118	179	
DOMESTIC TRADE													
Retail sales: value	billion roubles	252.4											
	billion manat		206.2	1042.9	16.2	28.0	53.9	108.0	174.7	220.2	283.7	364.3	
Retail sales value: total[2]	billion manat			4666.7					777.9	1011.2	1296.2	1581.5	
Retail sales: volume	1990=100	15.1	7.4	6.7	11.0	7.8	9.4	7.2	7.5	6.3	7.5	7.2	
LABOUR													
Employment													
Total	thousands	2710	2587	2600	2603	2621	2577	2548	2610	2630	2590	2570	
Industry	thousands	392	374	375	370	364	375	387	370	365	375	390	
Manufacturing	thousands	340	330	330									
Unemployment													
Total registered	thousands	13.0	22.4	26.4	20.8	22.1	23.0	23.7	24.5	26.0	27.3	27.8	
Beneficiaries	thousands	5.9	4.1	4.2	4.8	4.6	3.6	3.4	4.1	5.0	4.4	3.6	
Non-beneficiaries	thousands	7.1	18.3	22.2	16.0	17.5	19.4	20.4	20.5	21.0	22.9	24.3	
Unemployment	% of labour force	0.48	0.83	0.99	0.77	0.80	0.83	0.90	0.87	0.97	1.03	1.10	
WAGES													
Monthly earnings													
Total	roubles	20225											
	manat		15365	58703	5919	9053	14822	31667	43320	55582	62423	73487	
Industry	roubles	28019											
	manat		21009	99668	7911	11116	20237	44772	68129	101251	102777	126515	
Manufacturing	roubles	27000											
	manat		18932	89700									
PRICES													
Consumer prices[3]													
Total	PP=100	1080.9	1763.3	511.8									
Food	PP=100	1131.0	1793.3	522.4									
Goods less food	PP=100	907.8	1185.8	408.0									
Total goods[4]	PP=100	1023.3	1674.5	502.0									
Services	PP=100	1479.5	3353.7	601.3									
DOMESTIC FINANCE													
Personal deposits	million roubles	49698											
	billion manat		37.1	61.0	6.4	8.9	21.5	37.1	70.0	77.7	78.9	61.0	
FOREIGN FINANCE													
US$ exchange rate end period	rouble/US$	1247											
	manat/US$		4182	4440	174	1000	1650	4182	4380	4453	4435	4440	
Rouble exchange rate end period	manat/rouble		1.210	0.950	0.100	0.516	0.710	1.210	0.900	0.990	0.990	0.950	
Rouble exchange rate per. ave.	manat/rouble		0.448	0.974	0.084	0.242	0.543	0.923	1.037	0.883	1.000	0.977	

Footnotes appear at the end of the table.

 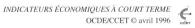

1995									1996		
Apr	May	Jun	Jul	Aug	Sep	Oct	Nov	Dec	Jan	Feb	Mar
												PRODUCTION INDUSTRIELLE
												Total[1]	1990=100
												Industries manufacturières	1990=100
												Industries extractives	1990=100
												Quantités produites
3.5	0.5	1.7	0.2	2.0	2.6	2.2	0.5	0.4	0.1	0.1		Acier brut	milliers de tonnes
11	21	19	22	29	20	20	20	10	9	10		Ciment	milliers de tonnes
1.5	1.3	1.1	1.1	1.1	1.1	1.4	1.6	1.7	1.8	1.6		Électricité	mrd kw-heures
0.0	0.1	0.2	0.2	0.3	0.2	0.2	0.2	0.2	0.2	0.1		Engrais minéral	millions de tonnes
5.1	1.3	2.2	0.7	3.4	0.7	0.0	2.3	1.1	0.0			Réfrigérateurs	milliers
												CONSTRUCTION
												Logements
												Achevés : total	milliers
												Achevés : surface	milliers de m²
												COMMERCE INTÉRIEUR
												Ventes de détail : valeur	milliards de roubles
69.3	72.1	78.7	86.0	90.3	88.6	98.9	101.6	105.3	90.5	93.7			milliards de manat
304.5	317.2	389.4	417.8	460.4	399.7	499.0	577.6	460.6	430.9	441.8		Ventes de détail en valeur : total[2]	milliards de manat
7.5	6.8	6.4	6.5	8.2	7.0	7.3	6.0	7.5	7.4			Ventes de détail : volume	1990=100
												MAIN-D'OEUVRE
												Emploi
												Total	milliers
												Industrie	milliers
												Industries manufacturières	milliers
												Chômage
25.4	26.0	26.5	26.9	27.3	27.6	27.5	27.7	28.3	28.1	28.7		Chômeurs inscrits : total	milliers
4.6	5.0	5.3	5.3	4.1	3.7	3.5	3.2	4.0	2.8	3.0		Allocataires	milliers
20.8	21.0	21.2	21.6	23.2	23.9	24.0	24.5	24.3	25.3	25.7		Non allocataires	milliers
0.90	1.00	1.00	1.00	1.00	1.10	1.10	1.10	1.10	1.10	1.10		Chômage	% de main-d'oeuvre
												SALAIRES
												Gains mensuels
												Total	roubles
													manat
												Industrie	roubles
													manat
												Industries manufacturières	roubles
													manat
												PRIX
												Prix à la consommation[3]
105.6	104.1	99.4	99.7	100.2	105.4	101.4	102.5	104.7	102.1	103.1		Total	PP=100
105.9	104.7	98.4	98.7	98.8	106.0	101.6	103.0	106.1	102.7	103.7		Alimentation	PP=100
105.1	102.3	103.0	103.5	103.0	102.3	101.4	101.0	100.6	100.1	100.1		Biens sauf alimentation	PP=100
105.8	104.4	99.1	99.4	99.4	105.4	101.5	102.7	105.3	102.3	103.1		Biens : total[4]	PP=100
104.6	102.1	101.6	102.4	106.0	105.2	100.6	100.9	100.1	100.2	103.0		Services	PP=100
												FINANCES INTERNES
												Dépôts personnels	millions de roubles
72.5	75.9	77.7	78.0	77.5	78.9	71.9	64.2	61.0					milliards de manat
												FINANCES EXTÉRIEURES
												Taux de change du $É-U fin période	rouble/$É-U
4405	4426	4453	4487	4486	4435	4440	4440	4440	4445	4438			manat/$É-U
0.870	0.880	0.990	0.990	1.010	0.990	0.990	0.970	0.950	0.950	0.920		Taux de change du rouble fin pér.	manat/rouble
0.880	0.860	0.910	0.980	1.020	1.000	0.990	0.980	0.960	0.950	0.930		Taux de change du rouble moy. pér.	manat/rouble

Les notes se trouvent en fin de tableau.

AZERBAIJAN (continued)

		1993	1994	1995	1994 Q1	Q2	Q3	Q4	1995 Q1	Q2	Q3	Q4	1996 Q1
FOREIGN TRADE													
Imports													
Total	million US$		777.9	667.7	268.8	209.3	181.1	118.7	140.7	124.9	160.2	241.9	
from countries other than NIS	million US$	241.0	292.1	439.4	90.9	70.0	76.6	54.6	80.0	90.6	111.7	157.1	
from NIS	million US$		485.8	228.3	177.9	139.3	104.5	64.1	60.7	34.3	48.5	84.8	
Exports													
Total	million US$		636.8	547.4	152.8	184.7	176.4	122.9	88.5	113.0	168.8	177.1	
to countries other than NIS	million US$	350.9	362.6	329.8	76.0	105.6	102.1	78.9	56.2	83.0	112.0	78.6	
to NIS	million US$		274.2	217.6	76.8	79.1	74.3	44.0	32.3	30.0	56.8	98.5	
Net trade													
Total	million US$		-141.1	-120.3	-116.0	-24.6	-4.7	4.2	-52.2	-11.9	8.6	-64.8	
with countries other than NIS	million US$	109.9	70.5	-109.6	-14.9	35.6	25.5	24.3	-23.8	-7.6	0.3	-78.5	
with NIS	million US$		-211.6	-10.7	-101.1	-60.2	-30.2	-20.1	-28.4	-4.3	8.3	13.7	
GROSS CAPITAL FORMATION													
Total	billion roubles	289.8											
	billion manat		603.1	546.4	12.8	23.5	31.7	535.1	93.8	126.8	158.7	167.1	
Total: volume	1990=100	44.0	119.0	33.0									
Construction and installation	billion roubles	159.2											
	billion manat		112.3	309.5	8.9	15.8	20.6	67.0	52.5	65.4	92.9	98.7	

A new currency, the manat, was introduced on the 1st January 1994.

Statistics include the Nahichivan region but exclude Karabakh.

For notes concerning these series, refer to *Short-term Economic Indicators: Transition Economies, Sources and Definitions* (April 1996) and the *Methodological Notes* at the end of this publication.

(1) The sub-annual indices previously published are currently being assessed by the OECD Secretariat: for further information see the industrial production subject table in the "Recent trends" section.

(2) Total retail sales including estimates of sales by non registered enterprises and private persons in informal markets.

(3) Laspeyres index from January 1993; new consumer price index from January 1994. Annual 1994 figure represents December 1994 with respect to December 1993.

(4) New consumer price index from January 1995.

1995									1996					
Apr	May	Jun	Jul	Aug	Sep	Oct	Nov	Dec	Jan	Feb	Mar			
												COMMERCE EXTÉRIEUR		
												Importations		
46.2	40.6	38.1	52.8	59.1	48.3	72.9	91.4	77.6				Total		*millions de $É-U*
33.8	31.3	25.5	39.8	39.6	32.3	43.3	58.9	54.9				depuis autres que les NEI		*millions de $É-U*
12.4	9.3	12.6	13.0	19.5	16.0	29.6	32.5	22.7				depuis les NEI		*millions de $É-U*
												Exportations		
42.0	27.3	43.7	76.8	44.1	47.9	71.0	54.3	51.8				Total		*millions de $É-U*
26.5	18.5	38.0	58.1	28.6	25.3	31.9	25.8	20.9				vers autres que les NEI		*millions de $É-U*
15.5	8.8	5.7	18.7	15.5	22.6	39.1	28.5	30.9				vers les NEI		*millions de $É-U*
												Solde commercial		
-4.2	-13.3	5.6	24.0	-15.0	-0.4	-1.9	-37.1	-25.8				Total		*millions de $É-U*
-7.3	-12.8	12.5	18.3	-11.0	-7.0	-11.4	-33.1	-34.0				avec autres que les NEI		*millions de $É-U*
3.1	-0.5	-6.9	5.7	-4.0	6.6	9.5	-4.0	8.2				avec les NEI		*millions de $É-U*
												FORMATION BRUTE DE CAPITAL		
												Total		*milliards de roubles*
														milliards de manat
												Total : volume		*1990=100*
												Construction et installation		*milliards de roubles*
														milliards de manat

Une nouvelle monnaie, le manat, a été introduite le 1er janvier 1994.

Les statistiques incluent la région de Nahichivan, mais excluent celle du Karabakh.

Pour les notes sur ces séries, veuillez consulter *Indicateurs économiques à court terme : Economies en transition ,Sources et définitions* (avril 1996) et les *Notes méthodologiques* à la fin de cette publication.

1) Les indices mensuels et trimestriels précédemment publiés sont actuellement examinés par le Secrétariat de l'OCDE: pour plus de détails, voir le tableau sujet sur la production industrielle dans la partie "Tendances récentes".

2) Ventes de détail totales, comprenant les ventes effectuées par les entreprises non inscrites au registre du commerce et par les personnes privées sur les marchés informels.

3) Indice de Laspeyres à partir de janvier 1993; nouvel indice des prix à la consommation depuis janvier 1994. La donnée annuelle pour 1994 correspond à la valeur de déc. 1994 par rapport à celle de déc. 1993.

4) Nouvel indice des prix à la consommation depuis janvier 1995.

BELARUS

		1993	1994	1995	1994 Q1	1994 Q2	1994 Q3	1994 Q4	1995 Q1	1995 Q2	1995 Q3	1995 Q4	1996 Q1
INDUSTRIAL PRODUCTION													
Total[1]	1990=100	83.1	68.9	61.0									
Manufacturing	1990=100	83.4	68.4										
Mining	1990=100	68.1	78.3										
Commodity output													
Natural gas	million m³	291.3	294.0	265.7	74.1	73.2	74.5	72.2	67.9	67.2	66.9	63.7	
Crude petroleum	thousand tonnes	2004	2000	1932	493	498	504	505	483	483	487	479	
Crude steel	thousand tonnes	946	873	741	187	212	229	245	169	190	194	188	
Cement	thousand tonnes	1907	1488	1236	254	419	474	305	224	290	409	313	
Electricity	bln kilowatt hours	33.4	31.4	24.9	8.5	7.0	6.8	9.1	8.1	5.2	4.9	6.7	
Metal cutting machines	thousands	9.2	6.1	4.7	1.3	1.5	1.8	1.5	1.2	1.1	1.3	1.1	
Lorries	thousands	30.8	21.3	12.8	5.0	5.7	5.0	5.7	2.7	3.5	2.9	3.7	
Mineral fertiliser	million tonnes	2.6	3.0	3.4	0.6	0.7	0.8	1.0	0.9	0.9	0.8	0.8	
Refrigerators	thousands	737.7	742.0	745.1	190.0	174.0	187.0	191.0	190.0	173.0	193.0	189.1	
BUSINESS SURVEYS - MANUFACT.													
Order books / Demand													
Total: level	balance					-54	-43	-32	-40	-75	-72	-67	-76
Export: level	balance					-29	-24	-25	-29	-45	-37	-36	-43
Production													
Tendency	balance					-70	-47	-15	-14	-42	-44	-11	-35
Future tendency	balance					-33	-17	-22	-4	-16	-23	-7	-3
Rate of capacity utilisation	%					53	51	54	55	51	46	50	47
Stocks													
Finished goods: level	balance					27	1	-10	-11	33	34	20	23
CONSTRUCTION													
Dwellings													
Completed: total	thousands	59.1	50.9	25.0	4.5	13.0	6.2	27.2	3.5	3.6	4.4	13.5	
Completed: area	thousand m²	3824	3403	1822	303	816	421	1863	263	265	310	984	
DOMESTIC TRADE													
Retail sales: value	billion roubles	3661.3											
	bln old blr roubles				3602.4	7869.6							
	bln blr roubles		6652.5	37426.1			1587.6	3855.5	6497.1	8836.5	10670.1	11422.4	
Retail sales value: total[2]	bln blr roubles			46118.0					7825.2	10906.8	13257.2	14128.8	
Retail sales: volume	1990=100	58.9	46.1	34.2	50.8	56.0	48.1	50.2	39.3	36.5	37.9	37.1	
LABOUR													
Employment													
Total	thousands	4824	4696	4600	4705	4716	4715	4648	4600	4650	4610	4540	
Industry	thousands	1430	1365	1340	1388	1367	1358	1346	1355	1345	1340	1320	
Manufacturing	thousands	1371	1300	1275									
Unemployment													
Total registered	thousands	56.4	90.1	115.9	77.0	86.8	95.8	100.8	108.4	110.0	117.9	127.1	
Beneficiaries	thousands	28.5	46.9	58.9	40.1	45.5	50.0	51.8	55.6	55.6	58.9	65.3	
Non-beneficiaries	thousands	27.9	43.3	57.0	36.9	41.3	45.8	49.1	52.8	54.4	59.0	61.8	
Unemployment	% of labour force	1.13	1.85	2.39	1.60	1.80	1.93	2.07	2.20	2.27	2.47	2.63	
WAGES													
Monthly earnings													
Total	'000 roubles	62.4											
	'000 old blr roubles				229.6	496.1							
	'000 blr roubles		98.2	749.7			104.1	216.1	461.1	746.5	859.7	931.3	
Industry	'000 roubles	69.5											
	'000 old blr roubles				266.5	575.0							
	'000 blr roubles		119.9	854.2			125.7	269.8	573.3	806.8	983.1	1053.5	
Manufacturing	'000 roubles	63.0											
	'000 blr roubles		106.3	760.2									
PRICES													
Consumer prices[3]													
Total	PP=100	1676.8	2321.0	809.3									
Food	PP=100	1706.8	2584.4	764.1									
Goods less food	PP=100	1620.2	2018.1	772.9									
Total goods	PP=100	1663.2	2324.0	764.2									
Services	PP=100	1831.9	2284.1	1349.1									
DOMESTIC FINANCE													
Personal deposits	billion roubles	220.2											
	bln old blr roubles				361.2	591.9							
	bln blr roubles		130.2	1189.6			92.6	130.2	521.0	1073.6	1404.3	1189.6	

Footnotes appear at the end of the table.

 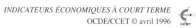

Indicateur	Unité	1995 Apr	May	Jun	Jul	Aug	Sep	Oct	Nov	Dec	1996 Jan	Feb	Mar
PRODUCTION INDUSTRIELLE													
Total[1]	1990=100												
Industries manufacturières	1990=100												
Industries extractives	1990=100												
Quantités produites													
Gaz naturel	millions de m³	22.0	22.7	22.5	22.6	22.6	21.7	21.0	20.8	21.9	22.1	19.9	
Pétrole brut	milliers de tonnes	159	164	160	165	164	158	163	157	159	158	148	
Acier brut	milliers de tonnes	75	59	55	72	65	58	60	60	68	58	60	
Ciment	milliers de tonnes	92	89	109	134	132	143	147	101	65	50	64	
Électricité	mrd kw-heures	2.1	1.7	1.4	1.4	1.7	1.8	2.1	2.2	2.4	2.5		
Machines à usiner les métaux	milliers	0.5	0.2	0.4	0.4	0.5	0.4	0.4	0.5	0.2	0.5	0.4	
Camions	milliers	0.8	1.2	1.5	1.0	0.8	1.1	1.7	1.3	0.7	0.7	0.6	
Engrais minéral	millions de tonnes	0.3	0.3	0.3	0.2	0.3	0.3	0.3	0.2	0.3	0.3	0.2	
Réfrigérateurs	milliers	51.9	57.3	64.2	58.4	68.9	65.9	69.5	62.2	57.4	64.1	62.7	
ENQUÊTES DE CONJONCTURE - IND. MANUF.													
Carnets de commandes / Demande													
Total : niveau	solde												
À l'exportation : niveau	solde												
Production													
Tendance	solde												
Perspectives	solde												
Taux d'utilisation des capacités	%												
Stocks													
Produits finis : niveau	solde												
CONSTRUCTION													
Logements													
Achevés : total	milliers												
Achevés : surface	milliers de m²												
COMMERCE INTÉRIEUR													
Ventes de détail : valeur	milliards de roubles												
	mrd anciens roub blr												
	mrd roubles blr	2534.1	2997.7	3202.0	3358.6	3720.9	3554.4	3694.8	3621.2	4026.6	3625.3	3838.5	
Ventes de détail en valeur : total[2]	mrd roubles blr	3154.7	3691.8	3940.6	4202.8	4614.6	4388.9	4571.8	4559.6	4934.0	4825.9	4896.1	
Ventes de détail : volume	1990=100	31.6	36.9	39.1	43.0	45.4	37.0	40.2	35.7	36.3	39.4		
MAIN-D'OEUVRE													
Emploi													
Total	milliers												
Industrie	milliers												
Industries manufacturières	milliers												
Chômage													
Chômeurs inscrits : total	milliers	109.2	109.7	111.2	114.9	118.5	120.2	123.3	127.0	131.1	143.2	156.7	
Allocataires	milliers	56.1	55.6	55.2	55.9	59.6	61.1	62.6	64.7	68.7	76.5	84.5	
Non allocataires	milliers	53.1	54.1	56.0	59.0	58.9	59.1	60.7	62.3	62.4	66.7	72.2	
Chômage	% de main-d'oeuvre	2.20	2.30	2.30	2.40	2.50	2.50	2.60	2.60	2.70	3.00	3.30	
SALAIRES													
Gains mensuels													
Total	'000 roubles												
	'000 anciens roubles blr												
	'000 roubles blr												
Industrie	'000 roubles												
	'000 anciens roubles blr												
	'000 roubles blr												
Industries manufacturières	'000 roubles												
	'000 roubles blr												
PRIX													
Prix à la consommation[3]													
Total	PP=100	114.5	103.4	102.5	105.2	103.0	105.2	103.4	103.7	103.9	105.6	104.0	
Alimentation	PP=100	105.9	102.2	99.9	99.7	101.5	104.9	103.8	104.1	105.3	106.9	104.5	
Biens sauf alimentation	PP=100	117.5	105.9	106.8	103.6	107.6	106.7	105.2	102.5	101.5	103.6	102.5	
Biens : total	PP=100	109.9	103.5	102.8	100.9	103.5	106.2	103.7	103.2	104.1	105.5	104.0	
Services	PP=100	160.1	103.1	101.2	129.1	100.6	100.9	102.0	106.2	102.9	105.9	103.9	
FINANCES INTERNES													
Dépôts personnels	milliards de roubles												
	mrd anciens roub blr												
	mrd roubles blr	711.1	746.8	1073.6	1434.0	1574.4	1404.3	1209.7	1188.3	1189.6			

Les notes se trouvent en fin de tableau.

BELARUS *(continued)*

		1993	1994	1995	1994 Q1	Q2	Q3	Q4	1995 Q1	Q2	Q3	Q4	1996 Q1
FOREIGN FINANCE													
US$ exchange rate end period	*old blr rouble/US$*	6990			15500	26800							
	blr rouble/US$		10600	11500			5630	10600	11550	11500	11500	11500	
Rouble exchange rate end period	*old blr rouble/rouble*	4.51			8.80	13.82							
	blr rouble/rouble		2.92	2.47			2.40	2.92	2.28	2.50	2.54	2.47	
Rouble exchange rate per. ave.	*old blr rouble/rouble*				5.410	11.160							
	blr rouble/rouble		1.46	2.52			1.65	2.53	2.74	2.28	2.55	2.52	
FOREIGN TRADE													
Imports													
Total	*million US$*		3066.5	4688.7	694.1	785.0	753.8	833.4	967.0	1109.4	1212.5	1399.8	
from countries other than NIS[4]	*million US$*	778.7	974.9	1453.7	216.6	278.1	233.1	246.9	234.2	372.0	412.5	435.0	
from NIS	*million US$*		2091.6	3235.0	477.5	506.9	520.7	586.5	732.8	737.4	800.0	964.8	
Exports													
Total	*million US$*		2510.0	4260.6	531.1	531.1	675.3	772.5	837.6	986.2	1199.3	1237.5	
to countries other than NIS[4]	*million US$*	757.9	1031.5	1693.8	226.9	215.2	283.1	306.3	353.4	435.1	466.5	438.8	
to NIS	*million US$*		1478.5	2566.8	304.2	315.9	392.2	466.2	484.2	551.1	732.8	798.7	
Net trade													
Total	*million US$*		-556.5	-428.1	-163.0	-253.9	-78.5	-60.9	-129.4	-123.2	-13.2	-162.3	
with countries other than NIS[4]	*million US$*	-20.8	56.6	240.1	10.3	-62.9	50.0	59.4	119.2	63.1	54.0	3.8	
with NIS	*million US$*		-613.1	-668.2	-173.3	-191.0	-128.5	-120.3	-248.6	-186.3	-67.2	-166.1	
GROSS CAPITAL FORMATION													
Total	*billion roubles*	1166.6											
	bln old blr roubles				1554.7	4156.4							
	bln blr roubles		4507.8	21930.8	1554.7	4156.4	747.8	3189.6	3424.0	3868.2	5208.7	9429.9	
Total: volume	*1990=100*	63.0	56.0	41.0									
Construction and installation	*billion roubles*	728.8											
	bln old blr roubles				1114.6	2727.5							
	bln blr roubles		2522.5	11981.1	1114.5	2727.5	491.9	1646.4	1751.3	2867.5	3191.7	4170.6	

An interim currency, the Belarussian rouble, was introduced on the 26th July 1993. It was redenominated by a factor of 10 on the 20th August 1994.

For notes concerning these series, refer to *Short-term Economic Indicators: Transition Economies, Sources and Definitions* (April 1996) and the *Methodological Notes* at the end of this publication.

(1) The sub-annual indices previously published are currently being assessed by the OECD Secretariat: for further information see the industrial production subject table in the "Recent trends" section.

(2) Total retail sales including estimates of sales by non registered enterprises and private persons in informal markets.

(3) Laspeyres index from January 1993; new consumer price index from January 1994.

(4) The 1993 figure includes certain customs data not allocated in the quarterly data.

1995									1996					
Apr	May	Jun	Jul	Aug	Sep	Oct	Nov	Dec	Jan	Feb	Mar			
												FINANCES EXTÉRIEURES		
												Taux de change du $É-U fin période		*ancien roub blr/$É-U*
11500	11500	11500	11500	11500	11500	11500	11500	11500	11500	11500				*rouble blr/$É-U*
												Taux de change du rouble fin pér.		*ancien rouble blr/rouble*
2.20	2.23	2.50	2.55	2.58	2.54	2.55	2.50	2.47	2.43	2.38				*rouble blr/rouble*
												Taux de change du rouble moy. pér.		*ancien rouble blr/rouble*
2.26	2.21	2.37	2.50	2.59	2.56	2.54	2.53	2.48	2.46	2.41				*rouble blr/rouble*
												COMMERCE EXTÉRIEUR		
												Importations		
349.9	395.7	363.8	346.9	416.3	449.3	459.0	447.9	492.9				Total		*millions de $É-U*
92.2	135.1	144.7	131.1	126.2	155.2	145.0	121.0	169.0				depuis autres que les NEI[4]		*millions de $É-U*
257.7	260.6	219.1	215.8	290.1	294.1	314.0	326.9	323.9				depuis les NEI		*millions de $É-U*
												Exportations		
289.6	311.0	385.6	364.3	400.6	434.4	424.1	354.6	458.8				Total		*millions de $É-U*
147.4	147.0	140.7	144.9	151.8	169.8	150.7	128.3	159.8				vers autres que les NEI[4]		*millions de $É-U*
142.2	164.0	244.9	219.4	248.8	264.6	273.4	226.3	299.0				vers les NEI		*millions de $É-U*
												Solde commercial		
-60.3	-84.7	21.8	17.4	-15.7	-14.9	-34.9	-93.3	-34.1				Total		*millions de $É-U*
55.2	11.9	-4.0	13.8	25.6	14.6	5.7	7.3	-9.2				avec autres que les NEI[4]		*millions de $É-U*
-115.5	-96.6	25.8	3.6	-41.3	-29.5	-40.6	-100.6	-24.9				avec les NEI		*millions de $É-U*
												FORMATION BRUTE DE CAPITAL		
												Total		*milliards de roubles*
														mrd anciens roub blr
														mrd roubles blr
												Total : volume		*1990=100*
												Construction et installation		*milliards de roubles*
														mrd anciens roub blr
														mrd roubles blr

Une monnaie provisoire, le rouble Bélarus, a été introduite le 26 juillet 1993. Une nouvelle dénomination a été introduite le 20 août 1994 par quoi le nouveau rouble Bélarus est égal à 10 anciens roubles Bélarus.
Pour les notes sur ces séries, veuillez consulter *Indicateurs économiques à court terme : Economies en transition, Sources et définitions* (avril 1996) et les *Notes méthodologiques* à la fin de cette publication.

1) Les indices mensuels et trimestriels précédemment publiés sont actuellement examinés par le Secrétariat de l'OCDE: pour plus de détails, voir le tableau sujet sur la production industrielle dans la partie "Tendances récentes".

2) Ventes de détail totales, comprenant les ventes effectuées par les entreprises non inscrites au registre du commerce et par les personnes privées sur les marchés informels.

3) Indice de Laspeyres à partir de janvier 1993; nouvel indice des prix à la consommation depuis janvier 1994.

4) La donnée annuelle de 1993 inclut certaines données douanières non ventilées par trimestre.

KAZAKSTAN

		1993	1994	1995	1994 Q1	1994 Q2	1994 Q3	1994 Q4	1995 Q1	1995 Q2	1995 Q3	1995 Q4	1996 Q1
INDUSTRIAL PRODUCTION													
Total[1]	1990=100	72.8	52.3	48.2									
Manufacturing	1990=100	71.8	51.4										
Mining	1990=100	77.0											
Commodity output													
Brown coal	thousand tonnes	4672	4814	3627	1303	1176	1012	1288	985	389	914	1339	
Black coal	million tonnes	107.2	99.8	79.5	26.6	25.3	24.0	23.8	23.5	15.5	18.4	22.1	
Natural gas	million m³	6711	4488	5916	1210	1099	988	1135	1251	1246	1155	1615	
Crude petroleum	thousand tonnes	19288	18544	17935	4213	4616	4915	4661	3786	4670	4726	4763	
Crude steel	thousand tonnes	4644	2969	3028	602	893	739	731	820	814	696	694	
Cement	thousand tonnes	3945	2033	1772	392	557	629	454	322	494	536	421	
Electricity	bln kilowatt hours	76.2	65.2	65.7	19.0	15.1	13.3	17.7	19.3	15.3	13.1	18.0	
Mineral fertiliser	thousand tonnes	304	126	197	35	31	16	45	35	54	53	55	
CONSTRUCTION													
Dwellings													
Completed: total	thousands	48.0	28.4	18.6	4.4	6.8	6.5	10.7	3.8	4.7	3.4	6.7	
Completed: area	thousand m²	3856	2322	1548	429	524	460	910	314	380	279	574	
DOMESTIC TRADE													
Retail sales: value	million tenge	4608	50383	110643	4261	9644	14281	22197	21239	26296	28107	35001	
Retail sales value: total[2]	million tenge			156600					30628	36776	39989	49207	
Retail sales: volume	1990=100	40.7	20.4	15.8	26.0	30.7	16.9	18.2	14.2	17.6	13.5	17.6	
LABOUR													
Employment													
Total	thousands	6926	6582	6350	6760	6720	6569	6279	6600	6500	6300	6000	
Industry	thousands	1305	1202	1140	1251	1239	1186	1130	1185	1180	1125	1070	
Manufacturing	thousands	1046	960	920									
Unemployment													
Total registered	thousands	38.4	55.1	101.3	45.9	51.4	56.6	66.4	81.3	92.9	103.3	127.8	
Beneficiaries	thousands	17.0	23.5	52.4	17.4	21.2	25.1	30.2	40.7	49.0	54.1	65.8	
Non-beneficiaries	thousands	21.4	31.6	48.9	28.5	30.2	31.5	36.2	40.6	43.9	49.1	62.0	
Unemployment	% of labour force	0.50	0.78	1.48	0.60	0.70	0.83	0.97	1.17	1.37	1.50	1.90	
WAGES													
Monthly earnings													
Total	'000 roubles	53.3											
	tenge		1711.5	5117.0	389.5	1047.3	2010.7	3398.7	3773.1	4690.5	5548.8	6455.6	
Industry	'000 roubles	72.7											
	tenge		2800.5	7944.8	607.4	1635.1	3379.1	5580.4	6410.8	7446.0	8162.3	9761.0	
Manufacturing	'000 roubles	65.4											
	tenge		2500	7100									
PRICES													
Consumer prices[3]													
Total	PP=100	1510.3	1977.4	276.2									
Food	PP=100	1268.8	1947.5	263.8									
Goods less food	PP=100	1327.1	1671.2	253.0									
Total goods	PP=100	1289.0	..	260.1									
Services	PP=100	1796.5	3589.9	432.8									
DOMESTIC FINANCE													
Personal deposits	million tenge	373.6	1583.3	6410.7	458.6	521.5	1299.4	1583.3	1732.8	4112.4	4830.9	6410.7	
FOREIGN FINANCE													
US$ exchange rate end period	tenge/US$	6.31	54.26	63.95	19.84	42.89	48.00	54.26	61.20	63.35	59.90	63.95	
Rouble exchange rate end period	tenge/rouble	0.0046	0.0162	0.0139	0.0112	0.0220	0.0189	0.0162	0.0126	0.0139	0.0134	0.0139	
Rouble exchange rate per. ave.	tenge/rouble		0.0160	0.0135	0.0077	0.0189	0.0212	0.0162	0.0139	0.0127	0.0134	0.0139	

Footnotes appear at the end of the table.

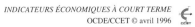

1995									1996		
Apr	May	Jun	Jul	Aug	Sep	Oct	Nov	Dec	Jan	Feb	Mar

PRODUCTION INDUSTRIELLE

												Total[1]	1990=100
												Industries manufacturières	1990=100
												Industries extractives	1990=100
												Quantités produites	
121	102	166	211	422	281	374	450	515	323	400		Lignite	milliers de tonnes
6.7	6.1	2.7	5.4	6.3	6.7	6.9	7.5	7.7	8.0	7.5		Houille	millions de tonnes
407	446	393	387	378	390	477	496	642	577	515		Gaz naturel	millions de m³
1486	1648	1536	1610	1587	1529	1600	1587	1576	1530	1474		Pétrole brut	milliers de tonnes
292	251	271	260	233	203	201	217	276	280	268		Acier brut	milliers de tonnes
189	133	172	187	170	179	152	147	122	69	80		Ciment	milliers de tonnes
5.5	5.2	4.6	4.2	4.3	4.6	5.4	5.8	6.8	6.6	6.2		Électricité	mrd kw-heures
20	20	15	17	18	19	20	17	18	17	22		Engrais minéral	milliers de tonnes

CONSTRUCTION
Logements

												Achevés : total	milliers
												Achevés : surface	milliers de m²

COMMERCE INTÉRIEUR

7765	8644	8822	8792	8863	9397	10348	10467	11740	8806	9116		Ventes de détail : valeur	millions de tenge
11933	12308	12535	13864	12315	13810	15567	16313	17327	14028	14427		Ventes de détail en valeur : total[2]	millions de tenge
17.0	17.0	17.9	13.2	13.0	14.0	14.9	16.4	19.6	14.1			Ventes de détail : volume	1990=100

MAIN-D'OEUVRE
Emploi

												Total	milliers
												Industrie	milliers
												Industries manufacturières	milliers
												Chômage	
90.3	92.5	95.8	98.3	103.1	108.4	116.1	127.8	139.6	157.7	186.5		Chômeurs inscrits : total	milliers
48.3	49.2	49.4	52.3	54.0	56.1	58.9	65.0	73.5	84.8	102.9		Allocataires	milliers
42.0	43.3	46.4	46.0	49.1	52.3	57.2	62.8	66.1	72.9	83.6		Non allocataires	milliers
1.30	1.40	1.40	1.40	1.50	1.60	1.70	1.90	2.10	2.40	2.90		Chômage	% de main-d'oeuvre

SALAIRES
Gains mensuels

												Total	'000 roubles
													tenge
												Industrie	'000 roubles
													tenge
												Industries manufacturières	'000 roubles
													tenge

PRIX
Prix à la consommation[3]

103.2	102.7	102.3	102.9	102.1	102.4	104.1	104.4	103.6	104.1	102.5		Total	PP=100
103.4	103.1	101.6	101.4	101.2	101.7	103.6	105.4	104.8	105.8	103.1		Alimentation	PP=100
102.3	101.8	101.3	101.4	102.1	101.8	101.7	101.7	101.2	100.9	100.9		Biens sauf alimentation	PP=100
103.0	102.6	101.5	101.4	101.5	101.7	103.0	104.2	103.7	104.2	102.4		Biens : total	PP=100
105.5	103.7	107.4	111.9	105.3	105.7	109.6	105.3	103.4	103.9	103.2		Services	PP=100

FINANCES INTERNES

3067.7	3696.1	4112.4	4311.6	4474.7	4830.9	5181.0	5668.1	6410.7				Dépôts personnels	millions de tenge

FINANCES EXTÉRIEURES

62.80	63.40	63.35	61.00	58.00	59.90	62.20	63.90	63.95	64.80	65.30		Taux de change du $É-U fin période	tenge/$É-U
0.0124	0.0129	0.0139	0.0139	0.0131	0.0134	0.0139	0.0140	0.0139	0.0139	0.0139		Taux de change du rouble fin pér.	tenge/rouble
0.0125	0.0122	0.0134	0.0139	0.0130	0.0134	0.0137	0.0140	0.0139	0.0138	0.0139		Taux de change du rouble moy. pér.	tenge/rouble

Les notes se trouvent en fin de tableau.

KAZAKSTAN *(continued)*

		1993	1994	1995	1994 Q1	Q2	Q3	Q4	1995 Q1	Q2	Q3	Q4	1996 Q1
FOREIGN TRADE													
Imports													
Total	million US$		3493.8	3742.1	868.8	1035.3	815.1	774.6	756.5	774.4	1031.3	1179.9	
from countries other than NIS[4]	million US$	494.2	1384.4	1172.3	350.7	374.0	321.9	337.8	301.1	311.7	311.6	247.9	
from NIS	million US$		2109.4	2569.8	518.1	661.3	493.2	436.8	455.4	462.7	719.7	932.0	
Exports													
Total	million US$		3230.7	4974.4	479.0	867.4	851.0	1033.3	803.5	1262.8	1623.6	1284.5	
to countries other than NIS[4]	million US$	1501.0	1356.9	2342.9	227.0	340.8	375.7	413.4	382.9	614.2	750.9	594.9	
to NIS	million US$		1873.8	2631.5	252.0	526.6	475.3	619.9	420.6	648.6	872.7	689.6	
Net trade													
Total	million US$		-263.1	1232.3	-389.8	-167.9	35.9	258.7	47.0	488.4	592.3	104.6	
with countries other than NIS[4]	million US$	1006.8	-27.5	1170.6	-123.7	-33.2	53.8	75.6	81.8	302.5	439.3	347.0	
with NIS	million US$		-235.6	61.7	-266.1	-134.7	-17.9	183.1	-34.8	185.9	153.0	-242.4	
GROSS CAPITAL FORMATION													
Total	billion roubles	2174.7											
	million tenge		80945	107680	2003	8492	15768	54683	15515	28114	31636	32415	
Total: volume	1990=100	32.0	28.0	20.0									
Construction and installation	billion roubles	1186.6											
	million tenge		35826	55024	1097	5006	8940	20784	8460	13571	16927	16066	

A new currency, the tenge, was introduced on the 15th November 1993.

For notes concerning these series, refer to *Short-term Economic Indicators: Transition Economies , Sources and Definistions*(April 1996) and the *Methodological Notes* at the end of this publication.

(1) The sub-annual indices previously published are currently being assessed by the OECD Secretariat: for further information see the industrial production subject table in the "Recent trends" section.

(2) Total retail sales including estimates of sales by non registered enterprises and private persons in informal markets.

(3) Laspeyres index from January 1993; new consumer price index from January 1994.

(4) The 1993 figure includes certain customs data not allocated in the quarterly data.

1995									1996					
Apr	May	Jun	Jul	Aug	Sep	Oct	Nov	Dec	Jan	Feb	Mar			
												COMMERCE EXTÉRIEUR		
												Importations		
258.8	257.8	257.8	331.2	258.7	441.4	489.3	415.2	275.4				Total	*millions de $É-U*	
116.7	107.8	87.2	135.6	71.6	104.4	90.7	96.8	60.4				depuis autres que les NEI[4]	*millions de $É-U*	
142.1	150.0	170.6	195.6	187.1	337.0	398.6	318.4	215.0				depuis les NEI	*millions de $É-U*	
												Exportations		
345.2	519.5	398.1	488.1	571.1	564.4	364.1	505.2	415.2				Total	*millions de $É-U*	
174.3	239.4	200.5	228.3	244.9	277.7	183.3	224.6	187.0				vers autres que les NEI[4]	*millions de $É-U*	
170.9	280.1	197.6	259.8	326.2	286.7	180.8	280.6	228.2				vers les NEI	*millions de $É-U*	
												Solde commercial		
86.4	261.7	140.3	156.9	312.4	123.0	-125.2	90.0	139.8				Total	*millions de $É-U*	
57.6	131.6	113.3	92.7	173.3	173.3	92.6	127.8	126.6				avec autres que les NEI[4]	*millions de $É-U*	
28.8	130.1	27.0	64.2	139.1	-50.3	-217.8	-37.8	13.2				avec les NEI	*millions de $É-U*	
												FORMATION BRUTE DE CAPITAL		
												Total	*milliards de roubles*	
													millions de tenge	
												Total : volume	*1990=100*	
												Construction et installation	*milliards de roubles*	
													millions de tenge	

Une nouvelle monnaie, le tenge, a été introduite le 15 novembre 1993.

Pour les notes sur ces séries, veuillez consulter *Indicateurs économiques à court terme : Economies en transition, Sources et définitions* (avril 1996) et les *Notes méthodologiques* à la fin de cette publication.

(1) Les indices mensuels et trimestriels précédemment publiés sont actuellement examinés par le Secrétariat de l'OCDE: pour plus de détails, voir le tableau sujet sur la production industrielle dans la partie "Tendances récentes".

(2) Ventes de détail totales, comprenant les ventes effectuées par les entreprises non inscrites au registre du commerce et par les personnes privées sur les marchés informels.

(3) Indice de Laspeyres à partir de janvier 1993; nouvel indice des prix à la consommation depuis janvier 1994.

(4) La donnée annuelle de 1993 inclut certaines données douanières non ventilées par trimestre.

KYRGYZ REPUBLIC

		1993	1994	1995	1994 Q1	1994 Q2	1994 Q3	1994 Q4	1995 Q1	1995 Q2	1995 Q3	1995 Q4	1996 Q1
INDUSTRIAL PRODUCTION													
Total[1]	1990=100	54.8	39.5	34.6									
Manufacturing	1990=100	52.1	32.1										
Mining	1990=100	56.1	50.1										
Commodity output													
Brown coal	thousand tonnes	959	550	346	157	140	95	158	110	45	63	128	
Black coal	thousand tonnes	712	298	155	81	74	48	95	48	32	36	39	
Natural gas	million m³	41.6	39.0	35.7	10.1	9.7	9.0	10.0	9.8	9.2	8.5	8.2	
Crude petroleum	thousand tonnes	87.6	88.2	88.5	17.8	28.1	22.1	20.0	20.8	24.0	23.4	20.3	
Cement	thousand tonnes	666	426	309	131	106	115	73	61	70	97	81	
Electricity	bln kilowatt hours	11.0	12.7	12.3	4.0	3.0	2.5	3.2	4.0	2.3	2.9	3.1	
Metal cutting machines	units	266	69	27	28	12	20	9	14	0	13	0	
CONSTRUCTION													
Dwellings													
Completed: total	thousands	7.4	4.9	3.6	0.5	1.1	1.2	2.1	0.3	0.6	1.3	1.4	
Completed: area	thousand m²	590	405	367	39	92	89	184	30	49	121	167	
DOMESTIC TRADE													
Retail sales: value	million som	1221	3679	4368	760	834	893	1192	991	1011	1122	1244	
Retail sales value: total[2]	million som			7345					1526	1669	1889	2261	
Retail sales: volume	1990=100	20.2	17.8	14.9	18.4	19.7	19.9	18.6	15.0	17.1	17.7	14.9	
LABOUR													
Employment													
Total	thousands	1681	1646	1640	1623	1690	1685	1584	1620	1690	1680	1570	
Industry	thousands	270	241	240	257	257	232	219	255	245	225	235	
Manufacturing	thousands	192	175	174									
Unemployment													
Total registered	thousands	2.7	7.6	32.9	3.6	6.1	8.8	11.8	18.3	28.2	38.3	46.6	
Beneficiaries	thousands	2.0	4.7	21.0	2.2	3.9	5.6	7.2	11.5	19.3	25.2	28.0	
Non-beneficiaries	thousands	0.7	2.9	11.9	1.4	2.2	3.2	4.7	6.8	9.0	13.1	18.5	
Unemployment	% of labour force	0.16	0.43	1.93	0.20	0.33	0.50	0.67	1.03	1.70	2.27	2.73	
WAGES													
Monthly earnings													
Total	som	85.9	233.4	390.3	174.1	210.8	242.5	306.2	337.3	365.1	391.7	467.1	
Industry	som	133.6	369.1	590.9	258.4	329.6	392.0	496.4	519.3	539.7	586.8	717.8	
Manufacturing	som	126	385	585									
PRICES													
Consumer prices[3]													
Total	PP=100	1391.0	378.1	151.6									
Food	PP=100	1267.8	314.8	143.8									
Goods less food	PP=100	1181.2	340.4	129.1									
Total goods	PP=100	1224.5	328.8	140.1									
Services	PP=100	2074.0	1183.0	209.4									
DOMESTIC FINANCE													
Personal deposits[4]	million som	25.4	68.2	98.3	30.9	33.8	39.8	68.2	89.6	93.2	95.3	98.3	
FOREIGN FINANCE													
US$ exchange rate end period	som/US$	8.03	10.60	11.20	11.70	11.30	10.50	10.60	10.90	10.60	10.86	11.20	
Rouble exchange rate end period	som/rouble	0.0064	0.0030	0.0024	0.0067	0.0057	0.0040	0.0030	0.0022	0.0023	0.0024	0.0024	
Rouble exchange rate per. ave.	som/rouble		0.0053	0.0024	0.0065	0.0064	0.0049	0.0034	0.0026	0.0022	0.0024	0.0024	
FOREIGN TRADE													
Imports													
Total	million US$		317.0	508.0	77.3	79.8	56.4	103.5	88.8	129.1	96.7	193.4	
from countries other than NIS	million US$	112.0	107.5	168.7	18.2	39.8	19.5	30.0	24.7	60.6	13.1	70.3	
from NIS	million US$		209.5	339.3	59.1	40.0	36.9	73.5	64.1	68.5	83.6	123.1	
Exports													
Total	million US$		340.1	408.0	56.8	86.7	99.6	97.0	75.3	98.5	123.0	111.2	
to countries other than NIS	million US$	112.1	117.2	139.7	7.5	19.0	47.9	42.8	28.6	38.6	38.4	34.1	
to NIS	million US$		222.9	268.3	49.3	67.7	51.7	54.2	46.7	59.9	84.6	77.1	
Net trade													
Total	million US$		23.1	-100.0	-20.5	6.9	43.2	-6.5	-13.5	-30.6	26.3	-82.2	
with countries other than NIS	million US$	0.1	9.7	-29.0	-10.7	-20.8	28.4	12.8	3.9	-22.0	25.3	-36.2	
with NIS	million US$		13.4	-71.0	-9.8	27.7	14.8	-19.3	-17.4	-8.6	1.0	-46.0	

Footnotes appear at the end of the table.

RÉPUBLIQUE KIRGHIZE

1995 Apr	May	Jun	Jul	Aug	Sep	Oct	Nov	Dec	1996 Jan	Feb	Mar	Indicateur	Unité
												PRODUCTION INDUSTRIELLE	
												Total[1]	*1990=100*
												Industries manufacturières	*1990=100*
												Industries extractives	*1990=100*
												Quantités produites	
12	10	23	17	19	27	41	46	41	37	26		Lignite	*milliers de tonnes*
7	9	16	14	9	13	12	12	15	20	14		Houille	*milliers de tonnes*
3.1	3.1	3.0	3.1	2.4	3.0	2.9	2.8	2.5	1.7	2.0		Gaz naturel	*millions de m³*
7.7	8.2	8.1	7.9	7.3	8.2	7.1	6.9	6.3	6.5	6.7		Pétrole brut	*milliers de tonnes*
21	22	27	34	31	32	26	25	30	21	25		Ciment	*milliers de tonnes*
0.8	0.6	0.9	1.6	0.9	0.4	0.7	0.9	1.5	1.6	1.4		Électricité	*mrd kw-heures*
0	0	0	6	7	0	0	0	0				Machines à usiner les métaux	*unités*
												CONSTRUCTION	
												Logements	
												Achevés : total	*milliers*
												Achevés : surface	*milliers de m²*
												COMMERCE INTÉRIEUR	
322	348	341	361	348	413	416	416	412	389	383		Ventes de détail : valeur	*millions de som*
546	565	558	584	612	693	729	742	790	706	605		Ventes de détail en valeur : total[2]	*millions de som*
16.8	21.2	15.1	17.9	17.0	19.2	18.2	13.5	15.3	14.6			Ventes de détail : volume	*1990=100*
												MAIN-D'OEUVRE	
												Emploi	
												Total	*milliers*
												Industrie	*milliers*
												Industries manufacturières	*milliers*
												Chômage	
24.9	28.0	31.8	36.0	38.3	40.7	43.2	46.1	50.4	54.1	64.7		Chômeurs inscrits : total	*milliers*
16.4	18.7	22.7	24.3	25.9	25.4	26.8	28.4	28.9	27.8	32.7		Allocataires	*milliers*
8.5	9.3	9.1	11.7	12.4	15.3	16.4	17.7	21.5	26.3	32.0		Non allocataires	*milliers*
1.50	1.70	1.90	2.10	2.30	2.40	2.60	2.70	2.90	3.10	3.80		Chômage	*% de main-d'oeuvre*
												SALAIRES	
												Gains mensuels	
												Total	*som*
												Industrie	*som*
												Industries manufacturières	*som*
												PRIX	
												Prix à la consommation[3]	
100.8	101.6	100.7	100.4	99.7	102.5	101.1	102.6	103.4	103.6	103.8		Total	*PP=100*
100.4	102.4	101.1	100.5	97.2	103.6	101.9	103.8	105.4	106.4	106.7		Alimentation	*PP=100*
100.9	99.5	100.3	100.7	104.8	99.5	98.0	99.9	101.1	100.0	100.0		Biens sauf alimentation	*PP=100*
100.6	101.6	100.8	100.6	99.3	102.4	101.1	102.8	103.7	104.1	104.2		Biens : total	*PP=100*
102.3	101.6	100.1	99.5	102.4	102.8	100.3	100.5	100.4	100.1	100.3		Services	*PP=100*
												FINANCES INTERNES	
91.1	93.1	93.2	95.5	95.0	95.3	96.4	97.5	98.3				Dépôts personnels[4]	*millions de som*
												FINANCES EXTÉRIEURES	
10.90	10.96	10.60	10.53	10.45	10.86	10.92	11.00	11.20	11.33	11.40		Taux de change du $É-U fin période	*som/$É-U*
0.0021	0.0022	0.0023	0.0024	0.0024	0.0024	0.0024	0.0024	0.0024	0.0024	0.0024		Taux de change du rouble fin pér.	*som/rouble*
0.0022	0.0022	0.0023	0.0023	0.0024	0.0024	0.0024	0.0024	0.0024	0.0024	0.0024		Taux de change du rouble moy. pér.	*som/rouble*
												COMMERCE EXTÉRIEUR	
												Importations	
												Total	*millions de $É-U*
												depuis autres que les NEI	*millions de $É-U*
												depuis les NEI	*millions de $É-U*
												Exportations	
												Total	*millions de $É-U*
												vers autres que les NEI	*millions de $É-U*
												vers les NEI	*millions de $É-U*
												Solde commercial	
												Total	*millions de $É-U*
												avec autres que les NEI	*millions de $É-U*
												avec les NEI	*millions de $É-U*

Les notes se trouvent en fin de tableau.

KYRGYZ REPUBLIC *(continued)*

		1993	1994	1995	1994 Q1	Q2	Q3	Q4	1995 Q1	Q2	Q3	Q4	1996 Q1
GROSS CAPITAL FORMATION													
Total	*billion roubles*	105.80											
	million som		1313.2	2908.6	71.4	199.0	212.8	830.0	391.3	611.2	721.6	1184.5	
Total: volume	*1990=100*	39.0	23.0	37.0									
Construction and installation	*billion roubles*	71.94											
	million som		747.4	2125.0	44.6	148.6	118.5	435.7	224.3	412.3	581.4	907.0	

A new currency, the som, was introduced on the 10th May 1993.

For notes concerning these series, refer to *Short-term Economic Indicators: Transition Economies, Sources and Definitions* (April 1996) and the *Methodological Notes* at the end of this publication.

(1) The sub-annual indices previously published are currently being assessed by the OECD Secretariat: for further information see the industrial production subject table in the "Recent trends" section.

(2) Total retail sales including estimates of sales by non registered enterprises and private persons in informal markets.

(3) New consumer price index from January 1994.

(4) From January 1995, compensation payments for price increases and interest on deposits are included.

1995									1996					
Apr	May	Jun	Jul	Aug	Sep	Oct	Nov	Dec	Jan	Feb	Mar			

FORMATION BRUTE DE CAPITAL
Total — *milliards de roubles*
millions de som
Total : volume — *1990=100*
Construction et installation — *milliards de roubles*
millions de som

Une nouvelle monnaie, le som, a été introduite le 10 mai 1993.
Pour les notes sur ces séries, veuillez consulter *Indicateurs économiques à court terme : Economies en transition, Sources et définitions* (avril 1996) et les *Notes méthodologiques* à la fin de cette publication.

1) Les indices mensuels et trimestriels précédemment publiés sont actuellement examinés par le Secrétariat de l'OCDE: pour plus de détails, voir le tableau sujet sur la production industrielle dans la partie "Tendances récentes".

2) Ventes de détail totales, comprenant les ventes effectuées par les entreprises non inscrites au registre du commerce et par les personnes privées sur les marchés informels.

3) Nouvel indice des prix à la consommation depuis janvier 1994.

4) A partir de janvier 1995, les dépôts personnels incluent les intérêts et les montants destinés à compenser les hausses de prix.

REPUBLIC OF MOLDOVA

		1993	1994	1995	1994 Q1	Q2	Q3	Q4	1995 Q1	Q2	Q3	Q4	1996 Q1
INDUSTRIAL PRODUCTION													
Total[1]	1990=100	65.0	47.0	44.2									
Manufacturing	1990=100	65.1	46.9										
Mining	1990=100	26.6	25.8										
Commodity output													
Cement[2]	thousand tonnes	553	39	49	3	11	24	1	1	0	0	48	
Electricity[3]	bln kilowatt hours	10.2	8.3	1.1	2.1	1.9	1.9	2.4	0.4	0.2	0.1	0.4	
Refrigerators	thousands	57.6	53.2	23.6	13.3	12.3	14.0	13.7	12.4	4.4	4.1	2.7	
CONSTRUCTION													
Dwellings[4]													
Completed: total	thousands	8.4	7.5	5.7	0.7	1.0	0.8	5.0	0.8	0.5	0.6	3.8	
Completed: area	thousand m²	666	582	415	59	77	68	379	57	46	58	254	
DOMESTIC TRADE													
Retail sales: value	million lei	602	1589	1991	288	371	473	457	463	499	472	557	
Retail sales: volume	1990=100	30.2	18.4	17.6	10.4	12.3	19.4	22.2	9.3	12.2	17.8	23.8	
LABOUR													
Employment													
Total	thousands	1688	1681	1670	1624	1733	1728	1639	1600	1740	1710	1630	
Industry	thousands	245	232	231	244	234	232	219	235	232	230	225	
Manufacturing	thousands	215	195	194									
Unemployment													
Total registered	thousands	11.7	18.5	23.5	16.8	17.5	19.0	20.5	22.8	22.9	23.3	24.8	
Beneficiaries	thousands	4.1	4.9	7.7	4.6	4.2	4.7	6.1	7.0	7.6	8.1	8.0	
Non-beneficiaries	thousands	7.5	13.5	15.8	12.1	13.3	14.3	14.4	15.8	15.3	15.2	16.9	
Unemployment	% of labour force	0.6	0.9	1.4	0.8	0.8	0.9	1.2	1.4	1.4	1.4	1.5	
WAGES													
Monthly earnings													
Total	lei	30.6	106.6	141.8	73.7	90.1	115.6	147.0	119.2	124.8	141.9	181.3	
Industry	lei	39.8	153.0	219.3	110.0	132.2	166.5	203.3	194.7	197.3	225.1	260.1	
Manufacturing	lei	36	151										
PRICES													
Consumer prices													
Total	PP=100	1283.7	586.8	130.0									
Food	PP=100	1269.8	553.0	130.0									
Goods less food	PP=100	1173.4	530.0	125.0									
Total goods	PP=100	1222.2	..	129.0									
Services	PP=100	1812.0	1162.0	140.0									
DOMESTIC FINANCE													
Personal deposits[5]	million lei	24.6	61.2	107.3	27.0	48.4	55.7	61.2	59.9	68.3	84.7	107.3	
FOREIGN FINANCE													
US$ exchange rate end period	leu/US$	3.64	4.27	4.50	3.98	4.08	4.20	4.27	4.43	4.54	4.53	4.50	
Rouble exchange rate end period	leu/rouble	0.0030	0.0010	0.0010	0.0022	0.0021	0.0017	0.0010	0.0009	0.0010	0.0010	0.0010	
Rouble exchange rate per. ave.	leu/rouble		0.0020	0.0010	0.0024	0.0022	0.0020	0.0013	0.0010	0.0010	0.0010	0.0010	
FOREIGN TRADE													
Imports													
Total	million US$		659.3	826.1	156.1	122.1	176.1	205.0	160.8	161.5	240.3	263.5	
from countries other than NIS	million US$	184.0	183.3	271.8	44.7	31.9	51.8	54.9	41.7	54.3	76.6	99.2	
from NIS	million US$		476.0	554.3	111.4	90.2	124.3	150.1	119.1	107.2	163.7	164.3	
Exports													
Total	million US$		565.4	745.5	114.4	116.5	170.3	164.2	137.7	156.4	181.2	270.2	
to countries other than NIS	million US$	178.0	159.9	278.6	24.5	29.9	40.4	65.1	66.2	54.5	67.3	90.6	
to NIS	million US$		405.5	466.9	89.9	86.6	129.9	99.1	71.5	101.9	113.9	179.6	
Net trade													
Total	million US$		-93.9	-80.6	-41.7	-5.6	-5.8	-40.8	-23.1	-5.1	-59.1	6.7	
with countries other than NIS	million US$	-6.0	-23.4	6.8	-20.2	-2.0	-11.4	10.2	24.5	0.2	-9.3	-8.6	
with NIS	million US$		-70.5	-87.4	-21.5	-3.6	5.6	-51.0	-47.6	-5.3	-49.8	15.3	

Footnotes appear at the end of the table.

	1995 Apr	May	Jun	Jul	Aug	Sep	Oct	Nov	Dec	1996 Jan	Feb	Mar		
PRODUCTION INDUSTRIELLE													Total[1]	1990=100
													Industries manufacturières	1990=100
													Industries extractives	1990=100
Quantités produites														
	0	0	0	0	0	0	15	30	2				Ciment[2]	milliers de tonnes
	0.1	0.1	0.0	0.0	0.0	0.1	0.1	0.1	0.2	0.2	0.2		Électricité[3]	mrd kw-heures
	1.7	2.5	0.2	1.5	0.1	2.5	0.8	0.8	1.1				Réfrigérateurs	milliers
CONSTRUCTION													Logements[4]	
													Achevés : total	milliers
													Achevés : surface	milliers de m²
COMMERCE INTÉRIEUR														
	175	148	168	146	155	169	170	175	202	139	142		Ventes de détail : valeur	millions de lei
	11.4	11.8	12.7	15.8	18.6	20.3	22.7	25.1	24.0	6.8			Ventes de détail : volume	1990=100
MAIN-D'OEUVRE													Emploi	
													Total	milliers
													Industrie	milliers
													Industries manufacturières	milliers
													Chômage	
	23.4	23.0	22.4	22.5	23.1	24.2	24.8	25.2	24.5	25.4	26.4		Chômeurs inscrits : total	milliers
	7.4	7.8	7.7	7.8	8.1	8.3	8.0	7.9	8.0	8.0	8.1		Allocataires	milliers
	16.0	15.2	14.7	14.7	15.0	15.9	16.8	17.3	16.5	17.4	18.3		Non allocataires	milliers
	1.5	1.4	1.3	1.4	1.4	1.4	1.5	1.5	1.4	1.5	1.6		Chômage	% de main-d'oeuvre
SALAIRES													Gains mensuels	
													Total	lei
													Industrie	lei
													Industries manufacturières	lei
PRIX													Prix à la consommation	
	100.6	100.4	100.2	100.2	100.2	102.6	102.7	106.0	102.9	103.5	102.5		Total	PP=100
	100.5	100.3	99.6	99.8	99.9	103.2	103.0	105.0	102.3	104.1	102.6		Alimentation	PP=100
	100.3	100.4	100.2	100.4	100.7	101.8	102.1	101.4	101.5	101.8	102.7		Biens sauf alimentation	PP=100
	100.5	100.3	99.9	100.1	100.2	102.6	102.6	103.9	102.2				Biens : total	PP=100
	101.6	101.0	102.4	101.1	100.3	102.4	103.3	123.9	107.9	106.4	101.4		Services	PP=100
FINANCES INTERNES														
	60.1	68.1	68.3	78.3	80.7	84.7	92.0	100.3	107.3				Dépôts personnels[5]	millions de lei
FINANCES EXTÉRIEURES														
	4.52	4.56	4.54	4.53	4.53	4.53	4.54	4.58	4.50	4.55	4.56		Taux de change du $É-U fin période	leu/$É-U
	0.0009	0.0009	0.0010	0.0010	0.0010	0.0010	0.0010	0.0010	0.0010	0.0010	0.0009		Taux de change du rouble fin pér.	leu/rouble
	0.0010	0.0010	0.0010	0.0010	0.0010	0.0010	0.0010	0.0010	0.0010	0.0010	0.0010		Taux de change du rouble moy. pér.	leu/rouble
COMMERCE EXTÉRIEUR													Importations	
	63.8	45.6	52.1	58.6	57.8	123.9	58.3	100.5	104.7				Total	millions de $É-U
	20.0	15.1	19.2	24.9	24.4	27.3	25.9	36.0	37.3				depuis autres que les NEI	millions de $É-U
	43.8	30.5	32.9	33.7	33.4	96.6	32.4	64.5	67.4				depuis les NEI	millions de $É-U
													Exportations	
	52.8	48.2	55.4	61.4	59.6	60.2	76.2	84.0	110.0				Total	millions de $É-U
	17.0	17.3	20.2	19.6	22.3	25.4	27.2	29.1	34.3				vers autres que les NEI	millions de $É-U
	35.8	30.9	35.2	41.8	37.3	34.8	49.0	54.9	75.7				vers les NEI	millions de $É-U
													Solde commercial	
	-11.0	2.6	3.3	2.8	1.8	-63.7	17.9	-16.5	5.3				Total	millions de $É-U
	-3.0	2.2	1.0	-5.3	-2.1	-1.9	1.3	-6.9	-3.0				avec autres que les NEI	millions de $É-U
	-8.0	0.4	2.3	8.1	3.9	-61.8	16.6	-9.6	8.3				avec les NEI	millions de $É-U

Les notes se trouvent en fin de tableau.

REPUBLIC OF MOLDOVA (continued)

		1993	1994	1995	1994 Q1	Q2	Q3	Q4	1995 Q1	Q2	Q3	Q4	1996 Q1
GROSS CAPITAL FORMATION													
Total[4]	billion roubles	122.3											
	million lei		712.4	571.8	61.9	123.9	142.3	384.3	70.6	141.4	118.5	241.3	
Total: volume	1990=100	38.0	18.0	14.0									
Construction and installation[4]	billion roubles	84.8											
	million lei		493.9	347.0	47.7	83.4	99.9	262.9	51.1	99.8	72.0	124.1	

A new currency, the leu, was introduced on the 29th November 1993.

For notes concerning these series, refer to *Short-term Economic Indicators: Transition Economies, Sources and Definitions* (April 1996) and the *Methodological Notes* at the end of this publication.

(1) The sub-annual indices previously published are currently being assessed by the OECD Secretariat: for further information see the industrial production subject table in the "Recent trends" section.

(2) From 1994 excludes the Pridnestrov region.

(3) From 1995, excludes the Pridnestrov region.

(4) From the fourth quarter of 1993, excludes the Pridnestrov region.

(5) Prior to May 1994, data cover deposits in savings banks only. Since then, commercial bank deposits are also included.

1995									1996			
Apr	May	Jun	Jul	Aug	Sep	Oct	Nov	Dec	Jan	Feb	Mar	

FORMATION BRUTE DE CAPITAL
Total[4]
                                           milliards de roubles
       millions de lei

Total : volume   *1990=100*
Construction et installation[4]   *milliards de roubles*
   millions de lei

Une nouvelle monnaie, le leu, a été introduite le 29 novembre 1993.
Pour les notes sur ces séries, veuillez consulter *Indicateurs économiques à court terme : Economies en transition, Sources et définitions* (avril 1996) et les *Notes méthodologiques* à la fin de cette publication.

(1) Les indices mensuels et trimestriels précédemment publiés sont actuellement examinés par le Secrétariat de l'OCDE: pour plus de détails, voir le tableau sujet sur la production industrielle dans la partie "Tendances récentes".
(2) Non compris la région de Pridnestrov à partir de 1994.
(3) Non compris la région de Pridnestrov à partir de 1995.
(4) Non compris la région de Pridnestrov à partir du quatrième trimestre de 1993.
(5) Avant mai 1994, cette série n'inclut que les dépôts dans les caisses d'épargne. Depuis mai 1994, elle inclut aussi les dépôts dans les banques commerciales.

RUSSIAN FEDERATION

		1993	1994	1995	1994 Q1	Q2	Q3	Q4	1995 Q1	Q2	Q3	Q4	1996 Q1
INDUSTRIAL PRODUCTION													
Total[1]	1990=100	64.8	51.3	49.8									
Manufacturing	1990=100	63.0	48.0	46.0									
Mining	1990=100	78.5	72.7										
Commodity output													
Brown coal	million tonnes	112	95	86	30	22	18	25	25	17	19	25	
Black coal	million tonnes	193	176	176	46	44	41	45	46	43	42	45	
Natural gas	billion m³	618	607	592	165	147	134	161	163	142	131	159	
Crude petroleum	million tonnes	333	310	298	76	77	79	78	74	74	76	74	
Crude steel	million tonnes	58.1	48.8	51.2	11.4	12.5	12.6	12.3	12.7	13.3	12.5	12.8	
Cement	million tonnes	49.9	37.2	36.4	7.4	9.3	11.3	9.2	7.1	9.7	11.4	8.2	
Electricity	bln kilowatt hours	937.0	859.0	845.2	260.0	187.0	172.0	240.0	247.0	185.0	176.0	237.2	
Mineral fertiliser	million tonnes	8.6	7.5	8.8	1.8	2.1	1.6	2.0	2.3	2.3	2.0	2.2	
Refrigerators	thousands	3478	2631	1744	756	654	650	571	501	418	454	371	
Metal cutting machines	thousands	38.0	18.2	16.1	6.0	3.8	3.6	4.8	4.9	4.0	3.5	3.7	
Lorries	thousands	525.3	145.6	115.1	38.5	35.0	32.3	39.8	33.6	29.3	27.4	24.8	
Passenger cars	thousands	956	798	835	168	201	206	223	206	211	213	205	
BUSINESS SURVEYS - MANUFACT.													
Order books / Demand													
Total: level	balance				-86	-83	-77	-73	-73	-83	-79	-89	-91
Export: level	balance				-37	-38	-36	-34	-32	-36	-34	-37	-41
Production													
Tendency	balance				-48	-53	-47	-21	-20	-26	-16	-23	-37
Future tendency	balance				-34	-41	-21	-7	-7	-6	5	-7	4
Rate of capacity utilisation	%				56	54	48	49	48	47	47	46	44
Stocks													
Finished goods: level	balance				46	37	14	1	1	11	6	19	24
CONSTRUCTION													
Dwellings													
Completed: total	thousands	682	611	658	61	106	106	337	65	113	112	369	
Completed: area	million m²	41.8	39.2	42.8	4.0	6.7	6.9	21.8	4.3	7.7	7.3	23.4	
DOMESTIC TRADE[2]													
Retail sales value: total	billion roubles	58762	213430	553467	36235	43578	54970	78647	95648	124148	151755	181916	
Retail sales volume: total	1990=100	95.2	95.3	88.4	89.0	83.1	99.4	100.7	80.1	77.8	90.0	96.0	
Retail sales volume: total[3] sa	1990=100				103.6	99.9	99.2	79.7	95.0	93.8	89.6	74.7	
LABOUR													
Employment													
Total	millions	70.9	68.5	67.1	69.4	68.7	68.2	67.6	67.0	67.1	67.2	67.1	
Industry	millions	20.8	18.6	17.2	19.3	18.7	18.3	18.2	17.4	17.2	17.1	17.1	
Manufacturing	millions	16.9	15.6	14.3									
Unemployment													
Total registered	thousands	728.2	1285.7	2033.4	988.8	1219.5	1380.6	1553.9	1823.4	1994.4	2083.3	2232.3	
Beneficiaries	thousands	477.3	1067.6	1754.3	796.3	1008.8	1155.0	1310.2	1562.6	1718.7	1798.8	1937.3	
Non-beneficiaries	thousands	250.8	218.1	279.0	192.5	210.7	225.6	243.7	260.9	275.7	284.5	295.0	
Unemployment	% of labour force	0.99	1.73	2.77	1.33	1.63	1.87	2.10	2.47	2.70	2.87	3.03	
WAGES													
Monthly earnings													
Total	'000 roubles	64.3	242.6	540.9	160.8	209.1	262.0	338.4	360.4	483.8	592.1	727.3	
Industry	'000 roubles	70.4	256.1	638.5	169.8	225.9	271.3	357.5	438.3	588.4	712.6	814.7	
Manufacturing	'000 roubles	58.4	210.7	523.2									
PRICES													
Consumer prices[4]													
Total	PP=100	940	315	231									
Food	PP=100	905	333	223									
Goods less food	PP=100	742	269	216									
Total goods	PP=100	833	295	220									
Services	PP=100	2411	622	332									
DOMESTIC FINANCE													
Personal deposits	billion roubles	4018	17557	46068	5168	7783	11773	17557	22168	30306	36241	46068	
FOREIGN FINANCE													
US$ exchange rate end period	rouble/US$	1247	3550	4640	1753	1985	2596	3550	4897	4538	4508	4640	

Footnotes appear at the end of the table.

 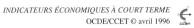

FÉDÉRATION DE RUSSIE

	1995 Apr	May	Jun	Jul	Aug	Sep	Oct	Nov	Dec	1996 Jan	Feb	Mar		
PRODUCTION INDUSTRIELLE														
Total[1]														*1990=100*
Industries manufacturières														*1990=100*
Industries extractives														*1990=100*
Quantités produites														
Lignite	5	6	6	6	6	7	8	8	9	9				*millions de tonnes*
Houille	15	14	14	14	14	14	15	15	15	14				*millions de tonnes*
Gaz naturel	49	47	43	44	44	43	51	52	56	57				*milliards de m³*
Pétrole brut	24	25	25	26	26	24	25	24	25	25				*millions de tonnes*
Acier brut	4.4	4.6	4.3	4.2	4.3	4.0	4.3	4.2	4.3	3.8				*millions de tonnes*
Ciment	2.9	3.3	3.5	4.0	3.9	3.5	3.5	2.7	2.0	1.6				*millions de tonnes*
Électricité	67.3	61.4	56.4	57.2	58.4	60.6	71.6	78.0	87.6	89.3				*mrd kw-heures*
Engrais minéral	0.9	0.8	0.6	0.6	0.7	0.6	0.7	0.7	0.8	0.7				*millions de tonnes*
Réfrigérateurs	152	106	160	170	147	137	140	121	110	76				*milliers*
Machines à usiner les métaux	1.3	1.3	1.4	1.2	0.8	1.5	1.2	1.4	1.1	1.0				*milliers*
Camions	9.5	8.7	11.1	10.0	9.2	8.2	7.1	7.7	10.0	8.3				*milliers*
Voitures particulières	70	68	73	70	76	67	77	66	62	54				*milliers*
ENQUÊTES DE CONJONCTURE - IND. MANUF.														
Carnets de commandes / Demande														
Total : niveau	-78	-86	-84	-80	-78	-80	-87	-91	-89	-90	-90	-94		*solde*
À l'exportation : niveau	-32	-41	-36	-34	-34	-34	-32	-39	-40	-39	-41	-44		*solde*
Production														
Tendance	-30	-24	-24	-24	-15	-9	-16	-28	-26	-39	-43	-29		*solde*
Perspectives	-5	-3	-9	2	10	3	-4	-13	-5	-1	6	6		*solde*
Taux d'utilisation des capacités														*%*
Stocks														
Produits finis : niveau	7	13	12	5	3	10	13	19	26	28	22	22		*solde*
CONSTRUCTION														
Logements														
Achevés : total														*milliers*
Achevés : surface														*millions de m²*
COMMERCE INTÉRIEUR[2]														
Ventes de détail en valeur : total	36433	42580	45135	47347	51040	53368	56940	59395	65581	59286	55187			*milliards de roubles*
Ventes de détail en volume : total	78.0	90.9	91.1	95.2	87.2	88.6	98.7	96.5	95.7	70.7				*1990=100*
Ventes de détail en volume : total[3]	89.5	98.1	93.8	94.5	88.1	86.2	79.5	84.7	59.8	106.4			*cvs*	*1990=100*
MAIN-D'OEUVRE														
Emploi														
Total														*millions*
Industrie														*millions*
Industries manufacturières														*millions*
Chômage														
Chômeurs inscrits : total	1985.6	1993.1	2004.4	2048.1	2097.7	2104.1	2142.2	2227.7	2327.0	2417.7	2567.5			*milliers*
Allocataires	1708.8	1720.7	1726.5	1764.2	1811.7	1820.6	1853.7	1932.4	2025.8	2099.0	2230.1			*milliers*
Non allocataires	276.8	272.4	277.9	283.9	286.0	283.5	288.5	295.3	301.2	318.7	337.4			*milliers*
Chômage	2.70	2.70	2.70	2.80	2.90	2.90	2.90	3.00	3.20	3.30	3.50			*% de main-d'oeuvre*
SALAIRES														
Gains mensuels														
Total														*'000 roubles*
Industrie														*'000 roubles*
Industries manufacturières														*'000 roubles*
PRIX														
Prix à la consommation[4]														
Total	109	108	107	105	105	105	105	105	103	104	103			*PP=100*
Alimentation	107	108	108	104	102	102	103	104	104	104	102			*PP=100*
Biens sauf alimentation	109	106	105	105	106	106	105	105	103	103	102			*PP=100*
Biens : total	108	108	106	105	104	104	104	104	103	104	102			*PP=100*
Services	112	111	109	110	108	107	109	107	103	108	106			*PP=100*
FINANCES INTERNES														
Dépôts personnels	24487	27330	30306	32257	34083	36241	38834	41860	46068	54916				*milliards de roubles*
FINANCES EXTÉRIEURES														
Taux de change du $É-U fin période	5100	4995	4538	4415	4435	4508	4504	4578	4640	4732	4815			*rouble/$É-U*

Les notes se trouvent en fin de tableau.

RUSSIAN FEDERATION (continued)

		1993	1994	1995	1994				1995				1996
					Q1	Q2	Q3	Q4	Q1	Q2	Q3	Q4	Q1
FOREIGN TRADE													
Imports													
Total	million US$		38650	46445	9086	9272	9008	11283	10111	11296	11443	13594	
from countries other than NIS	million US$	26807	28336	33177	7009	6748	6224	8355	7848	8494	7512	9322	
from NIS	million US$		10313	13269	2078	2524	2784	2928	2263	2802	3931	4273	
Exports													
Total	million US$		65531	77342	13161	16619	17307	18442	18063	19934	18720	20625	
to countries other than NIS	million US$	44297	51449	64344	10235	13131	13237	14845	14846	16914	15580	17004	
to NIS	million US$		14081	12998	2926	3488	4070	3598	3217	3021	3140	3620	
Net trade													
Total	million US$		26881	30897	4075	7347	8299	7160	7953	8638	7277	7030	
with countries other than NIS	million US$	17491	23113	31168	3227	6383	7013	6490	6999	8420	8067	7682	
with NIS	million US$		3768	-271	848	964	1286	670	954	219	-791	-652	
GROSS CAPITAL FORMATION													
Total	billion roubles	27124	108810	250182	12294	22099	26374	48043	29513	48378	66240	106051	
Total: volume	1990=100	45.0	34.0	30.0	31.0	29.0	31.0	41.0	24.0	25.0	28.0	37.0	
Construction and installation	billion roubles	16149	70278	164703	8430	15021	17683	29144	20074	31444	46304	66881	

For notes concerning these series, refer to *Short-term Economic Indicators: Transition Economies, Sources and Definitions* (April 1996) and the *Methodological Notes* at the end of this publication.

(1) The sub-annual indices previously published are currently being assessed by the OECD Secretariat: for further information see the industrial production subject table in the "Recent trends" section.

(2) Total retail sales including estimates of sales by non registered enterprises and private persons in informal markets.

(3) This series has been estimated by the OECD Secretariat.

(4) Annual data is calculated using December with respect to December of the previous year.

1995									1996					
Apr	May	Jun	Jul	Aug	Sep	Oct	Nov	Dec	Jan	Feb	Mar			
												COMMERCE EXTÉRIEUR		
												Importations		
3202	3966	4128	3515	3972	3956	4027	4670	4898				Total	*millions de $É-U*	
2376	3006	3112	2471	2579	2462	2690	3242	3390				depuis autres que les NEI	*millions de $É-U*	
826	960	1016	1044	1393	1494	1337	1428	1508				depuis les NEI	*millions de $É-U*	
												Exportations		
6337	6692	6905	5960	6245	6515	6567	6866	7192				Total	*millions de $É-U*	
5356	5686	5872	4949	5193	5437	5390	5664	5950				vers autres que les NEI	*millions de $É-U*	
982	1006	1033	1011	1052	1078	1177	1202	1242				vers les NEI	*millions de $É-U*	
												Solde commercial		
3135	2726	2777	2445	2273	2559	2540	2197	2294				Total	*millions de $É-U*	
2980	2680	2760	2478	2614	2975	2700	2422	2560				avec autres que les NEI	*millions de $É-U*	
156	46	17	-33	-341	-417	-160	-226	-266				avec les NEI	*millions de $É-U*	
												FORMATION BRUTE DE CAPITAL		
												Total	*milliards de roubles*	
												Total : volume	*1990=100*	
												Construction et installation	*milliards de roubles*	

Pour les notes sur ces séries, veuillez consulter *Indicateurs économiques à court terme : Economies en transition, Sources et définitions* (avril 1996) et les *Notes méthodologiques* à la fin de cette publication.

1) Les indices mensuels et trimestriels précédemment publiés sont actuellement examinés par le Secrétariat de l'OCDE: pour plus de détails, voir le tableau sujet sur la production industrielle dans la partie Tendances récentes".

2) Ventes de détail totales, comprenant les ventes effectuées par les entreprises non inscrites au registre du commerce et par les personnes privées sur les marchés informels.

3) Cette série a été estimée par le Secrétariat de l'OCDE.

4) Les données annuelles correspondent à la valeur de décembre par rapport à celle de décembre de l'année précédente.

TAJIKISTAN

		1993	1994	1995	1994 Q1	Q2	Q3	Q4	1995 Q1	Q2	Q3	Q4	1996 Q1
INDUSTRIAL PRODUCTION													
Total[1]	1990=100	67.4	46.6	44.2									
Manufacturing	1990=100	66.1											
Mining	1990=100	39.8											
Commodity output													
Coal	thousand tonnes	177	106	33	44	28	18	17	12	5	5	11	
Natural gas	million m³	48.7	33.0	38.5	11.1	7.9	5.8	8.2	9.7	7.9	8.7	12.2	
Crude petroleum	thousand tonnes	39.2	31.3	24.1	8.5	8.8	7.3	6.7	5.9	6.4	5.9	5.9	
Crude steel	tonnes	862											
Cement	thousand tonnes	235	178	78	51	65	38	24	16	19	23	20	
Electricity	bln kilowatt hours	17.7	17.0	14.8	3.7	4.4	5.7	3.2	3.6	3.3	4.4	3.5	
CONSTRUCTION													
Dwellings													
Completed: total	thousands	8.1	3.3	2.4	0.3	0.6	0.8	1.6	0.2	0.3	0.3	1.6	
Completed: area	thousand m²	523	198	143	21	42	30	105	14	17	18	94	
DOMESTIC TRADE													
Retail sales: value	billion roubles	206.46	470.93		80.28	114.06	119.13	157.46	126.00				
	mln tajik roubles			6746						1180	1770	2536	
Retail sales: volume	1990=100	16.5	11.3	2.7	8.7	12.5	8.1	9.4	10.4	4.0	2.6	1.5	
LABOUR													
Employment													
Total	thousands	1854	1800	1751	1700	1800	1810	1890	1650	1750	1770	1832	
Industry	thousands	219	200	190	200	204	202	194	190	195	192	183	
Unemployment													
Total registered	thousands	13.8	27.9	32.8	24.9	27.7	28.2	30.9	34.3	30.9	31.7	34.2	
Beneficiaries	thousands	5.0	4.7	10.8	4.3	4.7	4.9	4.8	5.7	6.8	12.0	18.6	
Non-beneficiaries	thousands	8.8	23.3	22.0	20.6	23.0	23.3	26.1	28.6	24.1	19.7	15.7	
Unemployment	% of labour force	0.68	1.50	1.78	1.33	1.50	1.53	1.63	1.90	1.70	1.73	1.80	
WAGES													
Monthly earnings													
Total	roubles	16155	36030		31962	37164	36574	38420	40787				
	tajik roubles			731						592	761	1163	
Industry	roubles	26902	65162		63805	69758	62138	64947	79200				
	tajik roubles			1559						1203	1703	2553	
Manufacturing	roubles	26000	64500										
	tajik roubles			1500									
PRICES													
Consumer prices[2]													
Total	PP=100	1584.5	101.1	543.1									
Food	PP=100	1795.8	84.4	563.0									
Goods less food	PP=100	1435.8	112.5	427.8									
Total goods[3]	PP=100	1613.0	333.8	600.0									
Services	PP=100	1400.0	300.3	413.8									
DOMESTIC FINANCE													
Personal deposits	billion roubles	47.2	173.4		139.8	143.7	154.9	173.4	206.4				
FOREIGN FINANCE													
US$ exchange rate end period	tajik rouble/US$			294						53	153	294	
Rouble exchange rate end period	tajik rouble/rouble			0.0600						0.0117	0.0341	0.0600	
Rouble exchange rate per. ave.	tajik rouble/rouble			0.0236						0.0106	0.0188	0.0552	
FOREIGN TRADE													
Imports													
Total	million US$		550.8	690.5	185.1	122.7	157.6	85.4					
from countries other than NIS	million US$	373.8	317.7	375.6	77.6	80.9	111.2	48.0	57.5	130.3			
from NIS	million US$		233.1	314.9	107.5	41.8	46.4	37.4					
Exports													
Total	million US$		413.1	707.4	99.4	133.4	77.7	102.6					
to countries other than NIS	million US$	263.1	320.1	506.0	73.7	108.1	59.7	78.6	99.5	156.2			
to NIS	million US$		93.0	201.4	25.7	25.3	18.0	24.0					
Net trade													
Total	million US$		-137.7	16.9	-85.7	10.7	-79.9	17.2					
with countries other than NIS	million US$	-110.7	2.4	130.4	-3.9	27.2	-51.5	30.6	42.0	25.9			
with NIS	million US$		-140.1	-113.5	-81.8	-16.5	-28.4	-13.4					

Footnotes appear at the end of the table.

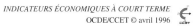

		1995									1996		
		Apr	May	Jun	Jul	Aug	Sep	Oct	Nov	Dec	Jan	Feb	Mar
PRODUCTION INDUSTRIELLE													
Total[1]	*1990=100*												
Industries manufacturières	*1990=100*												
Industries extractives	*1990=100*												
Quantités produites													
Charbon	*milliers de tonnes*	2	1	2	2	1	2	3	4	4	1	1	
Gaz naturel	*millions de m³*	2.7	2.6	2.6	2.7	2.9	3.1	3.6	4.1	4.5	4.5	3.8	
Pétrole brut	*milliers de tonnes*	2.3	2.0	2.1	2.2	1.7	2.0	2.1	1.9	1.9	1.9	1.8	
Acier brut	*tonnes*												
Ciment	*milliers de tonnes*	5	3	11	14	0	9	12	3	5	3	3	
Électricité	*mrd kw-heures*	0.7	1.2	1.4	1.4	1.7	1.3	1.2	1.2	1.1	1.2	1.1	
CONSTRUCTION													
Logements													
Achevés : total	*milliers*												
Achevés : surface	*milliers de m²*												
COMMERCE INTÉRIEUR													
Ventes de détail : valeur	*milliards de roubles*	43.64											
	mln roubles tadjiks		383	351	403	504	693	793	778	936	885	964	
Ventes de détail : volume	*1990=100*	8.5	4.8	3.2	3.0	1.8	2.5	1.7	0.9	1.5	1.7		
MAIN-D'OEUVRE													
Emploi													
Total	*milliers*												
Industrie	*milliers*												
Chômage													
Chômeurs inscrits : total	*milliers*	29.8	32.1	30.9	29.2	30.7	35.2	30.5	34.7	37.5	38.3	39.0	
Allocataires	*milliers*	5.0	6.3	9.2	8.9	10.0	17.1	13.4	22.4	19.9	21.0	21.2	
Non allocataires	*milliers*	24.8	25.8	21.7	20.3	20.7	18.1	17.1	12.3	17.6	17.3	17.8	
Chômage	*% de main-d'oeuvre*	1.60	1.80	1.70	1.60	1.70	1.90	1.60	1.80	2.00	2.10	2.20	
SALAIRES													
Gains mensuels													
Total	*roubles*												
	roubles tadjiks												
Industrie	*roubles*												
	roubles tadjiks												
Industries manufacturières	*roubles*												
	roubles tadjiks												
PRIX													
Prix à la consommation[2]													
Total	*PP=100*	120.9	127.9	108.2	106.7	178.1	162.9	156.9	123.1	167.5			
Alimentation	*PP=100*	129.9	154.9	87.8	106.7	184.1	165.5	156.9	122.3	185.3			
Biens sauf alimentation	*PP=100*	106.8	105.2	134.3	113.5	207.3	164.6	163.5	121.6	111.6			
Biens : total[3]	*PP=100*	125.6	145.7	106.8	107.8	188.3	165.2	156.6	122.1	169.5			
Services	*PP=100*	113.2	136.3	111.0	99.1	109.8	136.4	145.8	137.1	132.9			
FINANCES INTERNES													
Dépôts personnels	*milliards de roubles*	213.4											
FINANCES EXTÉRIEURES													
Taux de change du $É-U fin pér.	*rouble tadjik/$É-U*		51	53	57	58	153	241	290	294	300	280	
Taux de change du rouble fin pér.	*rouble tadjik/rouble*		0.0102	0.0117	0.0128	0.0131	0.0341	0.0534	0.0632	0.0600	0.0550	0.0540	
Taux de change du rouble moy. pér.	*rouble tadjik/rouble*		0.0100	0.0112	0.0126	0.0132	0.0305	0.0456	0.0585	0.0616	0.0571	0.0540	
COMMERCE EXTÉRIEUR													
Importations													
Total	*millions de $É-U*												
depuis autres que les NEI	*millions de $É-U*	26.2	31.6	72.5									
depuis les NEI	*millions de $É-U*												
Exportations													
Total	*millions de $É-U*												
vers autres que les NEI	*millions de $É-U*	29.0	87.2	40.0									
vers les NEI	*millions de $É-U*												
Solde commercial													
Total	*millions de $É-U*												
avec autres que les NEI	*millions de $É-U*	2.8	55.6	-32.5									
avec les NEI	*millions de $É-U*												

Les notes se trouvent en fin de tableau.

TAJIKISTAN (continued)

		1993	1994	1995	1994 Q1	Q2	Q3	Q4	1995 Q1	Q2	Q3	Q4	1996 Q1
GROSS CAPITAL FORMATION													
Total	billion roubles	171.51	415.88		58.56	111.43	86.08	159.81	101.40				
	mln tajik roubles			5633.4						1188.8	1911.7	2448.4	
Total: volume	1990=100	49.0	28.0	21.0									
Construction and installation	billion roubles	116.60	303.78		43.45	82.27	66.39	111.67	70.80				
	mln tajik roubles			3829.5						878.7	1218.3	1673.5	

A new currency, the Tajik rouble, was introduced on the 10th May 1995.

For notes concerning these series, refer to *Short-term Economic Indicators: Transition Economies, Sources and Definitions* (April 1996) and the *Methodological Notes* at the end of this publication.

(1) The sub-annual indices previously published are currently being assessed by the OECD Secretariat: for further information see the industrial production subject table in the "Recent trends" section.

(2) Laspeyres index from January 1993; new consumer price index from January 1994. Annual 1994 figure represents December 1994 with respect to December 1993.

(3) New consumer price index from January 1995. Annual 1994 figure represents 1994 average with respect to 1993 average.

1995									1996				
Apr	May	Jun	Jul	Aug	Sep	Oct	Nov	Dec	Jan	Feb	Mar		
												FORMATION BRUTE DE CAPITAL	
												Total	*milliards de roubles*
													mln roubles tadjiks
												Total : volume	*1990=100*
												Construction et installation	*milliards de roubles*
													mln roubles tadjiks

Une nouvelle monnaie, le rouble tadjik, a été introduite le 10 mai 1995.

Pour les notes sur ces séries, veuillez consulter *Indicateurs économiques à court terme : Economies en transition, Sources et définitions* (avril 1996) et les *Notes méthodologiques* à la fin de cette publication.

(1) Les indices mensuels et trimestriels précédemment publiés sont actuellement examinés par le Secrétariat de l'OCDE: pour plus de détails, voir le tableau sujet sur la production industrielle dans la partie "Tendances récentes".

(2) Indice de Laspeyres à partir de janvier 1993; nouvel indice des prix à la consommation depuis janvier 1994. La donnée annuelle de 1994 correspond à la valeur de déc. 1994 par rapport à celle de déc. 1993.

(3) Nouvel indice des prix à la consommation depuis janvier 1995. La donnée annuelle de 1994 correspond à la valeur moyenne de 1994 par rapport à celle de 1993.

TURKMENISTAN

		1993	1994	1995	1994 Q1	Q2	Q3	Q4	1995 Q1	Q2	Q3	Q4	1996 Q1
INDUSTRIAL PRODUCTION													
Total[1]	1990=100	92.8	69.6	64.8									
Manufacturing	1990=100	94.0											
Mining	1990=100	84.2											
Commodity output													
Natural gas	million m³	65154	35636	32266	11520	9059	8630	6427	10049	..	..	..	
Crude petroleum	thousand tonnes	3928	3738	3776	924	939	959	916	924	..	..	..	
Crude steel	tonnes	911	1349	1100	281	354	375	339	281	..	..	..	
Cement	thousand tonnes	1118	690	437	259	151	155	124	134	..	..	..	
Electricity	mln kilowatt hours	12.6	10.6	9.8	3.9	2.0	1.9	2.8	3.1	..	..	..	
Mineral fertiliser	thousand tonnes	126.2	86.1	68.5	35.9	24.6	18.4	7.2	13.2	..	..	..	
CONSTRUCTION													
Dwellings													
Completed: total	thousands	18.8	16.6		2.3	4.5	4.8	4.9					
Completed: area	thousand m²	1962	1682		245	466	471	501					
DOMESTIC TRADE													
Retail sales: value	million manat	1019	11707	55217	1379	2189	3080	5048	5687	..	..	..	
Retail sales value: total[2]	million manat			85110					8220	..	..	..	
Retail sales: volume	1990=100	48.1	20.9		40.2	31.0	17.6	19.1					
LABOUR													
Employment													
Total	thousands	1642	1665	1680	1620	1650	1680	1710	1650	1670	1690	1710	
Industry	thousands	171	166	167	152	153	151	144	170	167	170	162	
Manufacturing	thousands	129	125	128									
WAGES													
Monthly earnings[3]													
Total	manat	132.9	1300.0	6683.0	761.8	873.6	1645.8	1918.8	3542.0	4077.0	8622.0	10492.0	
Industry	manat	169.5	1250.0		763.4	808.1	1500.0	1927.5	4400.0	4664.0	9800.0		
Manufacturing	manat	160.0	1110.0										
PRICES													
Consumer prices[4]													
Total	PP=100	1874.7	2814.0										
Food	PP=100	1911.5	1949.0										
Goods less food	PP=100	1807.5	3490.0										
Total goods	PP=100	1854.5											
Services	PP=100	1906.6	2138.0										
DOMESTIC FINANCE													
Personal deposits	million manat	82.7	284.1		105.0	120.9	175.3	284.1					
FOREIGN FINANCE[5]													
US$ exchange rate end period	manat/US$	2.0	75.0	200.0	10.0	10.0	10.0	75.0	75.0	75.0	200.0	200.0	
Rouble exchange rate end period	manat/rouble	0.0017	0.0231	0.0431	0.0059	0.0059	0.0059	0.0231	0.0154	0.0164	0.0447	0.0431	
Rouble exchange rate per. ave.	manat/rouble		0.0081	0.0247	0.0031	0.0059	0.0059	0.0175	0.0194	0.0152	0.0205	0.0440	
FOREIGN TRADE													
Imports													
Total	million US$		672.9	720.0	136.3	221.3	189.0	342.4	87.6	170.1	148.3	314.0	
from countries other than NIS	million US$	501.4	328.4	91.7	46.3	100.8	70.7	110.6	29.6	23.7	18.8	19.6	
from NIS[6]	million US$		344.5	628.3	90.0	120.5	118.3	231.8	58.0	146.4	129.5	294.4	
Exports													
Total	million US$		1721.6	1736.5	525.5	397.2	439.6	449.9	535.7	456.2	309.1	435.5	
to countries other than NIS	million US$	1049.0	412.0	564.1	163.3	60.8	70.5	117.4	177.3	223.1	37.5	126.2	
to NIS[6]	million US$		1309.6	1172.4	362.2	336.4	369.1	332.5	358.4	233.1	271.6	309.3	
Net trade													
Total	million US$		1048.7	1016.5	389.2	175.9	250.6	107.5	448.1	286.1	160.8	121.5	
with countries other than NIS	million US$	547.6	83.6	472.4	117.0	-40.0	-0.2	6.8	147.7	199.4	18.7	106.6	
with NIS[6]	million US$		965.1	544.1	272.2	215.9	250.8	100.7	300.4	86.7	142.1	14.9	

Footnotes appear at the end of the table.

		1995									1996		
		Apr	May	Jun	Jul	Aug	Sep	Oct	Nov	Dec	Jan	Feb	Mar
PRODUCTION INDUSTRIELLE													
Total[1]	1990=100												
Industries manufacturières	1990=100												
Industries extractives	1990=100												
Quantités produites													
Gaz naturel	millions de m³	..	..	..	..	..	..	..	..	3692	3646	3583	
Pétrole brut	milliers de tonnes	..	..	..	..	..	..	..	..	323	318	306	
Acier brut	tonnes	..	..	..	..	..	..	..	..	100	86	90	
Ciment	milliers de tonnes	..	..	..	..	..	..	..	..	40	37	40	
Électricité	mln kw-heures	..	..	..	..	..	..	..	..	1.3	1.3	1.2	
Engrais minéral	milliers de tonnes	..	..	..	..	..	..	..	..	5.5	5.2	4.3	
CONSTRUCTION													
Logements													
Achevés : total	milliers												
Achevés : surface	milliers de m²												
COMMERCE INTÉRIEUR													
Ventes de détail : valeur	millions de manat	..	..	..	..	..	..	..	..	12226			
Ventes de détail en valeur: total[2]	millions de manat	..	..	..	..	..	..	..	..	18500			
Ventes de détail : volume	1990=100												
MAIN-D'OEUVRE													
Emploi													
Total	milliers												
Industrie	milliers												
Industries manufacturières	milliers												
SALAIRES													
Gains mensuels[3]													
Total	manat												
Industrie	manat												
Industries manufacturières	manat												
PRIX													
Prix à la consommation[4]													
Total	PP=100												
Alimentation	PP=100												
Biens sauf alimentation	PP=100												
Biens : total	PP=100												
Services	PP=100												
FINANCES INTERNES													
Dépôts personnels	millions de manat												
FINANCES EXTÉRIEURES[5]													
Taux de change du $É-U fin période	manat/$É-U	75.0	75.0	75.0	75.0	75.0	200.0	200.0	200.0	200.0	2400.0	2316.0	
Taux de change du rouble fin pér.	manat/rouble	0.0148	0.0150	0.0164	0.0165	0.0169	0.0447	0.0444	0.0438	0.0431	0.5080	0.4850	
Taux de change du rouble moy. pér.	manat/rouble	0.0149	0.0148	0.0158	0.0165	0.0169	0.0280	0.0444	0.0441	0.0434	0.5142	0.5201	
COMMERCE EXTÉRIEUR													
Importations													
Total	millions de $É-U	33.8	57.3	79.0	41.5	34.4	72.4	74.0	148.4	91.6			
depuis autres que les NEI	millions de $É-U	2.1	19.4	2.2	6.0	2.4	10.4	7.9	8.0	3.7			
depuis les NEI[6]	millions de $É-U	31.7	37.9	76.8	35.5	32.0	62.0	66.1	140.4	87.9			
Exportations													
Total	millions de $É-U	107.3	264.5	84.4	93.3	105.3	110.5	109.0	264.7	61.8			
vers autres que les NEI	millions de $É-U	60.6	125.3	37.2	12.0	13.8	11.7	12.1	72.0	42.1			
vers les NEI[6]	millions de $É-U	46.7	139.2	47.2	81.3	91.5	98.8	96.9	192.7	19.7			
Solde commercial													
Total	millions de $É-U	73.5	207.2	5.4	51.8	70.9	38.1	35.0	116.3	-29.8			
avec autres que les NEI	millions de $É-U	58.5	105.9	35.0	6.0	11.4	1.3	4.2	64.0	38.4			
avec les NEI[6]	millions de $É-U	15.0	101.3	-29.6	45.8	59.5	36.8	30.8	52.3	-68.2			

Les notes se trouvent en fin de tableau.

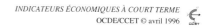

TURKMENISTAN (continued)

		1993	1994	1995	1994 Q1	Q2	Q3	Q4	1995 Q1	Q2	Q3	Q4	1996 Q1
GROSS CAPITAL FORMATION													
Total	*billion roubles*	1261.0											
	million manat		12961.6		1549.5	2365.4	4224.6	4822.1					
Total: volume	*1990=100*	193.0											
Construction and installation	*billion roubles*	794.2											
	million manat		5846.3		641.0	1274.5	1468.4	2462.4					

A new currency, the manat, was introduced on the 1st November 1993.

For notes concerning these series, refer to *Short-term Economic Indicators: Transition Economies, Sources and Definitions* (April 1996) and the *Methodological Notes* at the end of this publication.

(1) The sub-annual indices previously published are currently being assessed by the OECD Secretariat: for further information see the industrial production subject table in the "Recent trends" section.

(2) Total retail sales including estimates of sales by non registered enterprises and private persons in informal markets.

(3) The minimum wage was increased from 250 to 1000 manat on the 1st January 1995.

(4) Laspeyres index from January 1993; new consumer price index from January 1994.

(5) Figures refer to the official exchange rates which are periodically changed by the Turkmen National Bank.

(6) Quarterly data for 1994 are derived from statistical reports and do not correspond to the annual figure, revised on the basis of customs declarations.

1995									1996			
Apr	May	Jun	Jul	Aug	Sep	Oct	Nov	Dec	Jan	Feb	Mar	

FORMATION BRUTE DE CAPITAL
Total — *milliards de roubles*
millions de manat
Total : volume — *1990=100*
Construction et installation — *milliards de roubles*
millions de manat

Une nouvelle monnaie, le manat, a été introduite le 1er novembre 1993.

Pour les notes sur ces séries, veuillez consulter *Indicateurs économiques à court terme : Economies en transition, Sources et définitions* (avril 1996) et les *Notes méthodologiques* à la fin de cette publication.

1) Les indices mensuels et trimestriels précédemment publiés sont actuellement examinés par le Secrétariat de l'OCDE: pour plus de détails, voir le tableau sujet sur la production industrielle dans la partie "Tendances récentes".

2) Ventes de détail totales, comprenant les ventes effectuées par les entreprises non inscrites au registre du commerce et par les personnes privées sur les marchés informels.

3) Le salaire minimum a été augmenté de 250 à 1000 manat le 1er janvier 1995.

4) Indice de Laspeyres à partir de janvier 1993; nouvel indice des prix à la consommation depuis janvier 1994.

5) Taux de change officiels périodiquement modifiés par la Banque Nationale du Turkménistan.

6) Les données trimestrielles de 1994 sont tirées de rapports statistiques et ne correspondent pas à la donnée annuelle révisée à partir des déclarations en douane.

UKRAINE

					1994				1995				1996
		1993	1994	1995	Q1	Q2	Q3	Q4	Q1	Q2	Q3	Q4	Q1
INDUSTRIAL PRODUCTION													
Total[1]	1990=100	82.0	59.6	52.7									
Manufacturing	SPPY=100	91.4	70.3	85.4									
Mining	SPPY=100	81.4	79.5	89.2									
Electricity	SPPY=100	94.1	87.5	94.6									
Construction material	SPPY=100	85.6	62.4										
Commodity output													
Coal	million tonnes	115.8	94.6	83.6	27.7	24.9	20.8	21.2	23.8	21.2	19.4	19.2	
Natural gas	million m³	19221	18316	18121	4593	4589	4551	4583	4442	4449	4586	4644	
Crude petroleum	thousand tonnes	4248	4198	4010	1038	1062	1049	1049	1008	1004	1003	995	
Crude steel	thousand tonnes	32610	24081	22309	5702	6820	6270	5289	5197	6133	5612	5367	
Cement	thousand tonnes	15012	11435	7621	1987	3064	3715	2657	1607	1951	2453	1610	
Passenger cars	thousands	140.1	93.6	59.8	24.6	31.5	19.2	18.3	19.8	15.7	12.1	12.1	
CONSTRUCTION													
Dwellings													
Completed: total	thousands	189.0	146.5	111.9	14.8	25.9	27.7	78.1	13.1	22.5	18.8	57.5	
Completed: area	thousand m²	12311	10073	8028	1019	1779	1905	5370	978	1559	1320	4171	
DOMESTIC TRADE													
Retail sales: value	'000 bln karbovanets	43.8	337.0	1149.1	44.2	57.5	74.7	160.6	195.3	249.0	334.2	370.7	
Retail sales: volume	PP=100	65.0	86.4	86.8									
LABOUR													
Employment													
Total	millions	23.4	22.2										
Material branches	millions	16.9	15.8										
Industry	thousands	6012	5856	5398	6015	5864	5783	5653	5533	5457	5359	5247	
Unemployment[2]													
Total registered	thousands	78.9	93.0	94.9	98.6	99.0	90.8	83.7	85.0	86.0	94.1	114.5	
Beneficiaries	thousands	43.4	48.8	56.1	46.8	49.1	51.3	47.8	49.0	51.5	56.9	67.1	
WAGES													
Monthly earnings													
Total	'000 karbovanets	155.4	1377.2	7345.0	790.2	955.6	1160.8	2623.1	4257.8	6327.2	8059.7	10915.0	
Industry	'000 karbovanets	185.6	1539.9	7901.0	954.7	1058.7	1304.7	2810.8	4705.1	6586.9	8654.3	11873.0	
Manufacturing	'000 karbovanets	153.5	1316.0										
PRICES[3]													
Wholesale prices													
Total	PP=100	4061.7	874.0	272.0									
Consumer prices													
Total[4]	PP=100	4618.8	501.1	281.7	141.9	115.9	112.4	271.2	159.5	116.0	125.7	121.2	
Food[4]	PP=100	5243.2	473.2	250.1	125.0	113.4	106.8	312.6	151.6	110.7	116.0	128.5	
Goods less food[4]	PP=100	4034.2	473.1	220.0	152.2	115.2	116.0	232.6	143.7	111.9	119.6	114.3	
Total goods[5]	PP=100	4596.9											
Services[4]	PP=100	4606.8	881.4	584.4	205.2	129.6	120.2	275.9	244.0	138.0	154.0	112.8	
DOMESTIC FINANCE													
Personal deposits[6]	bln karbovanets	2415	21401	50428	5591	10217	13348	21401	27236	33537	35837	50428	
FOREIGN FINANCE													
US$ exchange rate end period	karbovanets/US$	12610	108855	179497	12610	16607	24700	108855	132648	142150	165340	179497	
FOREIGN TRADE													
Imports													
Total	million US$	9532.6	10745.3	11335.5	2491.5	2711.6	3114.5	2427.7	2257.2	2525.5	3072.0	3480.8	
from non-FSU countries	million US$	2430.9	2742.1	4010.1	649.5	605.3	748.2	739.1	715.4	835.1	1195.0	1264.6	
from FSU countries	million US$	7101.7	8003.2	7325.4	1842.0	2106.3	2366.3	1688.6	1541.8	1690.4	1877.0	2216.2	
Exports													
Total	million US$	7817.3	10272.1	11566.5	2041.5	2601.4	2939.8	2689.4	1976.5	2605.2	3375.7	3609.1	
to non-FSU countries	million US$	3115.3	4347.2	5356.5	848.0	1203.1	1174.8	1121.3	1011.5	1336.7	1473.3	1535.0	
to FSU countries	million US$	4702.0	5924.9	6210.0	1193.5	1398.3	1765.0	1568.1	965.0	1268.5	1902.4	2074.1	
Net trade													
Total	million US$	-1715.3	-473.2	231.0	-450.0	-110.2	-174.7	261.7	-280.7	79.7	303.7	128.3	
with non-FSU countries	million US$	684.4	1605.1	1346.4	198.5	597.8	426.6	382.2	296.1	501.6	278.3	270.4	
with FSU countries	million US$	-2399.7	-2078.3	-1115.4	-648.5	-708.0	-601.3	-120.5	-576.8	-421.9	25.4	-142.1	

Footnotes appear at the end of the table.

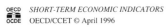

	1995									1996			
	Apr	May	Jun	Jul	Aug	Sep	Oct	Nov	Dec	Jan	Feb	Mar	
PRODUCTION INDUSTRIELLE													
Total[1]													1990=100
Industries manufacturières													PCAP=100
Industries extractives													PCAP=100
Électricité													PCAP=100
Matériaux de construction													PCAP=100
Quantités produites													
Charbon	7.7	6.9	6.6	6.7	6.3	6.4	6.3	6.4	6.5	6.2	6.1		millions de tonnes
Gaz naturel	1469	1510	1470	1517	1540	1529	1549	1530	1565	1555	1445		millions de m³
Pétrole brut	333	341	330	340	337	326	334	327	334	334	313		milliers de tonnes
Acier brut	2066	2157	1910	2064	1891	1657	1854	1697	1816	1648	1505		milliers de tonnes
Ciment	676	556	719	837	848	768	694	542	374	242	184		milliers de tonnes
Voitures particulières	5.4	5.3	5.0	4.3	3.3	4.5	5.2	3.6	3.3	1.6	0.9		milliers
CONSTRUCTION													
Logements													
Achevés : total	5.2	5.0	12.3	4.0	6.8	8.0	3.6	4.4	49.5				milliers
Achevés : surface	363	348	848	282	480	558	259	321	3591				milliers de m²
COMMERCE INTÉRIEUR													
Ventes de détail : valeur	72.4	83.3	89.6	97.6	112.7	118.8	125.6	116.1	128.8	112.2	118.4		'000 mrd karbovanets
Ventes de détail : volume	93.4	111.3	103.2	105.4	109.9	96.0	97.5	87.6	107.1	83.0	102.2		PP=100
MAIN-D'OEUVRE													
Emploi													
Total													millions
Branches matérielles													millions
Industrie	5461	5426	5402	5379	5350	5339	5302	5254	5204				milliers
Chômage[2]													
Chômeurs inscrits : total	87.9	85.4	84.6	89.2	94.6	98.5	103.9	112.6	126.9	139.2	172.1		milliers
Allocataires	51.9	51.5	51.0	53.6	57.1	60.1	61.6	65.3	74.4	82.7	97.0		milliers
SALAIRES													
Gains mensuels													
Total	5567.0	6276.8	7109.0	7573.0	8001.0	8689.0	9620.0	10329.0	12250.0				'000 karbovanets
Industrie	5960.0	6482.9	7334.0	7910.0	8628.0	9422.0	10635.0	11146.0	13473.0				'000 karbovanets
Industries manufacturières													'000 karbovanets
PRIX[3]													
Prix de gros													
Total	105.1	107.1	108.6	104.3	106.5	109.9	108.4	104.2	102.6	103.4	102.9		PP=100
Prix à la consommation													
Total[4]	105.8	104.6	104.8	105.2	104.6	114.2	109.1	106.2	104.6	109.4	107.4		PP=100
Alimentation[4]	104.8	104.6	101.0	99.9	104.3	111.3	112.0	107.9	106.3	106.8	104.4		PP=100
Biens sauf alimentation[4]	104.9	103.2	103.4	103.6	106.5	108.4	105.8	104.7	103.2	103.1	103.1		PP=100
Biens : total[5]													PP=100
Services[4]	110.2	107.1	116.9	119.5	103.4	124.6	106.1	104.1	102.1	119.3	115.7		PP=100
FINANCES INTERNES													
Dépôts personnels[6]	29363	30732	33537	35156	35529	35837	36905	41016	50428	51616			mrd karbovanets
FINANCES EXTÉRIEURES													
Taux de change du $É-U fin période	131403	130481	142150	143674	160897	165340	174403	177883	179497	182800			karbovanets/US$
COMMERCE EXTÉRIEUR													
Importations													
Total	764.1	850.8	910.6	959.5	946.4	1166.1	908.7	1134.5	1437.6				millions de $É-U
depuis autres que ex-URSS	233.9	294.0	307.2	390.7	330.9	473.4	312.4	364.4	587.8				millions de $É-U
depuis ex-URSS	530.2	556.8	603.4	568.8	615.5	692.7	596.3	770.1	849.8				millions de $É-U
Exportations													
Total	730.5	852.7	1022.0	1154.6	1012.9	1208.2	1051.1	1134.6	1423.4				millions de $É-U
vers autres que ex-URSS	398.4	473.6	464.7	526.8	420.0	526.5	431.0	482.2	621.8				millions de $É-U
vers ex-URSS	332.1	379.1	557.3	627.8	592.9	681.7	620.1	652.4	801.6				millions de $É-U
Solde commercial													
Total	-33.6	1.9	111.4	195.1	66.5	42.1	142.4	0.1	-14.2				millions de $É-U
avec autres que ex-URSS	164.5	179.6	157.5	136.1	89.1	53.1	118.6	117.8	34.0				millions de $É-U
avec ex-URSS	-198.1	-177.7	-46.1	59.0	-22.6	-11.0	23.8	-117.7	-48.2				millions de $É-U

Les notes se trouvent en fin de tableau.

		1993	1994	1995	1994				1995				1996
					Q1	Q2	Q3	Q4	Q1	Q2	Q3	Q4	Q1
GROSS CAPITAL FORMATION													
Total	*'000 bln karbovanets*	29.3	229.9	797.2	18.1	33.0	42.6	136.2	89.4	171.8	207.4	328.6	
Total: volume	*1990=100*	52.5	40.6	26.4									
Construction and installation	*'000 bln karbovanets*	20.9	161.3	563.7	14.0	24.5	29.7	93.1	67.1	122.2	152.4	222.0	

For notes concerning these series, refer to *Short-term Economic Indicators: Transition Economies, Sources and Definitions* (April 1996) and the *Methodological Notes* at the end of this publication.

(1) The sub-annual indices previously published are currently being assessed by the OECD Secretariat: for further information see the industrial production subject table in the "Recent trends" section.

(2) Quarterly data refer to the end of the period through first quarter 1994; afterward to period averages.

(3) From 1994 annual data is calculated using December with respect to December of the previous year.

(4) Modified Laspeyres index from January 1994. New indices are consumer price indices whereas the preceding ones were retail price indices.

(5) Retail price index.

(6) Prior to 1994 data cover deposits in savings banks only. Since then commercial bank deposits are also included.

1995									1996						
Apr	May	Jun	Jul	Aug	Sep	Oct	Nov	Dec	Jan	Feb	Mar				
												FORMATION BRUTE DE CAPITAL			
												Total			*'000 mrd karbovanets*
												Total : volume			*1990=100*
												Construction et installation			*'000 mrd karbovanets*

Pour les notes sur ces séries, veuillez consulter *Indicateurs économiques à court terme : Economies en transition, Sources et définitions* (avril 1996) et les *Notes méthodologiques* à la fin de cette publication.

1) Les indices mensuels et trimestriels précédemment publiés sont actuellement examinés par le Secrétariat de l'OCDE: pour plus de détails, voir le tableau sujet sur la production industrielle dans la partie "Tendances récentes".

2) Les chiffres trimestriels se rapportent à la fin de la période considérée jusqu'au premier trimestre de 1994. Ils se rapportent à la moyenne de la période ensuite.

3) A partir de 1994, les données annuelles correspondent à la valeur de décembre par rapport à celle de décembre de l'année précédente.

4) Indice de Laspeyres modifié à partir de janvier 1994. Les nouveaux indices sont des indices de prix à la consommation alors que les précédents étaient des indices de prix de détail.

5) Indice des prix de détail.

6) Avant 1994 cette série n'inclut que les dépôts dans les caisses d'épargne. Depuis 1994, elle inclut aussi les dépôts dans les banques commerciales.

UZBEKISTAN

					1994				1995				1996
		1993	1994	1995	Q1	Q2	Q3	Q4	Q1	Q2	Q3	Q4	Q1
INDUSTRIAL PRODUCTION													
Total[1]	*1990=100*	98.1	99.7	99.9									
Manufacturing	*1990=100*	98.8	100.4										
Mining	*1990=100*	91.7	92.3										
Commodity output													
Brown coal	*thousand tonnes*	3655	3734	3005	904	967	1009	894	662	701	807	835	
Black coal	*thousand tonnes*	152	111	73	33	24	24	29	33	5	12	23	
Natural gas	*million m³*	45036	47182	47951	13297	11323	9940	12622	13217	11903	10633	12198	
Electricity	*bln kilowatt hours*	49.7	47.7	47.2	13.3	11.5	10.5	12.4	13.4	11.5	10.6	11.7	
Refrigerators	*thousands*	81.7	19.8	19.6	5.5	7.8	0.2	6.3	7.0	5.0	2.1	5.5	
Crude petroleum	*thousand tonnes*	2406	3874	5310	796	895	977	1206	1310	1290	1317	1393	
Crude steel	*thousand tonnes*	610	364	356	114	95	78	74	57	81	106	112	
Cement	*thousand tonnes*	5177	4780	3419	1060	1356	1283	985	783	828	967	841	
CONSTRUCTION													
Dwellings													
Completed: total	*thousands*	76.3	66.3	58.6	6.6	19.8	20.7	19.2	7.3	16.8	19.3	15.2	
Completed: area	*thousand m²*	6445	5342	4939	591	1761	1518	1472	562	1507	1598	1272	
DOMESTIC TRADE													
Retail sales: value	*billion roubles*	1389.8											
	bln sum-coupons				1664.2	4331.9							
	million sum		20633	74316			5552	9085	14085	17838	17314	23616	
Retail sales value: total[2]	*million sum*			104230					16491	24405	27757	35530	
Retail sales: volume	*1990=100*	71.1	58.2	48.0	47.9	63.5	52.1	74.7	36.4	49.5	47.6	68.6	
LABOUR													
Employment													
Total	*thousands*	8259	8276	8153	7651	8312	8860	8279	8165	8185	8180	8080	
Industry	*thousands*	1222	1106	1100	1125	1115	1100	1084	1120	1110	1100	1070	
Manufacturing	*thousands*	935	875	870									
Unemployment													
Total registered	*thousands*	14.2	19.1	28.8	16.7	19.3	19.3	21.2	27.6	32.8	28.4	26.4	
Beneficiaries	*thousands*	9.2	8.1	15.0	8.7	8.0	6.5	9.3	17.8	18.0	13.1	11.3	
Non-beneficiaries	*thousands*	5.0	11.0	13.8	8.0	11.3	12.8	11.8	9.8	14.8	15.3	15.1	
Unemployment	*% of labour force*	0.18	0.23	0.34	0.20	0.20	0.20	0.30	0.33	0.40	0.33	0.30	
WAGES													
Monthly earnings													
Total	*'000 roubles*	28.7											
	'000 sum-coupons				110.2	187.2							
	sum		265	1066			328	436	635	996	1114	1519	
Industry	*'000 roubles*	44.6											
	'000 sum-coupons				156.9	260.9							
	sum		389	1529			480	660	973	1475	1551	2118	
Manufacturing	*'000 roubles*	41.5											
	sum		400										
PRICES													
Consumer prices[3]													
Total	*PP=100*	1038.1	1650.0										
Food	*PP=100*	808.1	1354.0										
Goods less food	*PP=100*	1077.7	1029.0										
Total goods[4]	*PP=100*	907.8	1576.2										
Services	*PP=100*	1515.0	7130.0										
DOMESTIC FINANCE													
Personal deposits	*billion roubles*	632.0											
	bln sum-coupons				485.1	579.5							
	million sum		871	2555			838	871	930	1193	1554	2555	
FOREIGN FINANCE													
US$ exchange rate end period	*rouble/US$*	1247			1753								
	sum-coupon/US$					5372							
	sum/US$		25.0	35.5			17.0	25.0	26.1	30.0	33.5	35.5	
Rouble exchange rate end period	*sum-coupon/rouble*					2.74							
	sum/rouble		0.0071	0.0077			0.0069	0.0071	0.0054	0.0066	0.0074	0.0077	
Rouble exchange rate per. ave.	*sum/rouble*			0.0066			0.0054	0.0072	0.0060	0.0055	0.0071	0.0077	

Footnotes appear at the end of the table.

	1995									1996					
	Apr	May	Jun	Jul	Aug	Sep	Oct	Nov	Dec	Jan	Feb	Mar			
PRODUCTION INDUSTRIELLE															
Total[1]													1990=100		
Industries manufacturières													1990=100		
Industries extractives													1990=100		
Quantités produites															
Lignite	222	245	234	243	260	304	303	281	251	218	232		milliers de tonnes		
Houille	4	0	1	3	6	3	8	9	6	8	3		milliers de tonnes		
Gaz naturel	4244	4047	3612	3571	3540	3522	3921	4282	3995	4612	4350		millions de m³		
Électricité	4.2	3.8	3.5	3.5	3.7	3.4	3.7	4.0	4.0	4.4	4.1		mrd kw-heures		
Réfrigérateurs	2.4	1.0	1.6	0.2	0.9	1.0	2.0	1.6	1.9	2.4	1.3		milliers		
Pétrole brut	438	455	397	422	444	451	483	463	447	474	406		milliers de tonnes		
Acier brut	24	23	34	36	32	38	40	42	30	40	39		milliers de tonnes		
Ciment	249	292	287	286	350	331	287	312	242	245	171		milliers de tonnes		
CONSTRUCTION															
Logements															
Achevés : total													milliers		
Achevés : surface													milliers de m²		
COMMERCE INTÉRIEUR															
Ventes de détail : valeur													milliards de roubles		
													mrd sum-coupons		
	5426	5769	5577	5229	5700	6385	6887	7527	8372	7918	8777		millions de sum		
Ventes de détail en valeur: total[2]	6401	6864	7189	6977	7570	9069	10402	11191	12743	11733	12948		millions de sum		
Ventes de détail : volume	49.7	50.4	52.5	51.6	48.0	64.2	55.5	77.8	70.4				1990=100		
MAIN-D'OEUVRE															
Emploi															
Total													milliers		
Industrie													milliers		
Industries manufacturières													milliers		
Chômage															
Chômeurs inscrits : total	32.9	33.6	32.0	29.8	27.6	27.7	27.5	26.3	25.4	26.4	29.4		milliers		
Allocataires	20.6	18.2	15.3	14.7	13.4	11.1	10.0	11.3	12.5	13.9	15.9		milliers		
Non allocataires	12.3	15.4	16.7	15.1	14.2	16.6	17.5	15.0	12.9	12.5	13.5		milliers		
Chômage	0.40	0.40	0.40	0.40	0.30	0.30	0.30	0.30	0.30	0.30	0.40		% de main-d'oeuvre		
SALAIRES															
Gains mensuels															
Total													'000 roubles		
													'000 sum-coupons		
													sum		
Industrie													'000 roubles		
													'000 sum-coupons		
													sum		
Industries manufacturières													'000 roubles		
													sum		
PRIX															
Prix à la consommation[3]															
Total	116.7	106.2	97.9	100.1	100.9	106.5							PP=100		
Alimentation	122.5	109.0	92.5	92.6	100.8	106.5							PP=100		
Biens sauf alimentation	105.3	103.6	102.3	102.1	101.1	101.7							PP=100		
Biens : total[4]	115.8	107.3	94.7	95.3	100.8	105.1							PP=100		
Services	155.5	105.1	107.4	119.9	101.7	113.2							PP=100		
FINANCES INTERNES															
Dépôts personnels													milliards de roubles		
													mrd sum-coupons		
	970	1048	1193	1271	1351	1554	1751	2091	2555				millions de sum		
FINANCES EXTÉRIEURES															
Taux de change du $É-U fin période													rouble/$É-U		
													sum-coupon/$É-U		
	26.3	27.6	30.0	30.9	32.2	33.5	33.4	36.0	35.5	36.1	36.8		sum/$É-U		
Taux de change du rouble fin pér.	0.0052	0.0055	0.0066	0.0069	0.0073	0.0074	0.0076	0.0079	0.0077	0.0077	0.0077		sum-coupon/rouble		
	0.0052	0.0053	0.0061	0.0067	0.0072	0.0075	0.0076	0.0078	0.0078	0.0077	0.0077		sum/rouble		
Taux de change du rouble moy. pér.													sum/rouble		

Les notes se trouvent en fin de tableau.

		1993	1994	1995	1994 Q1	Q2	Q3	Q4	1995 Q1	Q2	Q3	Q4	1996 Q1
FOREIGN TRADE													
Imports													
Total	*million US$*		2483.5	2900.0	565.5	462.8	648.2	790.7	517.9	592.8	488.8	1300.5	
from countries other than NIS	*million US$*	958.0	1135.7	1650.0	188.8	246.6	273.0	412.4	297.9	319.3	172.0	860.8	
from NIS	*million US$*		1347.8	1250.0	376.7	216.2	375.2	378.3	220.0	273.5	316.8	439.7	
Exports													
Total	*million US$*		3043.9	3100.0	767.7	527.0	449.2	1276.3	499.0	779.7	577.8	1243.5	
to countries other than NIS	*million US$*	720.5	966.3	1825.0	228.1	212.5	225.1	277.4	320.3	337.2	342.2	825.3	
to NIS	*million US$*		2077.6	1275.0	539.6	314.5	224.1	998.9	178.7	442.5	235.6	418.2	
Net trade													
Total	*million US$*		560.4	200.0	202.2	64.2	-199.0	485.6	-18.9	186.9	89.0	-57.0	
with countries other than NIS	*million US$*	-237.5	-169.4	175.0	39.3	-34.1	-47.9	-135.0	22.4	17.9	170.2	-35.5	
with NIS	*million US$*		729.8	25.0	162.9	98.3	-151.1	620.6	-41.3	169.0	-81.2	-21.5	
GROSS CAPITAL FORMATION													
Total	*billion roubles*	1272.6											
	bln sum-coupons				804	1861							
	million sum		13045	82200			3421	6959	6396	17930	26189	31685	
Total: volume	*1990=100*	68.0	53.0	54.0									
Construction and installation	*billion roubles*	853.1											
	bln sum-coupons				575	1313							
	million sum		8731				2432	4412	4528	10729	13862		

A new currency, the sum-coupon, was introduced on the 15th November 1993. It was replaced by the sum on the 27th June 1994.

For notes concerning these series, refer to *Short-term Economic Indicators: Transition Economies, Sources and Definitions* (April 1996) and the *Methodological Notes* at the end of this publication.

(1) The sub-annual indices previously published are currently being assessed by the OECD Secretariat: for further information see the industrial production subject table in the "Recent trends" section.

(2) Total retail sales including estimates of sales by non registered enterprises and private persons in informal markets.

(3) New consumer price index from January 1994.

(4) New consumer price index from January 1995.

1995									1996					
Apr	May	Jun	Jul	Aug	Sep	Oct	Nov	Dec	Jan	Feb	Mar			

COMMERCE EXTÉRIEUR

Importations

193.2	134.8	264.8	90.4	151.7	246.7	448.7	451.8	400.0	Total	*millions de $É-U*
111.8	100.1	107.4	58.8	47.5	65.7	414.8	196.0	250.0	depuis autres que les NEI	*millions de $É-U*
81.4	34.7	157.4	31.6	104.2	181.0	33.9	255.8	150.0	depuis les NEI	*millions de $É-U*

Exportations

241.5	157.7	380.5	127.6	105.2	345.0	296.6	546.9	400.0	Total	*millions de $É-U*
92.6	119.8	124.8	59.2	51.7	231.3	244.3	306.0	275.0	vers autres que les NEI	*millions de $É-U*
148.9	37.9	255.7	68.4	53.5	113.7	52.3	240.9	125.0	vers les NEI	*millions de $É-U*

Solde commercial

48.3	22.9	115.7	37.2	-46.5	98.3	-152.1	95.1	0.0	Total	*millions de $É-U*
-19.2	19.7	17.4	0.4	4.2	165.6	-170.5	110.0	25.0	avec autres que les NEI	*millions de $É-U*
67.5	3.2	98.3	36.8	-50.7	-67.3	18.4	-14.9	-25.0	avec les NEI	*millions de $É-U*

FORMATION BRUTE DE CAPITAL

Total	*milliards de roubles*
	mrd sum-coupons
	millions de sum
Total : volume	*1990=100*
Construction et installation	*milliards de roubles*
	mrd sum-coupons
	millions de sum

Une nouvelle monnaie, le sum-coupon, a été introduite le 15 novembre 1993. Elle a été remplacée par le sum le 27 juin 1994.

Pour les notes sur ces séries, veuillez consulter *Indicateurs économiques à court terme : Economies en transition, Sources et définitions* (avril 1996) et les *Notes méthodologiques* à la fin de cette publication.

1) Les indices mensuels et trimestriels précédemment publiés sont actuellement examinés par le Secrétariat de l'OCDE: pour plus de détails, voir le tableau sujet sur la production industrielle dans la partie "Tendances récentes".

2) Ventes de détail totales, comprenant les ventes effectuées par les entreprises non inscrites au registre du commerce et par les personnes privées sur les marchés informels.

3) Nouvel indice des prix à la consommation depuis janvier 1994.

4) Nouvel indice des prix à la consommation depuis janvier 1995.

CENTRAL AND EASTERN EUROPE

INDICATORS BY SUBJECT

—

EUROPE CENTRALE ET ORIENTALE

INDICATEURS PAR SUJET

NATIONAL ACCOUNTS

General Introduction

The following section contains tables showing the expenditure components of Gross Domestic Product (GDP) at both current and constant prices for nine countries of Central and Eastern Europe: Bulgaria, Estonia, Hungary, Latvia, Lithuania, Poland, the Republic of Slovenia, Romania and the Slovak Republic.

In general, these estimates have been prepared by staff in the national statistical offices according to the principles of the System of National Accounts (SNA) rather than simple conversion from the MPS (Material Product System), even though the underlying data in many cases is still based on the data sources available under the old system of detailed reporting for state enterprises. Coverage of the private sector, especially of very small scale informal activity, is incomplete and based to greater or lesser extents on approximate estimates, as is the case in many OECD Member countries.

In accordance with the 1993 SNA, and to preserve continuity with earlier estimates, where possible final consumption is shown disaggregated into individual consumption and collective consumption. The former covers all consumption expenditure by households and non-profit institutions serving households and consumption expenditure by general government on services such as education and health benefiting particular households. Other government services such as public administration and defence are treated as collective consumption.

With the degree of inflation experienced in many transition countries in recent years, and the degree of structural change that has taken place, the preservation of a single base year for the constant price estimates may be of limited utility. In the case of Bulgaria and Romania, and Poland from 1993, each year's data is given in prices of the current and preceding year only.

A more extensive document, including estimates of GDP from the production approach, also at current and constant prices, has been released (OCDE/GD(95)89) and an updated publication containing these estimates is currently under preparation. Some of these data may also be incorporated into a future issue of this publication. Work on developing quarterly estimates of GDP is underway in all the countries covered here and it is intended to include these data in this publication as soon as appropriate.

COMPTES NATIONAUX

Introduction générale

La partie suivante contient des tableaux du produit intérieur brut (PIB) par catégorie de dépenses à prix courants et à prix constants pour neuf pays d'Europe centrale et orientale : la Bulgarie, l'Estonie, la Hongrie, la Lettonie, la Lituanie, la Pologne, la République de Slovénie, la Roumanie et la République slovaque.

Ces estimations, en général, ont été préparées par les offices nationaux de statistique selon les principes du Système du comptabilité nationale (SCN) au lieu d'être simplement converties du SPM (Système de produit matériel), ceci en dépit du fait que les données de base sont, dans de nombreux cas, toujours tirées des données disponibles dans l'ancien système des rapports détaillés des entreprises d'État. La couverture du secteur privé, notamment des activités informelles de petite taille, n'est pas complète; elle est basée selon les pays, sur des estimations approximatives, comme c'est le cas pour plusieurs pays Membres de l'OCDE.

Conformément au SCN de 1993, et afin de préserver la continuité avec les estimations précédentes, la consommation finale, dans la mesure du possible, est décomposée en consommation individuelle et en consommation collective. La consommation individuelle couvre toutes les dépenses de consommation des ménages et des institutions sans but lucratif au service des ménages ainsi que les dépenses de consommation du secteur des administrations publiques sur les services tels que l'éducation et la santé au bénéfice des ménages particuliers. Les autres services gouvernementaux comme les administrations publiques et la défense sont traités comme de la consommation collective.

Compte tenu du niveau d'inflation dans certains pays en transition au cours des dernières années et des changements structurels qui ont eu lieu, le maintien d'une seule année de base pour les estimations à prix constants peut être d'une utilité limitée. Pour la Bulgarie et la Roumanie, et la Pologne à partir de 1993, les données pour chaque année sont donc présentées uniquement aux prix de l'année courante et aux prix de l'année précédente.

Un document plus détaillé, incluant également des estimations du PIB du côté de la production à prix courants et à prix constants, a été publié (OCDE/GD(95)89) et une publication mise à jour qui contient ces estimations est actuellement en cours de préparation. Certaines données seront peut-être alors incorporées dans un numéro futur de cette publication. Le travail sur le développement des estimations trimestrielles du PIB se poursuit dans tous les pays ci-après et il est prévu d'inclure des données trimestrielles dans cette publication lorsque celles-ci seront assez solides.

BULGARIA

GDP BY EXPENDITURE

million levs

	1990[1]	%	1991	%	1992	%
Current prices						
Final consumption	33 585	74.0	99 254	73.1	172 590	85.9
Individual	30 298	66.8	88 813	65.4	154 929	77.1
of which final consumption exp. of						
Households[3]	25 330	55.8	73 164	53.9	131 195	65.3
Government[4]	4 969	10.9	15 387	11.3	23 174	11.5
NPISH[4]			262	0.2	560	0.3
Non-profit institutions	3 286	7.2	10 441	7.7	17 661	8.8
Collective	13 800	30.4	30 665	22.6	39 937	19.9
Gross fixed capital formation	9 652	21.3	24 635	18.2	32 577	16.2
Changes in inventories	4 148	9.1	6 030	4.4	7 360	3.7
Exports of goods and services[5]	10 560	23.3	58 976	43.5	94 630	47.1
less: imports of goods and services[5]	10 315	22.7	53 184	39.2	106 325	52.9
Statistical discrepancy	-2 240	-4.9				
GDP	45 390	100.0	135 711	100.0	200 832	100.0
GDP per capita, levs	5 206		15 721		23 516	
At prices of the previous year						
Final consumption	28 167	78.3	..	..	96 179	76.4
Individual	25 258	70.2	..	..	86 709	68.9
of which final consumption exp. of						
Households	21 128	58.7	..	..	73 903	58.7
Government[4]	4 130	11.5	..	..	12 520	9.9
NPISH[4]			..	..	286	0.2
Non-profit institutions	2 909	8.1	..	..	9 470	7.5
Collective	9 812	27.3	..	..	27 294	21.7
Gross fixed capital formation	8 415	23.4	..	..	22 830	18.1
Changes in inventories	1 397	3.9	..	..	4 464	3.5
Exports of goods and services			..	..		
less: imports of goods and services			..	..		
Statistical discrepancy[6]	-2 009	-5.6	..	..	2 396	1.9
GDP	35 970	100.0	..	..	125 869	100.0
GDP per capita, levs	4 126		..		14 738	

(1) Data for 1990 have been calculated by conversion from MPS estimates. From 1991 data are calculated according to the 1993 SNA.

(2) Preliminary data.

(3) For 1990 the imputed rent of owner occupied dwellings is valued at cost.

(4) For 1990 includes NPISH(Non-profit institutions serving households).

(5) For 1990 refers to exports and imports of goods only.

(6) For 1990-1994, refers to net exports and statistical discrepancy.

Source: National Statistical Institute

PIB PAR CATÉGORIE DE DÉPENSE

millions de levs

1993	%	1994[2]	%	
				Aux prix courants
276 022	92.3	493 879	90.9	Consommation finale
250 879	83.9	452 830	83.3	Consommation individuelle
				dont dépenses de consommation finale des
218 927	73.2	400 764	73.7	Ménages[3]
31 217	10.4	50 863	9.4	Administrations publiques[4]
735	0.2	1 203	0.2	ISBL[4]
25 143	8.4	41 049	7.6	Institutions sans but lucratif
45 678	15.3	46 157	8.5	Consommation collective
38 722	13.0	53 000	9.8	Formation brute de capital fixe
6 956	2.3	-6 843	-1.3	Variations de stocks
114 210	38.2	249 214	45.9	Exportations de biens et services[5]
136 976	45.8	245 776	45.2	moins: importations de biens et services[5]
				Écart statistique
298 934	100.0	543 474	100.0	**PIB**
35 284		64 148		**PIB par habitant**, levs
				Aux prix de l'année précédente
166 442	84.1	269 026	88.8	Consommation finale
150 418	76.0	247 059	81.5	Consommation individuelle
				dont dépenses de consommation finale des
130 249	65.8	218 381	72.1	Ménages
19 698	10.0	28 035	9.2	Administrations publiques[4]
471	0.2	643	0.2	ISBL[4]
16 024	8.1	21 967	7.2	Institutions sans but lucratif
31 859	16.1	27 285	9.0	Consommation collective
26 892	13.6	31 195	10.3	Formation brute de capital fixe
4 967	2.5	-3 910	-1.3	Variations de stocks
				Exportations de biens et services
				moins: importations de biens et services
-442	-0.2	6 782	2.2	Écart statistique[6]
197 859	100.0	303 093	100.0	**PIB**
23 354		35 775		**PIB par habitant**, leva

1) Les données de 1990 ont été calculées par conversion des estimations de la CPM. A partir de 1991 les données sont calculées selon le SCN 1993.

2) Données préliminaires.

3) Pour 1990 le loyer imputé des logements occupés par leur propriétaires est évaluées aux coûts.

4) Pour 1990, y compris les ISBL (Institutions sans but lucratif au service des ménages).

5) Pour 1990, se réfère aux exportations et aux importations des biens uniquement.

5) Pour 1990 à 1994, se réfère aux exportations nettes et à l'écart statistique.

ource: Institut national statistique

ESTONIA

GDP BY EXPENDITURE

million kroons

	1990[1]	%	1991[1]	%	1992[1]	%
Current prices						
Final consumption	619.5	77.7	1 295.5	70.7	10 254.9	71.9
Individual	..	..	..	..	..	..
of which final consumption exp. of						
Households	514.1	64.4	1 001.7	54.7	7 697.5	54.0
Government[2]	..	..	..	..	..	..
NPISH[3]	..	..	53.0	2.9	782.2	5.5
Collective[2]	105.4	13.2	240.8	13.1	1 775.2	12.5
Gross capital formation	241.1	30.2	447.7	24.4	3 738.0	26.2
Gross fixed capital formation	189.5	23.8	357.3	19.5	2 754.8	19.3
Changes in inventories	51.6	6.5	90.4	4.9	983.2	6.9
Exports of goods and services			583.8	31.9	7 893.2	55.4
less: imports of goods and services[4]	-62.9	-7.9	495.0	27.0	7 631.3	53.5
Statistical discrepancy						
GDP	797.7	100.0	1 832.0	100.0	14 254.8	100.0
GDP per capita, kroons	508		1 170		9 230	
Constant prices[5]						
Final consumption	..	..	..	..	..	..
Individual	..	..	..	..	..	..
of which final consumption exp. of						
Households	..	..	..	..	..	..
Government	..	..	..	..	..	..
NPISH[3]	..	..	..	..	..	..
Collective	..	..	..	..	..	..
Gross capital formation	..	..	..	..	..	..
Gross fixed capital formation	..	..	..	..	..	..
Changes in inventories	..	..	..	..	..	..
Exports of goods and services	..	..	..	..	..	..
less: imports of goods and services	..	..	..	..	..	..
GDP	..	..	1 832.0	100.0	1 571.0	100.0
GDP per capita, kroons	..		1 170		1 017	

(1) Data calculated by conversion from MPS estimates. From 1992 direct SNA estimates are made.

(2) General government expenditure has been broken into individual and collective consumption expenditure, in accordance with the classification of the functions of government use in the SNA, only since 1992. Data on individual consumption expenditure by government comprises expenditure on education, health and social security.

(3) Non-profit institutions serving households.

(4) Net exports for 1990.

(5) Constant price estimates are made from the production side, prior to the break in prices of 1991, thereafter in prices of 1993.

NOTE: The Estonian kroon was introduced on 20 June 1992. The conversion rate at introduction was 1 kroon to 10 roubles. Data for 1992 and previous years have been converted into kroons by the State Statistical Office of Estonia.

Source: State Statistical Office of Estonia.

 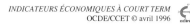

PIB PAR CATÉGORIE DE DÉPENSE

millions de couronnes

1992	%	1993	%	1994	%	
						Aux prix courants
9 344.3	71.0	17 010.7	77.1	24 467.8	81.3	Consommation finale
8 380.0	63.7	14 914.0	67.6	20 996.9	69.8	Consommation individuelle
						dont dépenses de consommation finale des
7 163.5	54.4	12 416.9	56.3	17 532.1	58.2	Ménages
1 119.5	8.5	2 377.1	10.8	3 319.2	11.0	Administrations publiques[2]
97.0	0.7	120.0	0.5	145.6	0.5	ISBL[3]
964.3	7.3	2 096.7	9.5	3 470.9	11.5	Consommation collective[2]
3 518.2	26.7	5 821.0	26.4	8 613.5	28.6	Formation brute de capital
2 754.8	20.9	5 280.0	23.9	7 827.5	26.0	Formation brute de capital fixe
763.4	5.8	541.0	2.5	786.0	2.6	Variations de stocks
7 893.2	60.0	15 197.0	68.9	23 799.0	79.1	Exportations de biens et services
7 121.3	54.1	16 124.9	73.1	27 034.2	89.8	moins: importations de biens et services[4]
-476.7	-3.6	156.1	0.7	256.8	0.9	Écart statistique
13 157.7	100.0	22 059.9	100.0	30 102.9	100.0	**PIB**
8 520		14 544		20 078		**PIB par habitant**, couronnes
						Aux prix constants[5]
..	..	..	..	..	..	Consommation finale
..	..	..	..	..	..	Consommation individuelle
						dont dépenses de consommation finale des
..	..	..	..	..	..	Ménages
..	..	..	..	..	..	Administrations publiques
..	..	..	..	..	..	ISBL[3]
..	..	..	..	..	..	Consommation collective
..	..	..	..	..	..	Formation brute de capital
..	..	..	..	..	..	Formation brute de capital fixe
..	..	..	..	..	..	Variations de stocks
..	..	..	..	..	..	Exportations de biens et services
..	..	..	..	..	..	moins: importations de biens et services
24 112.3	..	22 059.9	..	21 467.7	..	**PIB**
15 613		14 544		14 318		**PIB par habitant**, couronnes

1) Données calculées par conversion des estimations de la CPM. Depuis 1992 les estimations SCN sont faites directement.

2) Les dépenses des administrations publiques sont ventilées en consommation individuelle et consommation collective, en accord avec la classification des fonctions des administrations publiques utilisée dans le SCN, seulement depuis 1992. Les dépenses de consommation individuelle des administrations publiques couvrent les dépenses sur l'éducation, la santé et la sécurité sociale.

3) Institutions sans but lucratif au service des ménages.

4) Exportations nettes pour 1990.

5) Les estimations à prix constants sont calculées du côté de la production ; avant la rupture les estimations sont exprimées aux prix constants de 1991, ensuite aux prix constants de 1993.

NOTE: La couronne estonienne a été introduite le 20 juin 1992. Le taux de conversion à la date d'introduction était de 1 couronne pour 10 roubles. Les données pour 1992 et les années précédentes ont été converties en couronnes par l'Office statistique d'État de l'Estonie.

Source: Office statistique d'État de l'Estonie.

HUNGARY

GDP BY EXPENDITURE

billion forints

	1989	%	1990
Current prices			
Final consumption	1 207.3	70.1	1 504.3
Individual	1 029.6	59.8	1 282.5
Collective	177.7	10.3	221.8
Gross capital formation	458.1	26.6	530.4
Gross fixed capital formation	372.5	21.6	400.5
Changes in inventories	85.6	5.0	129.9
Exports of goods and services	620.9	36.0	650.7
less: imports of goods and services	563.5	32.7	596.1
GDP	1 722.8	100.0	2 089.3
GDP per capita, forints	165 685		201 577
Constant prices 1988			
Final consumption	1 057.6	72.5	1 029.4
Individual	893.6	61.3	861.1
Collective	164.0	11.2	168.3
Gross capital formation	365.2	25.0	349.8
Gross fixed capital formation	332.5	22.8	308.8
Changes in inventories	32.7	2.2	40.9
Exports of goods and services	536.8	36.8	508.1
less: imports of goods and services	500.7	34.3	479.4
GDP	1 458.9	100.0	1 407.9
GDP per capita, forints	140 300		135 831

Source: Hungarian Central Statistical Office and OECD (1994) "National Accounts for Hungary, Sources, Methods and Estimates".

PIB PAR CATÉGORIE DE DÉPENSE

milliards de forints

%	1991	%	
			Aux prix courants
72.0	1 894.7	82.1	Consommation finale
61.0	1 605.5	69.5	Consommation individuelle
10.0	289.3	12.5	Consommation collective
25.0	480.8	20.8	Formation brute de capital
19.0	440.9	19.1	Formation brute de capital fixe
6.0	39.9	1.7	Variations de stocks
31.0	834.9	36.2	Exportations de biens et services
28.0	902.0	39.1	moins: importations de biens et services
100.0	2 308.4	100.0	**PIB**
	223 120		**PIB par habitant**, forints
			Aux prix constants de 1988
73.0	977.1	78.8	Consommation finale
61.0	813.3	65.6	Consommation individuelle
12.0	163.8	13.2	Consommation collective
24.0	276.2	22.3	Formation brute de capital
21.0	276.6	22.3	Formation brute de capital fixe
2.0	-.4	0.0	Variations de stocks
36.0	492.5	39.7	Exportations de biens et services
34.0	505.4	40.7	moins: importations de biens et services
100.0	1 240.4	100.0	**PIB**
	119 895		**PIB par habitant**, forints

Source: Office central statistique hongrois et OCDE (1994) "Comptes nationaux de la Hongrie : Sources, méthodes et estimations".

HUNGARY

GDP BY EXPENDITURE

billion forints

	1991	%	1992	%	1993	%
Current prices						
Final consumption	2 011.5	80.5	2 477.6	84.2	3 131.3	88.2
Individual[2]	1 746.9	69.9	2 141.1	72.8	2 639.9	74.4
of which final consumption exp. of						
Households	1 354.1	54.2	1 670.8	56.8	2 061.5	58.1
Government	376.7	15.1	444.2	15.1	522.1	14.7
Non-profit institutions	16.1	0.6	26.1	0.9	56.3	1.6
Collective[3 4]	264.6	10.6	336.5	11.4	491.4	13.8
Gross capital formation	511.0	20.5	473.0	16.1	708.1	20.0
Gross fixed capital formation[5]	522.9	20.9	584.7	19.9	670.0	18.9
Changes in inventories	-11.9	-0.5	-111.7	-3.8	38.1	1.1
Exports of goods and services[6]	818.4	32.8	925.3	31.4	937.0	26.4
less: imports of goods and services[4 6]	842.6	33.7	933.3	31.7	1 228.1	34.6
GDP	2 498.3	100.0	2 942.6	100.0	3 548.3	100.0
GDP per capita, forints	241 476		285 040		344 707	
Constant prices 1991						
Final consumption	2 011.5	80.5	2 024.0	83.6	2 134.1	88.6
Individual[2]	1 746.9	69.9	1 746.3	72.1	1 780.0	73.9
of which final consumption exp. of						
Households	1 354.1	54.2	1 366.5	56.4	1 397.1	58.0
Government	376.7	15.1	356.9	14.7	342.7	14.2
Non-profit institutions	16.1	0.6	22.9	0.9	40.2	1.7
Collective[3 4]	264.6	10.6	277.7	11.5	354.1	14.7
Gross capital formation	511.0	20.5	406.9	16.8	538.6	22.4
Gross fixed capital formation[5]	522.9	20.9	509.1	21.0	519.5	21.6
Changes in inventories	-11.9	-0.5	-102.2	-4.2	19.1	0.8
Exports of goods and services[6]	818.4	32.8	835.6	34.5	750.9	31.2
less: imports of goods and services[4 6]	842.6	33.7	844.7	34.9	1 015.7	42.2
GDP	2 498.3	100.0	2 421.8	100.0	2 407.9	100.0
GDP per capita, forints	241 476		234 592		233 921	

(1) Preliminary data.

(2) Individual consumption also includes government housing services, subsidies on medicine, subsidised transport services for students and pensioners and consumption expenditure of non-profit institutions serving households.

(3) Collective consumption excludes financial and insurance services, treated as market services, and consumption expenditures of non-profit institutions serving households.

(4) In 1993 and 1994, imports of goods and collective consumption include a significant amount of military equipment imported from the Russian Federation.

(5) Gross fixed capital formation includes assets acquired as capital transfers in kind and under financial leasing, capital repairs and non-deductible VAT on capital goods.

(6) Contracted work is recorded on a gross basis in exports and imports of goods and services.

Source: Hungarian Central Statistical Office

PIB PAR CATÉGORIE DE DÉPENSE

milliards de forints

1994	%	1995[1]	%	
				Aux prix courants
3 678.8	84.3	4 384.0	79.7	Consommation finale
3 151.7	72.2	3 754.0	68.3	Consommation individuelle[2]
				dont dépenses de consommation finale des
2 458.3	56.3	3 754.0	68.3	Ménages
618.3	14.2			Administrations publiques
75.1	1.7			Institutions sans but lucratif
527.1	12.1	630.0	11.5	Consommation collective[3 4]
968.6	22.2	1 231.0	22.4	Formation brute de capital
878.5	20.1	1 120.0	20.4	Formation brute de capital fixe[5]
90.1	2.1	111.0	2.0	Variations de stocks
1 262.5	28.9	1 920.0	34.9	Exportations de biens et services[6]
1 545.1	35.4	2 035.0	37.0	moins: importations de biens et services[4 6]
4 364.8	100.0	5 500.0	100.0	**PIB**
425 365		540 000		**PIB par habitant**, forints
				Aux prix constants de 1991
2 085.2	84.1	..	..	Consommation finale
1 776.1	71.7	..	..	Consommation individuelle[2]
				dont dépenses de consommation finale des
1 394.7	56.3	..	..	Ménages
336.1	13.6	..	..	Administrations publiques
45.3	1.8	..	..	Institutions sans but lucratif
309.2	12.5	..	..	Consommation collective[3 4]
645.2	26.0	..	..	Formation brute de capital
584.3	23.6	..	..	Formation brute de capital fixe[5]
60.9	2.5	..	..	Variations de stocks
853.9	34.4	..	..	Exportations de biens et services[6]
1 105.5	44.6	..	..	moins: importations de biens et services[4 6]
2 478.8	100.0	2 516.0	100.0	**PIB**
241 568		247 024		**PIB par habitant**, forints

1) Données préliminaires.

2) La consommation individuelle inclut également les services de logement des administrations publiques, les subventions sur les médicaments et sur les services de transport pour étudiants et pensionnés ainsi que les dépenses de consommation des institutions sans but lucratif au service des ménages.

3) La consommation collective exclut les services financiers et d'assurance, traités comme des services marchands, ainsi que les dépenses de consommation des institutions sans but lucratif au service des ménages.

4) En 1993 et 1994, les importations de biens et la consommation collective incluent une quantité significative d'équipements militaires importés de la Fédération de Russie.

5) La formation brute de capital fixe inclut les actifs acquis sous forme de transferts en nature et sous crédit bail financier, ainsi que les réparations en capital et de la TVA non déductible sur les biens de capital.

6) Le travail de sous-traitance est enregistré sur une base brute dans les exportations et les importations de biens et de services.

Source: Office central statistique hongrois

LATVIA

GDP BY EXPENDITURE

thousand lats

	1990	%	1991	%	1992	%
Current prices						
Final consumption	38 235	61.2	80 990	56.5	521 240	51.9
Individual	36 925	59.1	76 250	53.2	472 895	47.1
of which final consumption exp. of						
Households	32 890	52.7	66 250	46.2	394 540	39.3
Government	4 035	6.5	10 000	7.0	77 015	7.7
NPISH[1]	0	0.0	0	0.0	1 340	0.1
Collective	1 310	2.1	4 740	3.3	48 345	4.8
Gross capital formation	25 030	40.1	48 345	33.7	414 225	41.2
Gross fixed capital formation	14 360	23.0	8 840	6.2	112 325	11.2
Changes in inventories	10 670	17.1	39 505	27.6	301 900	30.1
Exports of goods and services	29 785	47.7	50 520	35.2	803 080	79.9
less: imports of goods and services	30 610	49.0	36 530	25.5	733 990	73.1
GDP	62 440	100.0	143 325	100.0	1 004 555	100.0
GDP per capita, lats	23.4		53.8		381.7	
Constant prices 1993						
Final consumption	2 300 858	77.9	1 769 810	66.9	1 150 517	66.8
Individual	2 198 548	74.5	1 659 924	62.7	1 016 025	59.0
of which final consumption exp. of						
Households	1 983 432	67.2	1 467 824	55.5	828 832	48.1
Government	215 116	7.3	192 100	7.3	184 419	10.7
NPISH[1]	0	0.0	0	0.0	2 774	0.2
Collective	102 310	3.5	109 886	4.2	134 492	7.8
Gross capital formation	1 167 856	39.5	955 795	36.1	576 940	33.5
Gross fixed capital formation	932 832	31.6	336 423	12.7	239 717	13.9
Changes in inventories	235 024	8.0	619 372	23.4	337 223	19.6
Exports of goods and services	1 777 130	60.2	1 205 238	45.6	1 384 234	80.3
less: imports of goods and services	2 292 979	77.7	1 285 446	48.6	1 388 447	80.6
GDP	2 952 865	100.0	2 645 397	100.0	1 723 244	100.0
GDP per capita, lats	1 105.7		993.6		654.8	

(1) Non-profit institutions serving households.

NOTE: The Latvian rouble was introduced as legal tender on 7 May 1992. It was introduced at par with the FSU rouble which continued to be legal tender. On 20 July 1992 the Latvian rouble became the only legal tender. From 5 March 1993 Lats were gradually put into circulation, the conversion rate having been 1 lat to 200 Latvian roubles. From 18 October 1993 the Latvian rouble ceased to be legal tender and was completely withdrawn on 1 July 1994. All data have been converted into lats by the Central Statistical Bureau of Latvia.

Source: Central Statistical Bureau of Latvia

PIB PAR CATÉGORIE DE DÉPENSE

milliers de lats

1993	%	1994	%	1995	%	
						Aux prix courants
1 093 900	74.6	1 609 679	78.8	1 857 639	78.7	Consommation finale
971 616	66.2	1 446 174	70.8	1 658 320	70.2	Consommation individuelle
						dont dépenses de consommation finale des
767 122	52.3	1 194 520	58.5	1 363 993	57.8	Ménages
201 802	13.8	247 098	12.1	289 771	12.3	Administrations publiques
2 692	0.2	4 556	0.2	4 556	0.2	ISBL[1]
122 284	8.3	163 505	8.0	199 319	8.4	Consommation collective
134 615	9.2	390 810	19.1	518 116	21.9	Formation brute de capital
201 842	13.8	303 935	14.9	392 113	16.6	Formation brute de capital fixe
-67 227	-4.6	86 875	4.3	126 003	5.3	Variations de stocks
1 074 356	73.2	948 838	46.5	1 078 203	45.7	Exportations de biens et services
835 859	57.0	906 772	44.4	1 093 240	46.3	moins: importations de biens et services
1 467 012	100.0	2 042 555	100.0	2 360 718	100.0	**PIB**
567.3		801.7		938.7		**PIB par habitant**, lats
						Aux prix constants de 1993
1 093 900	74.6	1 115 419	75.5	..	..	Consommation finale
971 616	66.2	996 278	67.5	..	..	Consommation individuelle
						dont dépenses de consommation finale des
767 122	52.3	791 545	53.6	..	..	Ménages
201 802	13.8	201 955	13.7	..	..	Administrations publiques
2 692	0.2	2 778	0.2	..	..	ISBL[1]
122 284	8.3	119 141	8.1	..	..	Consommation collective
134 615	9.2	207 264	14.0	..	..	Formation brute de capital
201 842	13.8	203 446	13.8	..	..	Formation brute de capital fixe
-67 227	-4.6	3 818	0.3	..	..	Variations de stocks
1 074 356	73.2	984 044	66.6	..	..	Exportations de biens et services
835 859	57.0	830 204	56.2	..	..	moins: importations de biens et services
1 467 012	100.0	1 476 523	100.0	..	..	**PIB**
567.3		579.6		..		**PIB par habitant**, lats

) Institutions sans but lucratif au service des ménages.

OTE: Le rouble letton a été introduit comme moyen de paiement légal le 7 mai 1992. Il a été introduit à un taux de 1:1 avec le rouble de l'ex-URSS qui a continué d'être accepté comme moyen de paiement légal. Le 20 juillet 1992 le rouble letton est devenu le seul moyen de paiement légal. A partir du 5 mars 1993 le lat a été mis en circulation, le taux de conversion ayant été de 1 lat pour 200 roubles lettons. Le rouble letton a cessé d'être un moyen de paiement légal à partir du 18 octobre 1993. Il a été complétement retiré le 1er juillet 1994. Les données ont été converties en lats par le Bureau central de statistique de lettonie.

ource: Bureau central de statistique de lettonie.

LITHUANIA

GDP BY EXPENDITURE

	million roubles		millions de roubles		million litas	
	1990	%	1991	%	1992	%
Current prices						
Final consumption	9 658.2	74.9	28 108.5	66.5	2 780.9	82.1
Individual	..	..	..	..	2 621.3	77.4
of which final consumption exp. of						
Households	7 086.5	54.9	23 478.5	55.5	2 349.1	69.4
Government[1]	2 571.7	19.9	4 630.0	11.0	272.2	8.0
NPISH[2]	..	..	..	..	..	..
Collective[1]	..	..	..	..	159.6	4.7
Gross capital formation	4 375.4	33.9	10 602.4	25.1	299.7	8.8
Gross fixed capital formation	3 710.3	28.8	9 307.3	22.0	987.4	29.2
Changes in inventories	665.1	5.2	1 295.1	3.1	-687.7	-20.3
Exports of goods and services	6 988.6	54.2	12 300.1	29.1	1 077.5	31.8
less: imports of goods and services	8 125.0	63.0	8 728.9	20.6	771.4	22.8
GDP	12 897.2	100.0	42 282.1	100.0	3 386.7	100.0
GDP per capita	3 465	roubles	11 300	roubles	904	litas
Constant prices[4]						
Final consumption	9 011.2	76.0	7 952.5	52.6	..	..
Individual	..	..	..	..	..	..
of which final consumption exp. of						
Households	6 390.0	53.9	6 126.1	40.5	..	..
Government[1]	2 621.2	22.1	1 826.4	12.1	..	..
NPISH[2]	..	..	..	..	..	..
Collective[1]	..	..	..	..	..	..
Gross capital formation	3 607.7	30.4	3 835.0	25.4	..	..
Gross fixed capital formation	3 051.8	25.7	3 394.4	22.5	..	..
Changes in inventories	555.9	4.7	440.6	2.9	..	..
Exports of goods and services					..	..
less: imports of goods and services[3]	-756.0	-6.4	3 321.8	22.0	..	..
GDP[4]	11 862.9	100.0	15 109.3	100.0	15 948.4	100.0
GDP per capita	3 187	roubles	4 038	roubles	4 262	litas

(1) For 1990-91, data refer to total general government final consumption expenditure.

(2) Non-profit institutions serving households.

(3) Net exports.

(4) For 1990-91, at previous year prices. For 1992-94, derived from the production side at 1993 prices.

NOTE: The Lithuanian talonas was introduced as a separate temporary currency on 1 October 1992. It was replaced by the litas on 25 June 1993. The conversion rate at introductio
was 1 litas to 100 talonas. All data have been converted into litas by the Lithuanian Department of Statistics.

Source: Lithuanian Department of Statistics

PIB PAR CATÉGORIE DE DÉPENSE

millions de litas

1993	%	1994	%	
				Aux prix courants
9 493.9	85.5	15 385.2	90.6	Consommation finale
8 613.1	77.5	14 007.4	82.5	Consommation individuelle
				dont dépenses de consommation finale des
7 673.9	69.1	12 278.0	72.3	Ménages
939.2	8.5	1 716.6	10.1	Administrations publiques[1]
..	..	12.8	0.1	ISBL[2]
880.8	7.9	1 377.8	8.1	Consommation collective[1]
2 519.5	22.7	2 613.1	15.4	Formation brute de capital
2 700.3	24.3	3 500.0	20.6	Formation brute de capital fixe
-180.8	-1.6	-886.9	-5.2	Variations de stocks
9 566.9	86.1	9 360.8	55.1	Exportations de biens et services
10 472.4	94.3	10 378.4	61.1	moins: importations de biens et services
11 107.9	100.0	16 980.7	100.0	**PIB**
2 978 litas		4 564 litas		**PIB par habitant**
				Aux prix constants[4]
..	..	..	..	Consommation finale
..	..	..	..	Consommation individuelle
				dont dépenses de consommation finale des
..	..	..	..	Ménages
..	..	..	..	Administrations publiques[1]
..	..	..	..	ISBL[2]
..	..	..	..	Consommation collective[1]
..	..	..	..	Formation brute de capital
..	..	..	..	Formation brute de capital fixe
..	..	..	..	Variations de stocks
..	..	..	..	Exportations de biens et services
..	..	..	..	moins: importations de biens et services[3]
11 107.9	100.0	11 217.5	100.0	**PIB**[4]
2 978 litas		3 015 litas		**PIB par habitant**

1) De 1990 à 1991, les données se réfèrent aux dépenses de consommation finale totales des administrations publiques.

2) Institutions sans but lucratif au service des ménages.

3) Exportations nettes.

4) Pour 1990 à 1991 aux prix de l'année précédente. Pour 1992 à 1994, le PIB est calculé du côté de la production aux prix de 1993.

OTE: Le talonas lituanien a été adopté à titre de monnaie provisoire le 1er octobre 1992. Il a été remplacé par le litas le 25 juin 1993. Le taux de conversion à la date d'introduction était de 1 litas pour 100 talonas. Les données ont été converties en litas par le Département de statistiques de Lituanie.

ource: Département de statistiques de Lituanie.

GDP BY EXPENDITURE[1]

billion old zlotys[2]

	1990	%	1991	%
Current prices				
Final consumption	376 749	67.2	663 336	82.0
Individual	329 897	58.9	569 722	70.4
of which final consumption exp. of				
Households	268 670	48.0	480 009	59.3
Government and NPISH[3]	61 227	10.9	89 713	11.1
Collective	46 852	8.4	93 614	11.6
Gross capital formation	143 513	25.6	161 027	19.9
Gross fixed capital formation[4]	117 612	21.0	157 748	19.5
Changes in inventories	25 901	4.6	3 279	0.4
Exports of goods and services			190 257	23.5
less: imports of goods and services[5]	40 009	7.1	205 791	25.4
GDP	560 271	100.0	808 829	100.0
GDP per capita, thousand old zlotys	14 698		21 149	
Constant prices[6]				
Final consumption	376 749	67.2	404 860	77.7
Individual	329 897	58.9	344 032	66.0
of which final consumption exp. of				
Households	268 670	48.0	285 720	54.8
Government and NPISH[3]	61 227	10.9	58 312	11.2
Collective	46 852	8.4	60 828	11.7
Gross capital formation	143 513	25.6	114 654	22.0
Gross fixed capital formation[4]	117 612	21.0	112 432	21.6
Changes in inventories	25 901	4.6	2 222	0.4
Exports of goods and services			157 855	30.3
less: imports of goods and services[5]	40 009	7.1	156 163	30.0
GDP	560 271	100.0	521 206	100.0
GDP per capita, thousand old zlotys	14 698		13 628	

(1) Since 1990 total GDP according to 1993 SNA.

(2) The zloty was redenominated the 1st January 1995, with the new zloty equal to 10 000 old zlotys.

(3) Non-profit institutions serving households.

(4) Gross fixed capital formation includes intangible fixed assets from 1990.

(5) For 1990 data refer to net exports. Imports in 1990 and 1991 and exports in 1992 and 1993 are corrected by the estimated net purchases of residents and non-residents respective

(6) For 1990 to 1992 at constant prices of 1990. From 1993 in prices of the previous year.

Source: Polish Central Statistical Office

PIB PAR CATÉGORIE DE DÉPENSE[1]

milliards d' anciens zlotys[2]

1992	%	1993	%	1994	%	
						Aux prix courants
957 441	83.3	1 300 338	83.5	1 748 504	83.1	Consommation finale
831 323	72.3	1 148 552	73.7	1 592 984	75.7	Consommation individuelle
						dont dépenses de consommation finale des
709 553	61.7	982 000	63.0	1 353 886	64.3	Ménages
121 770	10.6	166 552	10.7	239 098	11.4	Administrations publiques et ISBL[3]
126 118	11.0	151 786	9.7	155 520	7.4	Consommation collective
174 370	15.2	242 283	15.6	333 634	15.9	Formation brute de capital
192 966	16.8	247 485	15.9	340 783	16.2	Formation brute de capital fixe[4]
-18 596	-1.6	-5 202	-0.3	-7 149	-0.3	Variations de stocks
272 418	23.7	357 326	22.9	505 829	24.0	Exportations de biens et services
254 787	22.2	342 147	22.0	483 894	23.0	moins: importations de biens et services[5]
1 149 442	100.0	1 557 800	100.0	2 104 073	100.0	**PIB**
29 961		40 505		54 590		**PIB par habitant**, milliers d'anciens zlotys
						Aux prix constants[6]
419 093	78.4	1 003 758	84.1	1 351 371	82.5	Consommation finale
354 615	66.3	881 053	73.8	1 222 414	74.6	Consommation individuelle
						dont dépenses de consommation finale des
292 330	54.7	746 450	62.6	1 024 120	62.5	Ménages
62 285	11.6	134 603	11.3	198 294	12.1	Administrations publiques et ISBL[3]
64 478	12.1	122 705	10.3	128 957	7.9	Consommation collective
99 736	18.6	196 616	16.5	264 045	16.1	Formation brute de capital
115 047	21.5	198 562	16.6	270 158	16.5	Formation brute de capital fixe[4]
-15 311	-2.9	-1 946	-0.2	-6 113	-0.4	Variations de stocks
174 872	32.7	281 251	23.6	404 084	24.7	Exportations de biens et services
158 812	29.7	288 504	24.2	380 695	23.2	moins: importations de biens et services[5]
534 889	100.0	1 193 121	100.0	1 638 805	100.0	**PIB**
13 942		31 023		42 518		**PIB par habitant**, milliers d'anciens zlotys

1) Depuis 1990 PIB total selon le SCN de 1993.

2) Une nouvelle dénomination du zloty a été introduite le 1er janvier 1995, le nouveau zloty équivalant à 10 000 anciens zlotys.

3) Institutions sans but lucratif au service des ménages.

4) La formation brute de capital fixe inclut les actifs fixes incorporels à partir de 1990.

5) Pour 1990 les données se réfèrent aux exportations nettes. Les importations pour 1990 et 1991 et les exportations pour 1992 et 1993 sont corrigées respectivement par une estimation des achats nettes des résidents et des non-résidents.

6) Pour 1990 à 1992, aux prix constants de 1990. Depuis 1993, aux prix constants de l'année précédente.

Source: Office central statistique polonais

REPUBLIC OF SLOVENIA

GDP BY EXPENDITURE

	million dinar[1]		million tolar[1]			
	1990	%	1991	%	1992	%
Current prices						
Final consumption	138 054	70.2	257 111	73.6	766 174	75.3
Individual	124 253	63.1	228 172	65.3	676 624	66.5
of which final consumption exp. of						
Households	101 954	51.8	187 019	53.5	546 718	53.7
Government	20 425	10.4	37 469	10.7	117 454	11.5
NPISH[3]	1 874	1.0	3 684	1.1	12 452	1.2
Collective	13 801	7.0	28 939	8.3	89 550	8.8
Gross capital formation	34 645	17.6	59 852	17.1	180 964	17.8
Gross fixed capital formation	36 917	18.8	72 016	20.6	187 450	18.4
Changes in inventories	-2 272	-1.2	-12 164	-3.5	-6 486	-0.6
Exports of goods and services[4]	178 580	90.8	291 877	83.5	642 772	63.1
less: imports of goods and services[4]	154 517	78.5	259 432	74.2	571 945	56.2
GDP	196 762	100.0	349 408	100.0	1 017 965	100.0
GDP per capita	98 475	dinar	174 547	tolar	510 054	tolar
Constant prices 1992						
Final consumption	..	..	..	..	766 174	75.3
Individual	..	..	..	..	676 624	66.5
of which final consumption exp. of						
Households	..	..	..	..	546 718	53.7
Government	..	..	..	..	117 454	11.5
NPISH[3]	..	..	..	..	12 452	1.2
Collective	..	..	..	..	89 550	8.8
Gross capital formation	..	..	..	..	180 964	17.8
Gross fixed capital formation	..	..	..	..	187 450	18.4
Changes in inventories	..	..	..	..	-6 486	-0.6
Exports of goods and services[4]	..	..	..	..	642 772	63.1
less: imports of goods and services[4]	..	..	..	..	571 945	56.2
GDP	..	..	..	..	1 017 965	100.0
GDP per capita	..		..		510 054	tolar

(1) The tolar was introduced on 8th October 1991 at a rate of 1:1 with the dinar.

(2) Preliminary data calculated from the production side.

(3) Non-profit institutions serving households.

(4) For 1990 including trade with other republics of the former Yugoslvia.

Source: Statistical Office of the Republic of Slovenia.

PIB PAR CATÉGORIE DE DÉPENSE

millions de tolar[1]

1993	%	1994	%	1995[2]	%	
						Aux prix courants
1 139 351	79.4	1 428 599	77.4	..	..	Consommation finale
1 010 006	70.4	1 269 889	68.8	..	..	Consommation individuelle
						dont dépenses de consommation finale des
820 955	57.2	1 041 119	56.4	..	..	Ménages
173 261	12.1	211 490	11.5	..	..	Administrations publiques
15 790	1.1	17 280	0.9	..	..	ISBL[3]
129 345	9.0	158 710	8.6	..	..	Consommation collective
287 577	20.0	374 879	20.3	..	..	Formation brute de capital
268 831	18.7	362 059	19.6	..	..	Formation brute de capital fixe
18 746	1.3	12 820	0.7	..	..	Variations de stocks
839 167	58.5	1 087 993	59.0	..	..	Exportations de biens et services[4]
831 000	57.9	1 046 797	56.7	..	..	moins: importations de biens et services[4]
1 435 095	100.0	1 844 674	100.0	2 198 517	100.0	**PIB**
720 936	tolar	927 485	tolar	1 108 347	tolar	**PIB par habitant**
						Aux prix constants de 1992
852 110	82.2	885 104	81.4	..	..	Consommation finale
758 389	73.1	790 417	72.7	..	..	Consommation individuelle
						dont dépenses de consommation finale des
622 698	60.1	653 962	60.1	..	..	Ménages
124 274	12.0	125 991	11.6	..	..	Administrations publiques
11 417	1.1	10 464	1.0	..	..	ISBL[3]
93 721	9.0	94 687	8.7	..	..	Consommation collective
218 351	21.1	237 883	21.9	..	..	Formation brute de capital
203 886	19.7	228 706	21.0	..	..	Formation brute de capital fixe
14 465	1.4	9 177	0.8	..	..	Variations de stocks
637 294	61.5	706 101	64.9	..	..	Exportations de biens et services[4]
670 803	64.7	741 455	68.2	..	..	moins: importations de biens et services[4]
1 036 952	100.0	1 087 633	100.0	1 125 865	100.0	**PIB**
520 924	tolar	546 852	tolar	567 587	tolar	**PIB par habitant**

1) Le tolar a été introduit le 8 octobre 1991 à un taux de conversion de 1:1 avec le dinar.

2) Données préliminaires calculées du côté de la production.

3) Institutions sans but lucratif au service des ménages.

4) Pour 1990 y compris les échanges avec d'autres républiques de l-ex Yougoslavie.

Source: Office statistique de la République de Slovénie

ROMANIA

GDP BY EXPENDITURE

billion lei

	1990	%	1991	%	1992	%
Current prices						
Final consumption	679.5	79.2	1 672.5	75.9	4 642.5	77.0
Households	557.7	65.0	1 323.7	60.1	3 750.8	62.2
General government and NPISH[3]	121.8	14.2	348.8	15.8	891.7	14.8
Gross capital formation	259.5	30.2	618.1	28.0	1 893.6	31.4
Gross fixed capital formation	169.8	19.8	317.0	14.4	1 156.9	19.2
Changes in inventories	89.7	10.5	301.1	13.7	736.7	12.2
Exports of goods and services	143.5	16.7	388.0	17.6	1 675.6	27.8
less: imports of goods and services	224.6	26.2	474.6	21.5	2 182.5	36.2
GDP	857.9	100.0	2 203.9	100.0	6 029.2	100.0
GDP per capita, lei	36 966		95 057		264 565	
At prices of the previous year						
Final consumption	614.1	81.3	599.4	80.2	1 579.1	78.5
Households	500.7	66.3	467.4	62.6	1 223.9	60.9
General government and NPISH[3]	113.4	15.0	132.0	17.7	355.2	17.7
Gross capital formation	211.8	28.0	187.9	25.2	542.7	27.0
Gross fixed capital formation	154.0	20.4	116.1	15.5	351.8	17.5
Changes in inventories	57.8	7.7	71.8	9.6	190.9	9.5
Exports of goods and services	101.2	13.4	117.8	15.8	399.2	19.9
less: imports of goods and services	172.0	22.8	158.1	21.2	510.3	25.4
GDP	755.1	100.0	747.0	100.0	2 010.7	100.0
GDP per capita, lei	32 537		32 220		88 231	

(1) Semi-definitive data.

(2) Estimated data.

(3) Non-profit institutions serving households.

Sources: National Commission for Statistics.

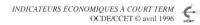

PIB PAR CATÉGORIE DE DÉPENSE

milliards de lei

1993	%	1994[1]	%	1995[2]	%	
						Aux prix courants
15 235.8	76.0	37 417.5	75.1	56 915.4	78.8	Consommation finale
12 670.3	63.2	30 641.3	61.5	47 796.4	66.2	Ménages
2 565.5	12.8	6 776.2	13.6	9 119.0	12.6	Administrations publiques et ISBL[3]
5 795.9	28.9	13 404.8	26.9	18 594.7	25.7	Formation brute de capital
3 583.7	17.9	9 823.9	19.7	15 729.4	21.8	Formation brute de capital fixe
2 212.2	11.0	3 580.9	7.2	2 865.3	4.0	Variations de stocks
4 611.6	23.0	12 389.2	24.9	19 175.8	26.5	Exportations de biens et services
5 607.5	28.0	13 416.7	26.9	22 437.0	31.1	moins: importations de biens et services
20 035.8	100.0	49 794.8	100.0	72 248.9	100.0	**PIB**
880 487		2 190 648		3 185 444		**PIB par habitant**, lei
						Aux prix de l'année précédente
4 700.2	76.8	15 892.1	76.3	42 488.1	79.9	Consommation finale
3 786.1	61.9	13 315.3	64.0	35 860.3	67.4	Ménages
914.1	14.9	2 576.8	12.4	6 627.8	12.5	Administrations publiques et ISBL[3]
1 837.3	30.0	5 697.1	27.4	13 469.0	25.3	Formation brute de capital
1 252.9	20.5	4 304.9	20.7	11 113.8	20.9	Formation brute de capital fixe
584.4	9.5	1 392.2	6.7	2 355.2	4.4	Variations de stocks
1 862.0	30.4	5 487.8	26.4	15 513.7	29.2	Exportations de biens et services
2 278.2	37.2	6 260.5	30.1	18 264.1	34.3	moins: importations de biens et services
6 121.3	100.0	20 816.5	100.0	53 206.7	100.0	**PIB**
269 008		916 429		2 345 876		**PIB par habitant**, lei

1) Données semi-définitives.

2) Estimations.

3) Institutions sans but lucratif au service des ménages.

Sources: Commission nationale de statistique.

SLOVAK REPUBLIC

GDP BY EXPENDITURE

billion koruny

	1990[1]	%	1991[1]	%	1992	%
Current prices						
Final consumption expenditure	210.8	75.8	229.4	71.7	249.6	75.1
Households	149.9	53.9	163.6	51.2	164.6	49.5
Government and NPISH[3]	60.9	21.9	65.8	20.6	85.0	25.6
Gross capital formation	92.3	33.2	99.9	31.2	95.7	28.8
Gross fixed capital formation	86.9	31.2	90.4	28.3	109.3	32.9
Changes in inventories	5.4	1.9	9.5	3.0	-13.6	-4.1
Exports of goods and services	73.8	26.5	148.1	46.3	233.7	70.3
less: imports of goods and services	98.8	35.5	157.6	49.3	246.8	74.3
GDP	278.1	100.0	319.8	100.0	332.2	100.0
GDP per capita, thousand koruny	52.4		58.2		63.4	
Constant prices 1993						
Final consumption expenditure	401.4	83.5	298.6	72.7	293.5	76.4
Households	296.9	61.7	212.7	51.8	199.1	51.8
Government and NPISH[3]	104.5	21.7	85.9	20.9	94.4	24.6
Gross capital formation	162.9	33.9	127.5	31.0	112.5	29.3
Gross fixed capital formation	176.3	36.7	131.9	32.1	125.9	32.8
Changes in inventories	-13.4	-2.8	-4.4	-1.1	-13.4	-3.5
Exports of goods and services	116.0	24.1	154.8	37.7	228.2	59.4
less: imports of goods and services	199.3	41.4	170.0	41.4	250.1	65.1
GDP	481.0	100.0	410.9	100.0	384.1	100.0
GDP per capita, thousand koruny	90.7		74.8		73.3	

(1) Data for 1990-91 have been calculated by conversion from MPS estimates.

(2) Preliminary data.

(3) Non-profit institutions serving households.

Source: Statistical Office of the Slovak Republic.

PIB PAR CATÉGORIE DE DÉPENSE

milliards de couronnes

1993	%	1994[2]	%	1995[2]	%	
						Aux prix courants
288.3	77.9	319.0	72.3	356.6	68.8	Dépense de consommation finale
196.0	53.0	222.6	50.4	252.6	48.8	Ménages
92.3	25.0	96.4	21.8	104.0	20.1	Administrations publiques et ISBL[3]
102.0	27.6	97.9	22.2	144.5	27.9	Formation brute de capital
120.7	32.6	130.0	29.5	150.6	29.1	Formation brute de capital fixe
-18.7	-5.1	-32.1	-7.3	-6.1	-1.2	Variations de stocks
227.8	61.6	287.8	65.2	324.7	62.7	Exportations de biens et services
248.2	67.1	263.4	59.7	307.8	59.4	moins: importations de biens et services
369.9	100.0	441.3	100.0	518.0	100.0	**PIB**
69.8		80.8		94.8		**PIB par habitant**, milliers de couronnes
						Aux prix constants de 1993
288.3	77.9	278.5	71.8	..	..	Dépense de consommation finale
196.0	53.0	195.9	50.5	..	..	Ménages
92.3	25.0	82.6	21.3	..	..	Administrations publiques et ISBL[3]
102.0	27.6	89.0	22.9	..	..	Formation brute de capital
120.7	32.6	114.6	29.5	..	..	Formation brute de capital fixe
-18.7	-5.1	-25.6	-6.6	..	..	Variations de stocks
227.8	61.6	260.0	67.0	..	..	Exportations de biens et services
248.2	67.1	239.5	61.7	..	..	moins: importations de biens et services
369.9	100.0	388.0	100.0	..	..	**PIB**
69.8		71.0		..		**PIB par habitant**, milliers de couronnes

1) Les données de 1990-1991 ont été calculées par conversion des estimations de la CPM.

2) Données préliminaires.

3) Institutions sans but lucratif au service des ménages.

Source: Office statistique de la République slovaque.

Purchasing Power Parities

The previous section shows GDP in local currency for 9 Central and Eastern European countries. Direct comparisons across countries in a common currency should be made using purchasing power parities (PPPs) which take into account different relative price levels as well as different currencies.

A project was completed during 1995, in which comparisons for 1993 were first made for each of 15 transition countries with Austria. These were then converted to allow comparison with all OECD Member countries, enabling the calculation of GDP per capita in US dollar terms for 1993. These figures were then extended to other years, using the same methodology by which PPPs for OECD countries for 1993 are extended to other years.

The table below shows GDP per capita in US dollars for the 9 Central and Eastern European countries for which accounts are shown in the previous section. The table also includes the purchasing power parities relative to the US dollar and per capita data in the form of volume indices.

These results differ markedly from GDP per capita figures derived by using exchange rates because these latter do not take into account relative price levels between the countries concerned.

GDP per capita figures are derived using the data in the preceding tables and will therefore change as GDP data change.

Parités de pouvoir d'achat

La précédente section présente le PIB en monnaie nationale de 9 pays d'Europe centrale et orientale. Des comparaisons directes entre pays devraient être faites en utilisant les parités de pouvoir d'achat (PPA), qui prennent en compte les niveaux des prix relatifs ainsi que les monnaies des différents pays.

Grâce à l'achèvement d'un projet en 1995, on dispose pour la première fois de comparaisons portant sur l'année 1993 entre chacun des 15 pays en transition et l'Autriche. Ces données ont ensuite été converties afin d'effectuer des comparaisons avec l'ensemble de pays Membres de l'OCDE permettant ainsi le calcul du PIB par habitant de ces pays en dollars des Etats-Unis pour l'année 1993. Enfin, les données ont été extrapolées à d'autres années, en utilisant une méthode d'extrapolation similaire à celle appliquée à 1993 pour les pays de l'OCDE.

Le tableau ci-dessous présente le PIB par habitant en dollars des Etats-Unis des 9 pays d'Europe centrale et orientale dont les comptes figurent dans la section précédente. Ce tableau reprend aussi les parités de pouvoir d'achat vis-à-vis du dollar des Etats-Unis et présente des statistiques par habitant sous forme d'indices de volume.

Ces résultats divergent sensiblement des chiffres de PIB par habitant calculés à partir des taux de change dans la mesure où ces derniers ne tiennent pas compte des différences de niveaux de prix relatifs entre les pays concernés.

Les données du PIB par habitant sont dérivées à partir des données des tableaux précédents. Elles seront donc modifiées au même rythme que les données du PIB.

Purchasing Power Parities
Parités de pouvoir d'achat

| | Purchasing Power Parities for GDP (U.S.$=1.00) | | | | Per capita real values of GDP in US$ | | | | Per capita volume indices for GDP (USA=100) | | | | |
	Parités de pouvoir d'achat du PIB ($É-U=1,00)				Valeurs réelles par habitant du PIB en $É-U				Indices de volume par habitant du PIB (É-U=100)				
	1991	1992	1993	1994	1991	1992	1993	1994	1991	1992	1993	1994	
Bulgaria		5.68	8.41	14.7		4141	4193	4386		18	17	17	Bulgarie
Estonia		2.14	3.84	5.24		3954	3828	3828		17	15	15	Estonie
Hungary	41.7	49.9	57.6	68.4	5794	5716	5980	6223	26	25	24	24	Hongrie
Latvia		0.11	0.185	0.249		3476	3070	3021		15	12	12	Lettonie
Lithuania		0.175	0.809	1.19		5166	3681	3831		22	15	15	Lituanie
Poland	5007	6770	8670	10827	4217	4420	4669	5037	19	19	19	20	Pologne
Rep. of Slovenia		57.5	78.1	93.1		8867	9233	9967		38	37	39	Rép. de Slovénie
Romania	25.3	74.2	238	554	3755	3567	3698	3954	17	15	15	15	Roumanie
Slovak Rep.	8.96	9.73	11.0	12.2	6744	6438	6299	6765	30	28	25	27	Rép. slovaque

METHODOLOGICAL NOTES

GENERAL ISSUES

In the past the statistics provided by the Central and Eastern European Countries and the New Independent States have differed in content, classification and methodology from similar data available in market economies. Like their economic systems, the statistical systems in these countries are now in a transitional phase. Many series have suffered, or will suffer, sharp discontinuities as changes in definitions, classifications and methods of data collection are introduced to bring them into line with the international standards used in OECD Member countries. In particular, statistical coverage of the new private sector is relatively poor and in all countries there is likely to be some understatement of output, sales, employment and investment by small private enterprises. This problem is not unique to the countries covered in this publication as coverage of small enterprises is also a problem for many OECD countries, but it is probable that error margins are somewhat larger for these countries than for most OECD countries.

Without an understanding of the basic approaches that have been used, analysis based on available data is likely to be misleading, because they do not conform to the underlying conventions that an analyst expects when working with apparently similar data for market economies.

The companion volume to this publication, *Short-term Economic Indicators: Transition Economies, Sources and Definitions* provides a full description of the general methodological differences that should be borne in mind when using the data. It includes detailed notes on the sources and methods used to compile the series presented and also indicates breaks in series. Before using the data in this publication, users are strongly advised to refer to the notes provided in that volume.

The series included in *Short-term Economic Indicators: Transition Economies* are similar to those published in the OECD's *Main Economic Indicators*. As far as possible the data are shown on a monthly, quarterly and annual basis. In some cases the quarterly and annual data are derived directly from the monthly data. In other cases the longer period data have a wider coverage and a consequence of extended coverage is that the longer period data are available progressively later.

Sources

Most data are supplied by statistical agencies and central banks in the countries concerned, although data are not always presented in the same form as in these countries' national publications.

The Interstate Statistical Committee of the Commonwealth of Independent States supplies the data for most of its member countries. Some countries however, prefer to supply data directly to the OECD.

NOTES MÉTHODOLOGIQUES

GÉNÉRALITÉS

Dans le passé, les statistiques fournies par les pays d'Europe centrale et orientale et par les Nouveaux États Indépendants différaient par leur contenu, leur classification et leur méthodologie des données similaires disponibles dans les économies de marché. A l'heure actuelle, le système statistique de ces pays traverse, tout comme leur système économique, une phase de transition. De nombreuses séries sont ou vont être affectées par des ruptures brutales, au fil des changements apportés aux définitions, aux classifications et aux modes de collecte des données pour les rendre conformes aux normes internationales en usage dans les pays Membres de l'OCDE. En particulier, le secteur privé, d'apparition récente, bénéficie d'une couverture statistique relativement médiocre et la production, les ventes, l'emploi et l'investissement des petites entreprises privées de ces pays sont vraisemblablement sous-estimés. Ce problème n'est pas limité aux pays considérés ici car la couverture des petites entreprises pose aussi des problèmes dans beaucoup de pays de l'OCDE; toutefois, il est probable que, dans la plupart des cas, les marges d'erreur sont un peu plus prononcées dans les pays cités que dans la plupart des pays de l'OCDE.

Sauf à bien appréhender les approches fondamentales utilisées, l'analyse des données disponibles risque d'induire en erreur, car ces données s'écartent des acceptions conventionnelles sur lesquelles s'appuie l'analyste occidental lorsqu'il examine des données apparemment semblables dans le contexte des économies de marché.

Le volume qui complète cette publication, *Indicateurs économiques à court terme : Économies en transition, Sources et définitions* donne une description complète des différences méthodologiques générales qu'il faut garder à l'esprit lorsque l'on étudie ces données. Il contient des notes détaillées sur les sources et méthodes utilisées pour élaborer les séries présentées et indique également les ruptures de série. Avant de travailler sur les données publiées ici, les utilisateurs sont instamment invités à se reporter aux notes contenues dans la publication citée.

Les séries présentées dans les *Indicateurs économiques à court terme : Économies en transition* sont semblables à celles qui figurent dans les *Principaux indicateurs économiques* de l'OCDE. Dans la mesure du possible, des chiffres mensuels, trimestriels et annuels sont fournis. Dans certains cas, les données trimestrielles et annuelles sont directement dérivées des données mensuelles. Il arrive aussi que les données de longue périodicité aient une couverture plus étendue que les autres, en conséquence de quoi, elles ne sont disponibles qu'avec du retard.

Sources

La plupart des données sont fournies par les instituts statistiques et les banques centrales des pays concernés, même si elles ne sont pas toujours présentées sous la même forme que dans les publications nationales de ces pays.

La Commission statistique inter-état de la Communauté des États Indépendants fournit les données pour la plupart des pays membres. Certains pays toutefois, préfèrent fournir directement leurs données à l'OCDE.

BUSINESS SURVEY ANNEX

—

ANNEXE DES ENQUÊTES DE CONJONCTURE

TABLE OF CONTENTS — TABLE DES MATIÈRES

Introduction

The OECD Centre for Co-operation with the Economies in Transition has been working with Eurostat and the Commission of the European Communities to develop a programme of business tendency surveys in transition countries since 1991. This programme is part of a larger OECD/EC-Eurostat project to assist transition countries in developing appropriate short-term indicators.

Business tendency surveys collect qualitative information from business managers on their assessment of the current economic situation and on their intentions and expectations for the immediate future. Such surveys are conducted in all OECD Member countries and they have proved a cost-effective means of generating timely information on short-term economic developments. Current economic information is of particular interest to countries in transition and a reliable system of both quantitative and qualitative short-term indicators is of prime importance.

Compared to traditional quantitative statistical surveys, business tendency surveys present many advantages as a source for short-term economic information. They collect information which is easier for enterprises to supply because the answers are not based on precise records and the returns can be submitted more quickly. Business tendency surveys cover a wide range of variables selected for their ability to monitor the business cycle and include information on variables not covered by quantitative statistics, such as capacity utilisation and views on the overall economic situation.

Member countries of the European Union have found it useful to standardise (or "harmonise") a number of the questions included in their business surveys so that the results are internationally comparable. Transition countries are being encouraged to use a number of standard questions to also make their survey results internationally comparable.

Business surveys covering the industrial sector (in most cases the manufacturing industry) have been conducted on a regular basis for several years in Hungary and Poland. Regular surveys were introduced during 1991 in the former CSFR, Estonia and Romania and in January 1992 in Bulgaria. The first business survey in manufacturing was conducted in Russia in January 1992. This survey, however was restricted to enterprises in the Moscow region, but a new survey has been introduced covering the western part of the Russian Federation including Moscow. Business surveys were introduced in Latvia and Lithuania during 1993, and in Belarus in 1994.

Business surveys in the construction sector are available for Bulgaria, Estonia, Hungary, Latvia, Poland, Romania and the Slovak Republic. Surveys in retail trade are available for all of the above countries with the exception of Latvia.

Selected business survey results have been included in the quarterly publication *Short-term Economic Indicators: Transition Economies* since April 1993. Business survey results in Bulgaria, Estonia, Hungary, Latvia, Lithuania, Poland, Romania, Slovak Republic, Belarus and the Russian Federation are now included on a regular basis. This annual Business Tendency Survey Annex, provides more detailed results from a wider range of surveys. The first such Annex was included in *Short-term Economic Indicators: Transition Economies*, Number 2/1995.

In particular, this Annex contains the full set of results from surveys conducted in manufacturing, construction, and retail trade. The complete set of questions for all three surveys corresponding to these results is also included in the following pages. Summary tables describing the survey characteristics in each country are provided in the accompanying publication *Short-term Economic Indicators: Transition Economies, Sources and Definitions*.

In most countries, surveys are conducted by the Central Statistical Office in the country concerned. In some countries, however, private research institutes conduct the surveys. In Estonia, the surveys are carried out by the Estonian Institute for Market Research; in Hungary by the Institute for Economic and Market Research and Informatics, Ltd. (KopintDatorg); in Russia, surveys are conducted by the Institute for the Economy in Transition and in Belarus by the Economic Institute in the Ministry of the Economy. In Poland, business surveys have been conducted for a number of years both by the CSO and by the Research Institute of Economic Development in the Warsaw School of Economics. Survey results described here refer to the CSO survey for manufacturing and construction and to the Research Institute of Economic Development survey for retail trade.

Terminology

The chief characteristics of business surveys is that instead of asking for exact figures, they usually ask for the respondents's assessment of the current business situation compared with the "normal" state, i.e. a question on levels, or they ask for judgement on the direction of changes, i.e. a question on **tendency**. Answers are typically given as "above normal/normal/below normal", or as "up/same/down". Questions may refer either to the present situation or to expectations, i.e. questions on **future tendency** for the next three to six months.

The answers received are usually weighted according to the size of the responding firm and, for convenience, the results are usually given as one figure. This is straightforward where a single figure is requested from respondents, i.e. **percentage** of capacity utilisation. Sometimes, respondents are asked to indicate one or several choices in a nominal list of alternatives, in which case the weighted **proportion** of firms selecting the alternative is given. This latter type of question is used for information concerning limits to production or investment, limits to improvement in business situation, and type of investment.

In the case of three-choice questions the data are generally presented in the form of a percent **balance**. "Normal" and "same" answers are ignored and the balance is obtained by taking the difference between the weighted percentages of respondents giving favourable and unfavourable answers. Negative balances indicate that unfavourable answers exceed favourable answers; positive balances show that favourable responses predominate. In the case of two-choice questions, i.e. do you plan fixed investment for this or next year -- "yes or no", the weighted **proportion** of firms indicating "yes" is given.

In the following section, the italicised title above each question refers to the title used in the tables in this Annex. In the tables, business survey series which refer to future tendency or prospects for some future period are located in all cases at the time period of the survey, not at the time period to which the forecast refers.

Introduction

Le Centre pour la coopération avec les économies en transition de l'OCDE travaille depuis 1991 avec Eurostat et la Commission des Communautés européennes à mettre au point un programme d'enquêtes de conjoncture dans les pays en transition. Ce programme fait partie d'un projet commun de plus grande ampleur destiné à aider les pays en transition à élaborer des indicateurs à court terme appropriés.

Les enquêtes de conjoncture servent à recueillir auprès des chefs d'entreprise des informations qualitatives sur leur appréciation de la situation économique du moment, ainsi que sur leurs intentions et prévisions pour l'avenir immédiat. Ce type d'enquête, qui existe dans tous les pays membres de l'OCDE, s'avère constituer un moyen rentable de disposer en temps utile de renseignements sur l'évolution économique à court terme. L'information économique sur la période courante présente un intérêt particulier pour les pays en transition et l'existence d'un système fiable d'indicateurs à court terme quantitatifs et qualitatifs est primordiale.

Par rapport aux enquêtes statistiques quantitatives classiques, les enquêtes de conjoncture présentent maints avantages en tant qu'outil d'information économique à court terme. Les renseignements qui y sont demandés sont plus faciles à fournir pour les entreprises car elles n'ont pas besoin pour répondre de s'appuyer sur des données chiffrées précises et les questionnaires remplis peuvent être renvoyés plus rapidement. Les enquêtes de conjoncture renseignent sur toute une série de variables choisies parce qu'elles permettent de suivre le cycle conjoncturel, y compris des variables dont les statistiques quantitatives ne rendent pas compte, comme l'utilisation des capacités et les opinions sur la situation économique générale.

Les pays membres de l'Union européenne ont jugé utile de normaliser (ou "harmoniser") un certain nombre des questions posées dans leurs enquêtes de conjoncture, de sorte que les résultats sont comparables au plan international. Les pays en transition sont encouragés à en faire autant pour que les résultats de leurs enquêtes se prêtent aussi à des comparaisons internationales.

Des enquêtes de conjoncture couvrant le secteur industriel (dans la plupart des cas, les industries manufacturières) sont effectuées périodiquement depuis plusieurs années en Hongrie et en Pologne, tandis que des enquêtes périodiques ont été instituées dans le courant de 1991 dans l'ex-République fédérative tchèque et slovaque, en Estonie et en Roumanie, puis en janvier 1992 en Bulgarie. En Russie, une première enquête de conjoncture a été menée dans l'industrie manufacturière en janvier 1992. Elle s'est toutefois limitée aux entreprises de la région de Moscou, mais une nouvelle enquête a été introduite et couvre en outre la partie ouest de la Russie. En Lettonie et en Lituanie, les enquêtes de conjoncture ont été mises en place pendant l'année 1993, et il en a été de même au Bélarus en 1994.

Pour le secteur de la construction, on dispose d'enquêtes de conjoncture pour la Bulgarie, l'Estonie, la Hongrie, la Lettonie, la Pologne, la Roumanie et la République slovaque. Pour le commerce de détail, il en existe dans tous les pays précités sauf la Lettonie.

Depuis avril 1993, une sélection de résultats des enquêtes de conjoncture est publiée dans les *Indicateurs économiques à court terme : Économies en transition* chaque trimestre. Les résultats des enquêtes de conjoncture des pays suivants : Bulgarie, Estonie, Hongrie, Lettonie, Lituanie, Pologne, Roumanie, République slovaque, Bélarus et la Fédération de Russie sont maintenant inclus régulièrement. Cette annexe annuelle consacrée aux enquêtes de conjoncture présente dans leur intégralité les résultats d'enquêtes menées dans l'industrie, la construction et le commerce de détail. Cette annexe a été publiée pour la première fois dans *Indicateurs économiques à court terme : Économies en transition*, numéro 2/1995.

Cette annexe contient, en particulier, les résultats complets des enquêtes conduites dans le secteur manufacturier, la construction et le commerce de détail. On trouvera dans la présente section le jeu complet des questions posées dans le cadre de ces trois enquêtes, ainsi que les différences qui existent par rapport aux questions harmonisées. Des tableaux récapitulatifs décrivant les caractéristiques des enquêtes dans chaque pays se trouvent dans la publication complémentaire *Indicateurs Economiques à Court terme: Economies en Transition, Sources et Définitions*.

Dans la plupart des pays, les enquêtes sont réalisées par l'Office central de statistique du pays concerné. Cependant, dans quelques pays, ce sont des instituts de recherche privés qui réalisent les enquêtes. En Estonie, les enquêtes sont réalisées par l'Institut estonien d'études de marché ; en Hongrie par l'Institut de recherche économique, d'études de marché et d'informatique (Kopint-Datorg) ; en Russie les enquêtes sont conduites par

OECD
OCDE
SHORT-TERM ECONOMIC INDICATORS
OECD/CCET © April 1996

A6

INDICATEURS ÉCONOMIQUES À COURT TERME
OCDE/CCET © avril 1996

l'Institut des économies en transition et au Bélarus par l'Institut d'études économiques du Ministère de l'économie. En Pologne, les enquêtes de conjoncture ont été réalisées pendant un certain nombre d'années aussi bien par l'Office central de statistique que par l'Institut de recherche sur le développement économique de la Faculté des sciences économiques de Varsovie. Les résultats dont il est fait état ici proviennent des enquêtes de l'Office central de statistique pour ce qui est de l'industrie manufacturière et du secteur de la construction et de celles menées à bien par l'Institut de recherche sur le développement économique pour ce qui est du commerce de détail.

Terminologie

Les enquêtes de conjoncture ont ceci de caractéristique, qu'elles visent à recueillir non pas des chiffres précis mais l'opinion des intéressés sur la situation présente, en comparaison avec la "normale", i.e. une question sur les niveaux, ou sur le sens dans lequel ce climat évolue, i.e. une question sur les **tendances**. Les réponses sont généralement "supérieur/égal/inférieur à la normale", ou "en augmentation/sans changement/en baisse". Les questions peuvent se référer soit à la situation présente soit aux anticipations i.e. une question sur les **perspectives** sur les trois à six prochains mois.

Les réponses reçues sont généralement pondérées par rapport à la taille de l'entreprise qui répond, et par conséquent, les résultats sont généralement présentés en un seul chiffre. Il est beaucoup plus simple de traiter les réponses quand un seul chiffre est demandé comme le **taux** d'utilisation des capacités. Cependant, quelquefois, on demande aux enquêtés de choisir une ou plusieurs réponses dans une liste qui leur est proposée, dans ce cas on calcule la **proportion** pondérée des entreprises ayant donné telle ou telle réponse. Ce dernier type de question est utilisé pour recueillir les informations concernant les limites de la production ou de l'investissement, les limites de l'amélioration de la situation économique, et le type d'investissement.

Dans le cas de question à choix multiple, les données sont généralement présentées sous la forme de **solde** des réponses obtenues pour les questions à triple choix. Les réponses "normale" ou "sans changement" ne sont pas prises en compte et l'on obtient le solde en calculant la différence entre les pourcentages de réponses favorables et de réponses défavorables. Un solde négatif indique que les réponses défavorables l'ont emporté, un solde positif que les réponses favorables sont les plus nombreuses. Pour les questions à double choix du type "pensez-vous réaliser des investissements cette année ou l'an prochain : oui - non ?" le **pourcentage** pondéré d'entreprises ayant répondu "oui" est donné.

Dans la section suivante, les titres en italique au-dessus de chaque question se rapportent aux titres des séries dans les tableaux de la présente annexe. Dans les tableaux, quand les séries des enquêtes de conjoncture se réfèrent aux perspectives, c'est dans tous les cas par rapport à la date de l'enquête et non à la période où la prévision doit être réalisée.

BULGARIA

		1993 Q1	Q2	Q3	Q4	1994 Q1	Q2	Q3	Q4	1995 Q1	Q2	Q3	Q4	1996 Q1
BUSINESS SURVEYS - MANUFACTURING														
Business situation														
Tendency	balance	-27	-32	-36	-36	-22	-20	-11	-4	4	4	12	16	9
Future tendency	balance	21	16	18	11	19	15	9	16	39	38	30	27	36
Order books / Demand														
Total: level	balance	-56	-67	-65	-59	-59	-53	-46	-39	-34	-34	-29	-22	-25
Export: level	balance	-45	-60	-59	-56	-57	-54	-48	-34	-33	-33	-27	-22	-29
Total: future tendency	balance	22	21	25	29	34	19	24	37	41	50	42	47	42
Export: future tendency	balance	32	30	29	25	28	24	24	26	33	35	35	32	33
Production														
Tendency	balance	-26	-29	-27	-21	-26	-18	-13	1	2	-2	4	6	-6
Future tendency	balance	15	7	18	8	20	15	13	21	36	32	32	35	33
Current capacity	balance	19	18	23	21	18	20	18	19	15	10	11	8	6
Rate of capacity utilisation	%	60	56	55	54	57	59	58	60	60	60	61	63	63
Limits to production														
None	proportion	6	3	3	4	3	3	4	4	4	3	5	5	4
Insufficient domestic demand	proportion	48	61	61	55	54	49	47	38	30	38	35	31	29
Insufficient foreign demand	proportion	35	48	48	47	39	37	36	29	23	23	23	21	20
Competitive imports	proportion	8	20	21	21	21	21	20	16	9	21	22	14	11
Shortage of skilled labour	proportion	2	2	2	3	3	4	4	4	4	5	3	4	4
Lack of appropriate equipment	proportion	3	1	2	1	3	2	3	4	5	5	4	4	2
Shortage of raw materials	proportion	19	17	15	18	21	23	25	28	30	28	25	29	25
Shortage of energy	proportion	1	1	0	0	0	0	1	0	1	1	0	0	0
Financial problems	proportion	47	52	56	55	50	44	49	47	45	45	46	52	56
Uncertainty in the economic environment	proportion	27	28	31	30	26	31	26	33	40	30	27	28	29
Stocks														
Finished goods: level	balance	22	37	38	24	22	18	9	-1	-4	10	10	-4	-7
Selling prices														
Future tendency	balance	71	63	54	64	78	82	76	73	67	62	63	62	68
Rate of increase: future tendency	balance	-16	-20	-24	-23	-26	-24	-26	-19	-17	-31	-32	-25	-33
Employment														
Future tendency	balance	-32	-41	-37	-37	-34	-31	-16	-17	-10	5	-4	-4	-8
Fixed investment														
Intentions	proportion		56		50		48		50		55		53	
Tendency	balance		-1		7		1		12		12		22	
Type of fixed investment														
Replacement of old equipment	proportion		65		69				72				74	
Extending prod. capacity w/unchanged product range	proportion		17		18				19				21	
Extending prod. capacity w/extended product range	proportion		20		23				21				23	
Automation of production process	proportion		28		33				39				38	
New production techniques	proportion		17		19				19				20	
Energy saving	proportion		15		13				14				14	
Pollution control	proportion		16		16				16				18	
Safety measures	proportion		13		14				15				16	
Other	proportion		7		7				8				8	
Limits to fixed investment														
Insufficient demand	proportion				31				21				17	
High cost of capital	proportion				37				49				49	
Insufficient credit guarantees	proportion				10				8				10	
Insufficient profits	proportion				36				28				29	
Fear of indebtedness	proportion												24	
Technical factors	proportion												3	
Other	proportion												17	

1995										1996					
Mar	Apr	May	Jun	Jul	Aug	Sep	Oct	Nov	Dec	Jan	Feb	Mar			
													ENQUÊTES DE CONJONCTURE - INDUST. MANUFACTUR.		
													État des affaires		
5	3	5	5	7	14	15	14	20	15	11	9	8	Tendance		*solde*
40	40	38	36	34	29	27	23	29	29	34	36	38	Perspectives		*solde*
													Carnets de commandes / Demande		
-31	-31	-37	-35	-34	-28	-25	-25	-19	-23	-20	-27	-27	Total : niveau		*solde*
-29	-32	-35	-33	-28	-29	-25	-26	-18	-22	-27	-31	-29	Exportations : niveau		*solde*
													Total : perspectives		*solde*
													Exportations : perspectives		*solde*
													Production		
-4	-3	-1	-2	-6	7	12	17	5	-5	1	-12	-6	Tendance		*solde*
30	41	33	21	25	35	37	32	39	35	28	36	36	Perspectives		*solde*
													Capacité actuelle		*solde*
													Taux d'utilisation des capacités		*%*
													Limites de la production		
5	3	3	4	4	5	6	5	5	4	4	3	4	Aucune		*proportion*
30	38	37	40	38	35	33	32	31	31	30	27	30	Demande intérieure insuffisante		*proportion*
22	24	23	23	24	23	22	23	20	20	17	21	21	Demande extérieure insuffisante		*proportion*
9	21	21	21	24	21	21	20	11	10	10	11	11	Importations compétitives		*proportion*
4	5	5	4	3	3	3	3	4	4	5	4	4	Pénurie de main-d'oeuvre qualifiée		*proportion*
6	6	5	4	2	5	4	3	4	5	2	2	2	Manque d'équipement approprié		*proportion*
27	29	28	28	23	25	26	27	31	30	26	26	24	Pénurie de matières premières		*proportion*
1	1	1	0	0	0	0	0	1	0	0	0	0	Pénurie d'énergie		*proportion*
44	44	44	47	48	43	47	45	55	56	56	56	55	Problèmes financiers		*proportion*
41	31	29	30	31	24	27	28	27	29	28	28	30	Environnement économique incertain		*proportion*
													Stocks		
-5	10	13	7	13	11	7	-1	-7	-5	-7	-8	-5	Produits finis : niveau		*solde*
													Prix de vente		
65	68	62	57	52	64	72	67	57	61	64	72	68	Perspectives		*solde*
-21	-29	-35	-30	-33	-31	-31	-32	-20	-23	-27	-37	-34	Taux d'augmentation : perspectives		*solde*
													Emploi		
													Perspectives		*solde*
													Investissements fixes		
													Intentions		*proportion*
													Tendance		*solde*
													Type d'investissement fixe		
													Remplacement d'équipements anciens		*proportion*
													Invest. de capacité: même gamme de produits		*proportion*
													Invest. de capacité: gamme de produits élargie		*proportion*
													Automatisation du procédé de production		*proportion*
													Nouvelles techniques de production		*proportion*
													Économies d'énergie		*proportion*
													Lutte contre la pollution		*proportion*
													Mesures de securité		*proportion*
													Autres		*proportion*
													Limites de l'investissement		
													Demande insuffisante		*proportion*
													Coût élevé du capital		*proportion*
													Garanties insuffisantes pour crédits		*proportion*
													Profits insuffisants		*proportion*
													Crainte d'endettement		*proportion*
													Facteurs techniques		*proportion*
													Autres		*proportion*

BULGARIA *(continued)*

		1993 Q1	Q2	Q3	Q4	1994 Q1	Q2	Q3	Q4	1995 Q1	Q2	Q3	Q4	1996 Q1
BUSINESS SURVEYS - CONSTRUCTION														
Business activity														
Tendency	*balance*	-46	-30	-20	-36	-44	-34	-29	-11	-19	-10	3	-1	-29
Duration of work in hand	*months*	5	5	4	3	5	5	4	4	4	4	5	4	4
Orders / Demand														
Level	*balance*	-60	-62	-55	-54	-64	-59	-60	-49	-50	-47	-36	-34	-42
Future tendency	*balance*	-15	17	-13	-35	1	-11	-7	-10	4	13	12	-3	7
Technical capacity														
With regard to expected demand: tendency	*balance*	1	22	19	21	10	14	21	10	10	19	18	10	14
Limits to production activity														
None	*proportion*	2	2	1	0	1	1	2	0	1	1	0	0	0
Insufficient demand	*proportion*	22	29	27	24	29	33	24	22	24	20	20	17	15
Weather conditions	*proportion*	45	14	3	10	14	2	2	4	16	12	2	10	39
Cost of materials	*proportion*	28	27	26	22	22	39	45	39	41	40	39	39	38
Financial problems	*proportion*	28	31	38	41	38	44	44	45	42	41	49	48	45
Shortage of skilled labour	*proportion*	5	4	5	6	6	6	5	6	6	10	10	10	8
Lack of appropriate equipment	*proportion*	1	1	0	1	1	1	1	1	1	2	3	2	2
Shortage of raw materials	*proportion*	4	3	7	3	3	3	2	4	3	13	5	6	4
Competition in own sector	*proportion*	15	25	25	20	22	22	24	26	27	30	29	32	29
Price expectations														
Future tendency	*balance*	80	81	66	70	76	80	86	85	89	85	86	85	86
Employment														
Future tendency	*balance*	-50	-40	-37	-53	-36	-42	-38	-27	-23	-19	-8	-17	-18
Financial situation														
Client delays in payment: total	*balance*	34	28	30	29	36	30	23	20	11	11	14	14	13
Client delays in payment: private	*balance*	16	13	17	16	26	23	15	16	9	7	5	9	10
Client delays in payment: public	*balance*	38	28	31	30	38	31	25	22	12	11	15	14	13
BUSINESS SURVEYS - RETAIL TRADE														
Business situation														
Tendency	*balance*		18	22	16	16	21	25	28	19	21	20	14	
Future tendency	*balance*		15	9	26	25	28	11	17	19	20	22	4	
Competition in own sector: tendency	*balance*		81	70	74	69	65	68	72	67	69	68	62	
Limits to improvement in business situation														
None	*proportion*		5	10	2	1	1	1	1	1	0	1	1	
Insufficient demand	*proportion*		38	35	38	37	31	31	33	35	35	26	27	
Supply	*proportion*		5	12	7	8	10	11	9	8	7	8	7	
Financial problems	*proportion*		43	46	48	47	55	57	54	50	44	51	54	
Sales surface	*proportion*		1	0	0	1	1	0	1	2	1	0	0	
Competition in own sector	*proportion*		50	53	50	49	45	49	47	49	55	46	49	
Intentions of placing orders														
Total: future tendency	*balance*		12	9	18	18	24	10	12	14	13	20	12	
Domestic: future tendency	*balance*		21	13	20	22	25	11	13	16	14	23	15	
Foreign: future tendency	*balance*		8	4	13	12	27	17	20	10	9	-8	-9	
Stocks														
Level	*balance*		-20	-25	-26	-32	-39	-37	-36	-34	-32	-44	-41	
Selling prices														
Tendency	*balance*		71	81	78	95	93	93	93	87	88	95	80	
Rate of increase: tendency	*balance*		3	13	18	57	57	64	43	14	5	21	12	
Future tendency	*balance*		82	92	92	96	95	97	94	83	88	95	93	
Rate of increase: future tendency	*balance*		10	16	18	46	44	50	43	12	6	17	18	
Employment														
Future tendency	*balance*		-46	-43	-35	-41	-30	-26	-33	-31	-27	-29	-31	
Financial situation														
Tendency	*balance*		0	7	-2	-1	-6	-1	4	0	5	13	-1	

1995										1996				
Mar	Apr	May	Jun	Jul	Aug	Sep	Oct	Nov	Dec	Jan	Feb	Mar		
													ENQUÊTES DE CONJONCTURE - CONSTRUCTION	
													Activité de l'entreprise	
-15	-14	-10	-5	-1	0	9	6	-2	-8	-12	-32	-42	Tendance	*solde*
													Durée des travaux commandés	*mois*
													Commandes / Demande	
-42	-49	-49	-44	-38	-37	-33	-33	-34	-35	-38	-41	-46	Niveau	*solde*
													Perspectives	*solde*
													Capacité technique	
													Tendance compte tenu de la demande prévue	*solde*
													Limites de la production	
0	0	1	1	0	1	0	0	0	1	0	0	0	Aucune	*proportion*
23	20	20	19	19	25	16	13	18	21	16	14	16	Demande insuffisante	*proportion*
8	11	15	11	1	1	5	2	8	19	26	46	46	Intempéries	*proportion*
46	41	40	38	40	32	44	37	43	36	38	38	38	Coût des matériaux	*proportion*
43	45	42	37	46	42	58	45	54	44	43	44	47	Problèmes financiers	*proportion*
5	9	10	11	10	11	10	10	11	8	7	8	10	Pénurie de main-d'oeuvre qualifiée	*proportion*
1	0	2	3	2	3	3	2	2	2	4	2	1	Manque d'équipement approprié	*proportion*
3	5	17	16	4	8	3	6	5	7	3	3	5	Pénurie de matières premières	*proportion*
29	40	25	24	36	26	24	38	27	32	38	23	25	Concurrence dans le secteur	*proportion*
													Pronostic sur les prix	
89	90	79	85	88	79	91	88	86	80	81	86	90	Perspectives	*solde*
													Emploi	
													Perspectives	*solde*
													Situation financière	
16	9	10	13	13	13	15	15	17	9	11	14	15	Retards de paiement de la clientèle : total	*solde*
15	7	5	9	6	3	5	9	13	4	8	11	11	Retards de paiement de la clientèle : privé	*solde*
18	10	9	15	13	15	17	15	17	10	12	12	16	Retards de paiement de la clientèle : public	*solde*
													ENQUÊTES DE CONJONCTURE - COMMERCE DE DÉTAIL	
													État des affaires	
31	21	21	16	27	17	20	24	19	18	23	8	10	Tendance	*solde*
22	21	20	17	18	18	23	13	27	25	12	-1	2	Perspectives	*solde*
73	69	68	64	74	70	64	67	68	68	65	63	59	Concurrence dans le secteur : tendance	*solde*
													Limites de l'amélioration des affaires	
1	0	1	1	0	0	0	0	2	0	1	1	0	Aucune	*proportion*
34	32	35	37	34	36	34	32	26	20	31	24	27	Demande insuffisante	*proportion*
9	9	8	7	8	5	7	6	6	13	7	9	4	Approvisionnement	*proportion*
53	57	47	47	47	42	44	47	56	50	48	55	60	Problèmes financiers	*proportion*
1	2	3	1	0	1	1	0	0	1	0	0	0	Surface de vente	*proportion*
46	49	49	49	56	57	52	54	42	41	57	45	46	Concurrence dans le secteur	*proportion*
													Commandes : intentions	
17	16	13	14	9	11	20	14	31	16	18	13	4	Total : perspectives	*solde*
17	17	15	16	9	13	20	17	31	20	19	23	4	Fournisseurs nationaux : perspectives	*solde*
19	19	15	-4	20	10	-3	-2	-6	-16	13	-25	-14	Fournisseurs étrangers : perspectives	*solde*
													Stocks	
-34	-32	-36	-33	-31	-32	-34	-34	-48	-49	-38	-41	-43	Niveau	*solde*
													Prix de vente	
93	92	87	82	83	87	94	94	97	94	94	75	71	Tendance	*solde*
38	21	13	8	-7	-6	27	22	23	17	21	7	8	Taux d'augmentation : tendance	*solde*
94	91	81	78	82	87	94	94	95	95	97	91	90	Perspectives	*solde*
38	23	10	4	-5	-8	30	21	24	6	15	19	19	Taux d'augmentation : perspectives	*solde*
													Emploi	
													Perspectives	*solde*
													Situation financière	
0	-3	1	1	-3	8	10	11	14	15	-3	0	-1	Tendance	*solde*

ESTONIA

		1993				1994				1995				1996
		Q1	Q2	Q3	Q4	Q1	Q2	Q3	Q4	Q1	Q2	Q3	Q4	Q1
BUSINESS SURVEYS - MANUFACTURING														
Order books / Demand														
Total: tendency	*balance*	-17	6	6	18	24	19	5	21	2	3	11	17	-30
Export: tendency	*balance*	12	7	1	12	26	6	1	19	14	-3	1	9	-17
Total: future tendency	*balance*									39	17	18	6	27
Export: future tendency	*balance*	30	15	18	18	23	12	29	17	28	10	8	12	18
Production														
Tendency	*balance*	-28	32	15	25	-1	20	-4	20	-3	13	7	3	-35
Future tendency	*balance*	35	4	16	9	51	12	21	10	63	16	10	5	52
Current capacity	*balance*	27	12	15	7	23	36	28	30	38	35	34	36	33
Rate of capacity utilisation	*%*	50	56	53	55	54	59	59	56	55	57	59	59	53
Limits to production														
None	*proportion*	0	2	3	7	2	2	6	6	4	4	2	2	3
Insufficient demand	*proportion*	72	68	51	54	54	61	59	52	55	60	55	57	63
Labour shortage	*proportion*	1	4	6	6	3	5	6	8	8	12	16	10	9
Lack of appropriate equipment	*proportion*	3	11	12	14	12	11	11	10	9	10	17	15	13
Shortage of raw materials	*proportion*	15	12	20	15	28	9	12	17	23	20	16	19	20
Financial problems	*proportion*	42	39	36	35	29	36	31	32	26	25	30	24	25
Stocks														
Finished goods: level	*balance*	31	35	19	18	1	23	22	9	10	18	13	12	16
Selling prices														
Future tendency	*balance*	12	14	21	35	43	8	47	37	14	2	28	37	9
Employment														
Future tendency	*balance*	-27	-16	-21	-15	-8	-16	-16	-9	-5	-13	-22	-22	-12
Fixed investment														
Intentions	*proportion*				70				88				94	
Future tendency	*balance*				40				34				37	
Type of fixed investment														
Replacement of old equipment	*proportion*												56	
Extending prod. capacity w/extended product range	*proportion*												38	
Automation of production process	*proportion*												63	
New production techniques	*proportion*												84	
Energy saving	*proportion*												60	
Pollution control / Safety measures[1]	*proportion*												38	
Limits to fixed investment														
Insufficient demand	*proportion*												29	
High cost of capital	*proportion*												48	
Insufficient credit guarantees	*proportion*												39	
Insufficient profits	*proportion*												77	
Fear of indebtedness	*proportion*												15	
Technical factors	*proportion*												6	
Other	*proportion*												6	

(1) "Pollution control" and "Safety measures" are grouped together.

1995										1996			
Mar	Apr	May	Jun	Jul	Aug	Sep	Oct	Nov	Dec	Jan	Feb	Mar

ENQUÊTES DE CONJONCTURE - INDUST. MANUFACTUR.

Carnets de commandes / Demande

Total : tendance	*solde*
Exportations : tendance	*solde*
Total : perspectives	*solde*
Exportations: perspectives	*solde*

Production

Tendance	*solde*
Perspectives	*solde*
Capacité actuelle	*solde*
Taux d'utilisation des capacités	*%*

Limites de la production

Aucune	*proportion*
Demande insuffisante	*proportion*
Pénurie de main d'oeuvre	*proportion*
Manque d'équipement approprié	*proportion*
Pénurie de matières premières	*proportion*
Problèmes financiers	*proportion*

Stocks

Produits finis : niveau	*solde*

Prix de vente

Perspectives	*solde*

Emploi

Perspectives	*solde*

Investissements fixes

Intentions	*proportion*
Perspectives	*solde*

Type d'investissement fixe

Remplacement d'équipments anciens	*proportion*
Invest. de capacité: gamme de produits élargie	*proportion*
Automatisation du procédé de production	*proportion*
Nouvelles techniques de production	*proportion*
Économies d'énergie	*proportion*
Lutte contre la pollution / Mesures de sécurité[1]	*proportion*

Limites de l'investissement

Demande insuffisante	*proportion*
Coût élevé du capital	*proportion*
Garanties insuffisantes pour crédits	*proportion*
Profits insuffisants	*proportion*
Crainte d'endettement	*proportion*
Facteurs techniques	*proportion*
Autres	*proportion*

1) "Lutte contre la pollution" et " mesures de sécurité" sont regroupés.

ESTONIA (continued)

		1993				1994				1995				1996
		Q1	Q2	Q3	Q4	Q1	Q2	Q3	Q4	Q1	Q2	Q3	Q4	Q1
BUSINESS SURVEYS - CONSTRUCTION														
Business activity														
Tendency	balance				16	-22	39	53	26	-16	34	49	-8	-28
Duration of work in hand	months				4	4	4	4	4	3	4	3	3	3
Orders / Demand														
Level	balance				-25	-32	15	30	-20	-15	-26	-4	-20	-41
Domestic: level	balance									-41	-20	-7	-17	-34
Foreign: level	balance									-16	-46	-29	-18	-37
Future tendency	balance				0	-41	44	39	11	50	35	0	-2	54
Technical capacity														
With regard to expected demand: tendency	balance									4	0	6	-8	1
Limits to production activity														
None	proportion				4	0	0	0	0	0	0	2	5	0
Insufficient demand	proportion				64	72	41	33	27	29	59	57	62	75
Weather conditions	proportion				28	48	0	3	12	6	0	2	24	42
Cost of labour	proportion									2	3	5	8	0
Shortage of skilled labour	proportion				40	20	33	30	12	13	19	32	30	12
Cost of materials	proportion									4	19	9	11	5
Shortage of raw materials	proportion				0	0	0	0	2	1	0	0	0	0
Lack of appropriate equipment	proportion				0	0	0	10	0	0	3	2	0	0
Cost of financing	proportion									10	22	18	11	8
Access to bank credit	proportion				40	36	30	30	12	11	19	18	19	7
Competition in own sector	proportion				36	60	48	53	35	24	59	61	68	57
Price expectations														
Future tendency	balance				64	91	89	77	69	75	63	64	69	56
Rate of increase: future tendency	balance									-6	-18	-17	0	-14
Employment														
Future tendency	balance				4	41	32	7	0	27	15	0	-19	39
Financial situation														
Tendency	balance				0	4	0	43	-7	-36	6	26	25	-29
Client delays in payment: total	balance									36	12	-3	18	37
Client delays in payment: private	balance									31	4	0	21	37
Client delays in payment: public	balance									43	17	-3	19	17
BUSINESS SURVEYS - RETAIL TRADE														
Business situation														
Tendency	balance		-8	2	-4	13	9	10	2	-9	11	-2	0	-14
Future tendency	balance		-3	31	35	48	18	45	29	41	20	20	29	43
Competition in own sector: tendency	balance		60	59	49	34	42	43	32	21	38	31	40	37
Limits to improvement in business situation														
None	proportion		2	2	4	2	0	3	4	1	0	4	3	4
Insufficient demand	proportion		21	22	47	47	56	58	51	48	47	40	49	60
Supply	proportion		6	4	10	7	15	18	11	14	13	7	7	10
Cost of labour	proportion		5	0	2	6	4	3	6	7	20	8	10	11
Cost of financing	proportion		22	22	31	32	19	33	26	30	18	26	29	23
Access to bank credit	proportion		10	8	12	13	13	13	17	28	24	28	22	23
Sales surface	proportion		14	16	29	34	42	33	43	35	42	30	22	29
Storage capacity	proportion		6	4	10	13	4	20	17	9	16	20	7	11
Competition in own sector	proportion		14	22	37	42	44	38	43	20	49	44	48	41
Intentions of placing orders														
Total: future tendency	balance								-13	47	10	26	9	49
Domestic: future tendency	balance		21	18	-6	32	18	30	-4	41	13	22	2	43
Foreign: future tendency	balance		29	16	11	38	22	22	-12	30	16	21	-5	43
Stocks														
Level	balance	7	2	5	2	1	5	-6	7	0	7	6	-2	-2
Selling prices														
Tendency	balance		62	76	76	87	75	68	81	76	53	38	56	67
Rate of increase: tendency	balance		-30	-7	-7	31	-16	-20	-15	10	-14	-6	31	31
Future tendency	balance		75	78	78	92	87	83	81	75	60	52	76	62
Rate of increase: future tendency	balance		-24	-12	-8	-6	-29	-44	0	-18	-7	14	23	22
Employment														
Future tendency	balance	-4	-8	2	4	15	-2	3	-2	7	-5	-6	4	2
Financial situation														
Tendency	balance		10	34	12	14	15	13	4	-31	9	10	4	-14

OECD/OCDE
SHORT-TERM ECONOMIC INDICATORS
OECD/CCET © April 1996

A14

INDICATEURS ÉCONOMIQUES À COURT TERME
OCDE/CCET © avril 1996

1995										1996			
Mar	Apr	May	Jun	Jul	Aug	Sep	Oct	Nov	Dec	Jan	Feb	Mar	

ENQUÊTES DE CONJONCTURE - CONSTRUCTION

Activité de l'entreprise

Tendance	*solde*
Durée des travaux commandés	*mois*

Commandes / Demande

Niveau	*solde*
Intérieurs : niveau	*solde*
Extérieures : niveau	*solde*
Perspectives	*solde*

Capacité technique

Tendance compte tenu de la demande prévue	*solde*

Limites de la production

Aucune	*proportion*
Demande insuffisante	*proportion*
Intempéries	*proportion*
Coût de la main d'oeuvre	*proportion*
Pénurie de main-d'oeuvre qualifiée	*proportion*
Coût des matériaux	*proportion*
Pénurie de matières premières	*proportion*
Manque d'équipement approprié	*proportion*
Coût de financement	*proportion*
Accès aux crédits bancaires	*proportion*
Concurrence dans le secteur	*proportion*

Pronostic sur les prix

Perspectives	*solde*
Taux d'augmentation : perspectives	*solde*

Emploi

Perspectives	*solde*

Situation financière

Tendance	*solde*
Retards de paiement de la clientèle : total	*solde*
Retards de paiement de la clientèle : privé	*solde*
Retards de paiement de la clientèle : public	*solde*

ENQUÊTES DE CONJONCTURE - COMMERCE DE DÉTAIL

État des affaires

Tendance	*solde*
Perspectives	*solde*
Concurrence dans le secteur : tendance	*solde*

Limites de l'amélioration des affaires

Aucune	*proportion*
Demande insuffisante	*proportion*
Approvisionnement	*proportion*
Coût de la main d'oeuvre	*proportion*
Coût de financement	*proportion*
Accès aux crédits bancaires	*proportion*
Surface de vente	*proportion*
Capacités de stockage	*proportion*
Concurrence dans le secteur	*proportion*

Commandes : intentions

Total : perspectives	*solde*
Fournisseurs nationaux : perspectives	*solde*
Fournisseurs étrangers : perspectives	*solde*

Stocks

Niveau	*solde*

Prix de vente

Tendance	*solde*
Taux d'augmentation : tendance	*solde*
Perspectives	*solde*
Taux d'augmentation : perspectives	*solde*

Emploi

Perspectives	*solde*

Situation financière

Tendance	*solde*

HUNGARY

		1993 Q1	Q2	Q3	Q4	1994 Q1	Q2	Q3	Q4	1995 Q1	Q2	Q3	Q4	1996 Q1
BUSINESS SURVEYS - MANUFACTURING														
Business situation														
Tendency	balance	-19	-22	-9	9	0	-1	4	22	8	12	33	40	15
Future tendency	balance	15	7	17	20	28	27	20	31	39	23	26	22	38
Order books / Demand														
Total: level	balance	-19	-22	-14	-15	-14	2	7	3	6	7	13	17	-5
Export: level[1]	balance	-30	-23	-21	-12	-13	11	-2	12	18	14	14	16	-4
Export: future tendency[1]	balance	17	13	19	23	32	34	17	37	52	35	32	42	35
Production														
Tendency	balance	-8	10	6	24	-3	24	16	37	9	28	24	22	-2
Future tendency	balance	34	12	17	23	37	34	23	33	38	30	31	22	50
Current capacity[2]	balance	34	32	30	24	29	13	19	9	9	11	12	8	13
Rate of capacity utilisation	%	69	69	71	73	72	75	75	76	76	76	78	79	77
Limits to production														
None	proportion	7	6	10	11	11	12	13	13	10	8	10	11	9
Insufficient domestic demand	proportion		56	52	57	59	55	55	51	49	54	49	54	61
Insufficient foreign demand	proportion		26	29	26	25	25	23	19	20	18	17	15	24
Competitive imports	proportion		4	5	4	6	5	6	4	6	6	6	4	4
Shortage of labour	proportion	2	3	4	4	4	7	7	8	4	7	9	4	5
Shortage of skilled labour	proportion	9	9	10	11	11	16	17	15	12	14	17	18	14
Shortage of raw materials	proportion	6	8	8	9	10	7	11	10	14	10	13	9	5
Financial problems	proportion	46	47	47	47	45	42	44	40	45	42	45	41	39
Unclear economic laws	proportion	14	11	11	14	12	11	11	15	17	17	16	19	13
Uncertainty in the economic environment	proportion	40	44	42	47	39	40	41	41	46	43	45	46	36
Stocks														
Finished goods: level	balance	5	8	13	-8	5	4	-5	-8	3	18	4	8	17
Employment														
Future tendency	balance	-46	-42	-43	-28	-24	-12	-22	-15	-28	-25	-22	-25	-30
BUSINESS SURVEYS - CONSTRUCTION														
Business activity														
Level	balance	-21	-8	7	6	0	17	17	22	-13	3	1	-6	-10
Duration of work in hand	months	4	4	4	4	5	5	4	5	4	4	4	4	4
Orders / Demand														
Total: level	balance	5	-16	-18	12	30	16	1	-8	5	-5	-12	2	-36
Total: future tendency	balance	0	-7	-10	26	40	34	-4	4	-9	-21	-31	-2	21
Limits to production activity														
Insufficient demand	proportion	70	51	42	41	38	34	31	34	40	39	43	40	45
Shortage of skilled labour	proportion	14	16	13	8	6	9	7	8	9	5	7	6	1
Lack of appropriate equipment	proportion	7	17	12	13	10	15	16	15	9	8	11	9	8
Cost of financing	proportion	56	63	30	27	33	32	32	27	43	46	50	46	47
Price expectations														
Future tendency	balance	24	43	67	74	70	63	67	81	85	72	67	86	68
Rate of increase: future tendency	balance		-67	-51	-36	-36	-39	-15	-13	8	-6	-21	-10	-36
Employment														
Future tendency	balance	-8	-24	-24	4	21	-1	-12	4	-10	-21	-17	-14	-8

(1) Concerns "Western" exports only.

(2) Revised according to the harmonised questions.

1995										1996		
Mar	Apr	May	Jun	Jul	Aug	Sep	Oct	Nov	Dec	Jan	Feb	Mar

ENQUÊTES DE CONJONCTURE - INDUST. MANUFACTUR.
État des affaires
Tendance — *solde*
Perspectives — *solde*
Carnets de commandes / Demande
Total : niveau — *solde*
Exportations : niveau[1] — *solde*
Exportations : perspectives[1] — *solde*
Production
Tendance — *solde*
Perspectives — *solde*
Capacité actuelle[2] — *solde*
Taux d'utilisation des capacités — *%*
Limites de la production
Aucune — *proportion*
Demande intérieure insuffisante — *proportion*
Demande extérieure insuffisante — *proportion*
Importations compétitives — *proportion*
Pénurie de main-d'oeuvre — *proportion*
Pénurie de main-d'oeuvre qualifiée — *proportion*
Pénurie de matières premières — *proportion*
Problèmes financiers — *proportion*
Lois économiques peu claires — *proportion*
Environnement économique incertain — *proportion*
Stocks
Produits finis : niveau — *solde*
Emploi
Perspectives — *solde*

ENQUÊTES DE CONJONCTURE - CONSTRUCTION
Activité de l'entreprise
Niveau — *solde*
Durée des travaux commandés — *mois*
Commandes / Demande
Total : niveau — *solde*
Total : perspectives — *solde*
Limites de la production
Demande insuffisante — *proportion*
Pénurie de main-d'oeuvre qualifiée — *proportion*
Manque d'équipement approprié — *proportion*
Coût de financement — *proportion*
Pronostic sur les prix
Perspectives — *solde*
Taux d'augmentation : perspectives — *solde*
Emploi
Perspectives — *solde*

1) Concerne seulement les exportations vers "l'Ouest".

2) Série révisée selon les questions harmonisées.

		1993				1994				1995				1996
		Q1	Q2	Q3	Q4	Q1	Q2	Q3	Q4	Q1	Q2	Q3	Q4	Q1
BUSINESS SURVEYS - RETAIL TRADE														
Business situation														
Tendency	*balance*	2	-2	8	13	3	14	0	23	0	-5	5	4	1
Future tendency	*balance*	16	-5	4	3	16	16	5	-16	-22	-3	3	-7	7
Competition in own sector: tendency	*balance*		46	54	56	49	51	48	53	53	46	60	47	51
Limits to improvement in business situation														
None	*proportion*	5	6	3	3	3	3	2	3	0	0	3	2	2
Insufficient demand	*proportion*	59	64	67	74	67	70	74	75	78	85	80	90	90
Cost of labour	*proportion*		17	15	25	22	21	17	21	12	14	16	13	17
Cost of financing	*proportion*	57	53	55	52	51	50	54	49	62	61	53	39	43
Access to bank credit	*proportion*		40	46	34	30	27	33	21	28	20	20	19	10
Sales surface	*proportion*		9	10	6	10	7	4	6	7	2	2	2	4
Storage capacity	*proportion*		5	10	4	3	7	4	7	6	2	1	2	1
Competition in own sector	*proportion*		35	33	48	44	51	56	45	52	55	56	55	55
Intentions of placing orders														
Total: future tendency	*balance*	9	-11	4	-20	-5	0	-1	-26	-19	-26	-2	-38	-13
Stocks														
Level	*balance*	5	9	9	23	21	20	17	18	27	38	31	18	38
Selling prices														
Tendency	*balance*	25	51	56	71	69	67	80	74	89	89	88	84	80
Rate of increase: tendency	*balance*		-22	-6	-21	-28	-18	7	-9	46	21	11	2	-10
Future tendency	*balance*	20	55	69	79	71	76	80	86	96	89	79	88	78
Rate of increase: future tendency	*balance*		-26	-8	-3	-34	-8	2	37	18	-24	-2	25	-29
Employment														
Future tendency	*balance*	-6	2	3	-16	-4	2	-9	-11	-10	-23	-15	-22	-23
Financial situation														
Tendency	*balance*	-9	-1	0	21	-9	5	7	23	-23	-27	3	3	-10

1995										1996		
Mar	Apr	May	Jun	Jul	Aug	Sep	Oct	Nov	Dec	Jan	Feb	Mar

ENQUÊTES DE CONJONCTURE - COMMERCE DE DÉTAIL
État des affaires

Tendance	*solde*
Perspectives	*solde*
Concurrence dans le secteur : tendance	*solde*

Limites de l'amélioration des affaires

Aucune	*proportion*
Demande insuffisante	*proportion*
Coût de la main d'oeuvre	*proportion*
Coût de financement	*proportion*
Accès aux crédits bancaires	*proportion*
Surface de vente	*proportion*
Capacités de stockage	*proportion*
Concurrence dans le secteur	*proportion*

Commandes : intentions

Total : perspectives	*solde*

Stocks

Niveau	*solde*

Prix de vente

Tendance	*solde*
Taux d'augmentation : tendance	*solde*
Perspectives	*solde*
Taux d'augmentation : perspectives	*solde*

Emploi

Perspectives	*solde*

Situation financière

Tendance	*solde*

LATVIA

		1993				1994				1995				1996
		Q1	Q2	Q3	Q4	Q1	Q2	Q3	Q4	Q1	Q2	Q3	Q4	Q1
BUSINESS SURVEYS - MANUFACTURING														
Business situation														
Tendency	*balance*		-38	-44	-33	-16	-37	-22	-25	-12	-23	-20	-17	-11
Future tendency	*balance*		9	6	11	20	14	16	17	28	25	17	13	22
Order books / Demand														
Total: level	*balance*		-71	-81	-64	-53	-65	-55	-64	-66	-54	-64	-56	-63
Export: level	*balance*		-47	-62	-44	-38	-43	-44	-44	-53	-35	-48	-46	-45
Total: future tendency	*balance*		-18	-3	-1	10	1	17	9	18	15	12	2	15
Export: future tendency	*balance*		7	-1	11	16	4	16	11	18	12	16	8	18
Production														
Tendency	*balance*		-51	-42	-20	8	-4	2	2	4	0	2	-1	5
Future tendency	*balance*		-15	-7	2	15	6	20	18	22	17	15	5	15
Current capacity	*balance*		42	54	41	39	35	30	36	49	34	42	39	31
Rate of capacity utilisation	*balance*		45	46	47	43	48	50	51	49	51	50	51	52
Limits to production														
None	*proportion*		1	2	1	0	1	2	1	3	2	1	1	1
Insufficient domestic demand	*proportion*		80	63	74	75	70	78	70	69	66	60	65	68
Insufficient foreign demand	*proportion*		36	32	37	33	29	31	37	43	36	33	38	41
Competitive imports	*proportion*		23	29	26	30	23	30	31	34	32	31	33	27
Shortage of skilled labour	*proportion*		6	13	9	4	4	7	9	8	10	8	8	11
Shortage of raw materials	*proportion*		22	22	23	24	32	19	21	21	23	21	23	21
Lack of appropriate equipment	*proportion*		26	39	39	22	38	33	41	39	35	33	38	37
Shortage of energy	*proportion*		4	2	3	3	4	2	4	5	4	1	2	2
Financial problems	*proportion*		67	55	64	56	65	58	52	54	52	63	54	58
Uncertainty in the economic environment	*proportion*		44	26	38	38	37	34	34	28	19	35	30	26
Unclear economic laws	*proportion*		44	27	44	42	38	30	25	24	23	24	27	28
Stocks														
Finished goods: level	*balance*		41	48	22	20	28	27	25	12	14	5	-8	22
Selling prices														
Future tendency	*balance*		40	16	52	60	35	37	42	48	30	33	53	41
Rate of increase: future tendency	*balance*		-46	-44	-11	-21	-37	-43	-9	0	-3	-12	9	4
Employment														
Future tendency	*balance*		-47	-52	-43	-25	-16	-15	-18	-13	-20	-14	-20	-8
Fixed investment														
Intentions	*proportion*		52		55		60		68		50		55	
Future tendency	*balance*		-41		6		11		10		4		13	
Type of fixed investment														
Replacement of old equipment	*proportion*				26				39				35		
Extending prod. capacity w/unchanged product range	*proportion*				9				8				8		
Extending prod. capacity w/extended product range	*proportion*				31				38				30		
Automation of production process	*proportion*				9				12				17		
New production techniques	*proportion*				21				29				22		
Energy saving	*proportion*				18				27				21		
Pollution control	*proportion*				14				11				8		
Safety measures	*proportion*				3				9				8		
Other	*proportion*				1				4				3		
Limits to fixed investment														
Insufficient demand	*proportion*				30				27				22		
High cost of capital	*proportion*				24				29				32		
Fear of indebtedness	*proportion*				23				28				22		
Insufficient credit guarantees	*proportion*				32				32				35		
Insufficient profits	*proportion*				43				50				47		
Technical factors	*proportion*				4				3				2		
Other	*proportion*				3				14				7		

1995										1996		
Mar	Apr	May	Jun	Jul	Aug	Sep	Oct	Nov	Dec	Jan	Feb	Mar

ENQUÊTES DE CONJONCTURE - INDUST. MANUFACTUR.

État des affaires

Tendance	*solde*
Perspectives	*solde*

Carnets de commandes / Demande

Total : niveau	*solde*
Exportations : niveau	*solde*
Total : perspectives	*solde*
Exportations : perspectives	*solde*

Production

Tendance	*solde*
Perspectives	*solde*
Capacité actuelle	*solde*
Taux d'utilisation des capacités	*solde*

Limites de la production

Aucune	*proportion*
Demande intérieure insuffisante	*proportion*
Demande extérieure insuffisante	*proportion*
Importations compétitives	*proportion*
Pénurie de main-d'oeuvre qualifiée	*proportion*
Pénurie de matières premières	*proportion*
Manque d'équipement approprié	*proportion*
Pénurie d'énergie	*proportion*
Problèmes financiers	*proportion*
Environnement économique incertain	*proportion*
Lois économiques peu claires	*proportion*

Stocks

Produits finis : niveau	*solde*

Prix de vente

Perspectives	*solde*
Taux d'augmentation : perspectives	*solde*

Emploi

Perspectives	*solde*

Investissements fixes

Intentions	*proportion*
Perspectives	*solde*

Type d'investissement fixe

Remplacement d'équipements anciens	*proportion*
Invest. de capacité: même gamme de produits	*proportion*
Invest. de capacité: gamme de produits élargie	*proportion*
Automatisation du procédé de production	*proportion*
Nouvelles techniques de production	*proportion*
Économies d'énergie	*proportion*
Lutte contre la pollution	*proportion*
Mesures de securité	*proportion*
Autres	*proportion*

Limites de l'investissement

Demande insuffisante	*proportion*
Coût élevé du capital	*proportion*
Crainte d'endettement	*proportion*
Garanties insuffisantes pour crédits	*proportion*
Profits insuffisants	*proportion*
Facteurs techniques	*proportion*
Autres	*proportion*

LATVIA (continued)

		1993				1994				1995				1996
		Q1	Q2	Q3	Q4	Q1	Q2	Q3	Q4	Q1	Q2	Q3	Q4	Q1
BUSINESS SURVEYS - CONSTRUCTION														
Business activity														
Tendency	balance			-17	-34	-38	5	39	3	-26	-4	-12	-34	-61
Duration of work in hand	months			3	3	3	4	4	2	3	4	2	2	2
Orders / Demand														
Total: level	balance			-75	-75	-70	-77	-49	-59	-73	-70	-72	-65	-88
Domestic: level	balance			-78	-80	-76	-77				-73	-72	-66	-91
Foreign: level	balance			-39	-32	-24	-24				-17	-15	-17	-25
Total: future tendency	balance			-44	-54	-31	51	1	41	-6	45	-30	-41	-38
Technical capacity														
With regard to expected demand: tendency	balance			25	32	14	11	16	-1	-1	4	7	8	13
Limits to production activity														
None	proportion			0	0	2	7	8	2	3	3	4	0	3
Insufficient demand	proportion			84	84	77	71	67	68	72	71	58	71	81
Weather conditions	proportion			1	2	3	5	3	3	10	4	0	5	19
Cost of labour	proportion			13	9	3	5	3	7	8	3	4	6	6
Shortage of skilled labour	proportion			16	22	7	7	18	12	8	7	5	5	1
Cost of materials	proportion			44	31	23	14	20	15	7	11	9	14	10
Shortage of raw materials	proportion			1	4	2	4	3	0	0	1	0	0	3
Lack of appropriate equipment	proportion			1	4	2	0	0	2	0	1	0	0	0
Cost of financing	proportion			39	38	30	27	23	30	17	27	45	33	22
Access to bank credit	proportion			13	11	10	13	2	7	7	4	5	6	6
Competition in own sector	proportion			14	22	21	25	28	32	27	33	29	32	22
Price expectations														
Future tendency	balance			29	48	46	38	27	31	31	41	23	40	51
Rate of increase: future tendency	balance								-8	10	-2	13	25	14
Employment														
Future tendency	balance			-43	-44	-28	14	-4	-24	-14	8	-29	-36	-29
Financial situation														
Tendency	balance			-6	-12	-14	-26	18	-6	-6	-34	-26	-22	-45
Client delays in payment: total	balance			-4	14	13	6	-6	-4	6	5	25	9	11
Client delays in payment: private	balance			-13	-5	-1	-9	-11	-8	7	9	9	-3	3
Client delays in payment: public	balance			12	19	17	5	-3	4	7	-1	27	9	21
BUSINESS SURVEYS - RETAIL TRADE														
Business situation														
Tendency	balance													-8
Future tendency	balance													17
Competition in own sector: tendency	balance													56
Limits to improvement in business situation														
None	proportion													6
Insufficient demand	proportion													51
Supply	proportion													5
Cost of labour	proportion													10
Cost of financing	proportion													28
Access to bank credit	proportion													20
Sales surface	proportion													11
Storage capacity	proportion													1
Competition in own sector	proportion													39
Other	proportion													11
Intentions of placing orders														
Total: future tendency	balance													3
Domestic: future tendency	balance													-2
Foreign: future tendency	balance													7
Stocks														
Level	balance													-10
Selling prices														
Tendency	balance													38
Rate of increase: tendency	balance													3
Future tendency	balance													52
Rate of increase: future tendency	balance													17
Employment														
Future tendency	balance													-19
Financial situation														
Tendency	balance													-23

1995										1996		
Mar	Apr	May	Jun	Jul	Aug	Sep	Oct	Nov	Dec	Jan	Feb	Mar

ENQUÊTES DE CONJONCTURE - CONSTRUCTION
Activité de l'entreprise
Tendance — *solde*
Durée des travaux commandés — *mois*
Commandes / Demande
Total : niveau — *solde*
Intérieures : niveau — *solde*
Extérieures : niveau — *solde*
Total : perspectives — *solde*
Capacité technique
Tendance compte tenu de la demande prévue — *solde*
Limites de la production
Aucune — *proportion*
Demande insuffisante — *proportion*
Intempéries — *proportion*
Coût de la main d'oeuvre — *proportion*
Pénurie de main-d'oeuvre qualifiée — *proportion*
Coût des matériaux — *proportion*
Pénurie de matières premières — *proportion*
Manque d'équipement approprié — *proportion*
Coût de financement — *proportion*
Accès aux crédits bancaires — *proportion*
Concurrence dans le secteur — *proportion*
Pronostic sur les prix
Perspectives — *solde*
Taux d'augmentation : perspectives — *solde*
Emploi
Perspectives — *solde*
Situation financière
Tendance — *solde*
Retards de paiement de la clientèle : total — *solde*
Retards de paiement de la clientèle : privé — *solde*
Retards de paiement de la clientèle : public — *solde*

ENQUÊTES DE CONJONCTURE - COMMERCE DE DÉTAIL
État des affaires
Tendance — *solde*
Perspectives — *solde*
Concurrence dans le secteur : tendance — *solde*
Limites de l'amélioration des affaires
Aucune — *proportion*
Demande insuffisante — *proportion*
Approvisionnement — *proportion*
Coût de la main d'oeuvre — *proportion*
Coût de financement — *proportion*
Accès aux crédits bancaires — *proportion*
Surface de vente — *proportion*
Capacités de stockage — *proportion*
Concurrence dans le secteur — *proportion*
Autres — *proportion*
Commandes : intentions
Total : perspectives — *solde*
Fournisseurs nationaux : perspectives — *solde*
Fournisseurs étrangers : perspectives — *solde*
Stocks
Niveau — *solde*
Prix de vente
Tendance — *solde*
Taux d'augmentation : tendance — *solde*
Perspectives — *solde*
Taux d'augmentation : perspectives — *solde*
Emploi
Perspectives — *solde*
Situation financière
Tendance — *solde*

LITHUANIA

		1993				1994				1995				1996
		Q1	Q2	Q3	Q4	Q1	Q2	Q3	Q4	Q1	Q2	Q3	Q4	Q1
BUSINESS SURVEYS - MANUFACTURING														
Business situation														
Tendency	*balance*	-42	-68	-45	-65	-48	-52	-41	-45	-27	-18	-21	-19	
Future tendency	*balance*	-16	-4	-6	1	-7	-19	-4	19	-2	-2	5	3	
Order books / Demand														
Total: level	*balance*	-47	-39	-61	-21	-48	-70	-43	-35	-30	-24	-18	-20	
Export: level	*balance*	-53	-47	-42	-29	-38	-60	-52	-43	-33	-33	-34	-32	
Total: future tendency	*balance*	1	-14	-2	-5	-18	-29	-5	14	8	3	7	7	
Export: future tendency	*balance*	-18	-4	3	-2	-8	-13	-2	-3	7	2	1	3	
Production														
Tendency	*balance*	-19	-7	-11	4	-21	-25	-11	-5	-11	2	8	-4	
Future tendency	*balance*	-1	-3	0	3	-4	-18	-11	-5	21	10	6	-9	
Current capacity	*balance*	32	54	48	71	58	56	43	41	39	27	37	30	
Rate of capacity utilisation	*%*	54	53	49	51	49	49	51	49	44	44	44	45	
Limits to production														
None	*proportion*			2	1	0	1	0	2	0	2	2	3	2
Insufficient domestic demand	*proportion*			54	45	61	74	66	56	53	60	63	56	61
Insufficient foreign demand	*proportion*			17	21	37	52	49	25	30	41	44	35	34
Competitive imports	*proportion*			20	6	15	17	19	8	10	11	11	10	8
Shortage of skilled labour	*proportion*			3	0	1	1	5	2	2	1	6	1	1
Shortage of raw materials	*proportion*			19	43	24	13	16	20	30	16	22	26	17
Lack of appropriate equipment	*proportion*			1	0	3	1	11	7	3	8	1	1	1
Financial problems	*proportion*			53	39	39	50	43	40	36	26	31	28	24
Uncertainty in the economic environment	*proportion*			41	24	26	18	21	29	29	19	19	17	17
Unclear economic laws	*proportion*			2	0	4	4	3	4	2	1	1	2	0
Stocks														
Finished goods: level	*balance*	38	37	31	25	23	30	16	6	-1	7	4	12	
Selling prices														
Future tendency	*balance*	97	63	49	67	52	45	50	54	60	41	47	51	46
Rate of increase: future tendency	*balance*				-40	-22	-21	-28						
Employment														
Future tendency	*balance*	-42	-41	-65	-50	-52	-58	-57	-37	-41	-40	-39	-36	

1995										1996			
Mar	Apr	May	Jun	Jul	Aug	Sep	Oct	Nov	Dec	Jan	Feb	Mar	
													ENQUÊTES DE CONJONCTURE - INDUST. MANUFACTUR.
													État des affaires
													Tendance · *solde*
													Perspectives · *solde*
													Carnets de commandes / Demande
-29	-19	-31	-23	-18	-23	-13	-21	-18	-20	-37	-38		Total : niveau · *solde*
-30	-34	-33	-31	-37	-33	-33	-34	-29	-32	-39	-31		Exportations : niveau · *solde*
													Total : perspectives · *solde*
													Exportations : perspectives · *solde*
													Production
12	-5	4	7	12	3	10	1	-2	-12	-12	-1		Tendance · *solde*
32	22	0	7	15	3	0	-6	-16	-4	14	27		Perspectives · *solde*
													Capacité actuelle · *solde*
													Taux d'utilisation des capacités · *%*
													Limites de la production
													Aucune · *proportion*
													Demande intérieure insuffisante · *proportion*
													Demande extérieure insuffisante · *proportion*
													Importations compétitives · *proportion*
													Pénurie de main-d'oeuvre qualifiée · *proportion*
													Pénurie de matières premières · *proportion*
													Manque d'équipement approprié · *proportion*
													Problèmes financiers · *proportion*
													Environnement économique incertain · *proportion*
													Lois économiques peu claires · *proportion*
													Stocks
9	14	2	4	0	0	12	13	11	12	13	19		Produits finis : niveau · *solde*
													Prix de vente
57	51	40	33	36	50	56	54	49	51	50	42	47	Perspectives · *solde*
													Taux d'augmentation : perspectives · *solde*
													Emploi
													Perspectives · *solde*

POLAND

		1993				1994				1995				1996
		Q1	Q2	Q3	Q4	Q1	Q2	Q3	Q4	Q1	Q2	Q3	Q4	Q1
BUSINESS SURVEYS - MANUFACTURING														
Business situation														
Tendency	*balance*	-25	-28	-23	-21	-21	-17	-8	-1	-5	0	5	4	
Future tendency	*balance*	9	0	8	-2	18	14	21	6	23	21	23	10	
Order books / Demand														
Total: tendency	*balance*	-11	-6	-6	-9	-8	9	16	13	-3	9	8	-1	
Export: tendency	*balance*	-7	-8	-6	-4	2	5	6	6	0	1	3	0	
Total: future tendency	*balance*	23	8	15	-2	32	27	28	10	37	30	28	13	
Export: future tendency	*balance*	15	8	12	7	25	15	22	14	23	17	20	12	
Production														
Tendency	*balance*	-8	-1	0	-4	-4	10	15	4	0	14	8	1	
Future tendency	*balance*	26	9	18	3	30	29	27	3	34	25	27	13	
Current capacity	*balance*								55	56	56	53	49	
Rate of capacity utilisation	*%*	62	62	62	64	64	66	65	70	68	69	69	71	
Stocks														
Finished goods: level	*balance*	3	5	2	-1	2	0	-9	-10	-4	-1	-4	-3	
Selling prices														
Future tendency	*balance*	32	26	26	24	32	26	33	33	32	20	21	18	
Employment														
Future tendency	*balance*	-26	-25	-24	-29	-25	-21	-17	-19	-13	-12	-12	-18	
BUSINESS SURVEYS - CONSTRUCTION														
Business activity														
Tendency	*balance*			14	3	-2	27	26	16	7	29	31	9	
Duration of work in hand	*months*			5	5	5	5	5	5	5	6	6	6	
Orders / Demand														
Total: tendency	*balance*			-1	-16	-15	19	17	-3	-8	20	27	4	
Total: future tendency	*balance*			-4	-21	35	38	16	-9	44	47	27	1	
Technical capacity														
With regard to expected demand: tendency	*balance*			10	13	16	13	9	7	6	5	-5	-4	
Limits to production activity														
None	*proportion*			3	2	1	3	3	3	2	3	5	4	
Insufficient demand	*proportion*			65	61	68	65	55	53	60	57	44	38	
Weather conditions	*proportion*			16	37	44	11	9	21	36	11	8	36	
Cost of materials	*proportion*			21	24	23	26	27	31	32	32	29	25	
Cost of financing	*proportion*			58	54	52	58	59	58	55	60	60	55	
Access to bank credit	*proportion*			25	21	19	20	19	17	16	19	16	12	
Shortage of skilled labour	*proportion*			18	14	9	12	19	17	13	16	27	24	
Shortage of raw materials	*proportion*			3	2	1	1	3	7	4	3	5	4	
Lack of appropriate equipment	*proportion*			8	8	6	7	8	9	7	8	13	11	
Competition in own sector	*proportion*			59	57	61	65	64	63	63	68	60	51	
Price expectations														
Future tendency	*balance*			33	28	44	34	32	35	47	38	31	30	
Employment														
Future tendency	*balance*			-25	-44	-10	2	-7	-30	-2	9	3	-25	
Financial situation														
Tendency	*balance*			-25	-29	-38	-22	-12	-14	-29	-16	-5	-9	
Client delays in payment: total	*balance*			26	29	22	26	21	18	18	22	23	20	

1995										1996			
Mar	Apr	May	Jun	Jul	Aug	Sep	Oct	Nov	Dec	Jan	Feb	Mar	

													ENQUÊTES DE CONJONCTURE - INDUST. MANUFACTUR.
													État des affaires
-4	-2	0	2	4	7	5	3	4	4	0	-11		Tendance
23	19	17	26	24	24	22	14	8	8	21	25		Perspectives
													Carnets de commandes / Demande
11	7	12	8	2	10	12	5	-5	-2	-10	-9		Total : tendance
11	1	1	2	-8	4	13	6	-2	-3	-8	-1		Exportations : tendance
38	34	27	30	30	32	23	15	9	16	34	43		Total : perspectives
20	23	13	14	21	22	17	13	9	15	22	22		Exportations : perspectives
													Production
21	7	16	20	-12	16	21	14	-3	-7	-6	-7		Tendance
41	33	19	24	24	30	27	21	7	10	20	40		Perspectives
57	55	58	55	52	54	53	48	48	52				Capacité actuelle
69	70	69	68	69	69	70	71	71	71	69	67		Taux d'utilisation des capacités
													Stocks
-2	-3	1	-1	-3	-4	-6	-1	-2	-5	0	1		Produits finis : niveau
													Prix de vente
28	18	19	22	16	24	22	14	13	28	24	25		Perspectives
													Emploi
-14	-14	-12	-11	-12	-11	-12	-18	-20	-17	-13	-12		Perspectives
													ENQUÊTES DE CONJONCTURE - CONSTRUCTION
													Activité de l'entreprise
22	26	30	30	36	30	27	22	9	-4	-33	-25		Tendance
6	6	6	6	6	6	6	6	6	6	6	6		Durée des travaux commandés
													Commandes / Demande
6	14	21	26	33	27	21	19	2	-10	-28	-6		Total : tendance
53	52	47	43	40	28	13	5	-3	2	43	58		Total : perspectives
													Capacité technique
8	4	6	4	-3	-5	-7	-5	-4	-2	-4	-3		Tendance compte tenu de la demande prévue
													Limites de la production
3	3	3	3	4	5	5	5	5	3	1	1		Aucune
61	60	57	54	49	43	40	37	38	39	44	44		Demande insuffisante
24	15	10	9	4	3	16	9	36	63	79	84		Intempéries
33	31	32	32	29	29	29	27	26	23	20	18		Coût des matériaux
57	60	61	60	61	61	59	59	56	50	39	38		Coût de financement
16	19	20	18	17	17	15	13	13	10	9	9		Accès aux crédits bancaires
13	15	16	17	25	28	29	30	24	18	11	9		Pénurie de main-d'oeuvre qualifiée
4	4	3	3	4	6	5	5	4	4	2	2		Pénurie de matières premières
7	8	8	9	12	13	13	13	12	9	6	5		Manque d'équipement approprié
64	67	70	68	66	58	57	55	53	45	44	43		Concurrence dans le secteur
													Pronostic sur les prix
45	39	39	37	34	33	27	26	29	34	46	47		Perspectives
													Emploi
10	9	9	10	9	3	-4	-15	-30	-30	-3	17		Perspectives
													Situation financière
-25	-20	-17	-10	-6	-5	-3	-5	-12	-11	-30	-39		Tendance
26	25	21	21	25	23	20	22	23	15	9	17		Retards de paiement de la clientèle : total

Right-hand unit column:

- Tendance — *solde*
- Perspectives — *solde*
- Total : tendance — *solde*
- Exportations : tendance — *solde*
- Total : perspectives — *solde*
- Exportations : perspectives — *solde*
- Tendance — *solde*
- Perspectives — *solde*
- Capacité actuelle — *solde*
- Taux d'utilisation des capacités — *%*
- Produits finis : niveau — *solde*
- Perspectives — *solde*
- Perspectives — *solde*
- Tendance — *solde*
- Durée des travaux commandés — *mois*
- Total : tendance — *solde*
- Total : perspectives — *solde*
- Tendance compte tenu de la demande prévue — *solde*
- Aucune — *proportion*
- Demande insuffisante — *proportion*
- Intempéries — *proportion*
- Coût des matériaux — *proportion*
- Coût de financement — *proportion*
- Accès aux crédits bancaires — *proportion*
- Pénurie de main-d'oeuvre qualifiée — *proportion*
- Pénurie de matières premières — *proportion*
- Manque d'équipement approprié — *proportion*
- Concurrence dans le secteur — *proportion*
- Perspectives — *solde*
- Perspectives — *solde*
- Tendance — *solde*
- Retards de paiement de la clientèle : total — *solde*

POLAND *(continued)*

		1993				1994				1995				1996
		Q1	Q2	Q3	Q4	Q1	Q2	Q3	Q4	Q1	Q2	Q3	Q4	Q1
BUSINESS SURVEYS - RETAIL TRADE														
Business situation														
Tendency	*balance*				-10	-20	11	47	42	-11	22	32	27	
Future tendency	*balance*					25	27	22	-16	37	41	26	-10	
Competition in own sector: tendency	*balance*				56	58	60	49	50	43	49	49	54	
Limits to improvement in business situation														
None	*proportion*				3	1	2	1	2	2	2	3	2	
Insufficient demand	*proportion*				37	60	61	56	54	56	57	49	59	
Supply	*proportion*				9	7	9	12	12	10	11	13	9	
Cost of labour	*proportion*				25	30	28	32	36	39	37	29	35	
Cost of financing	*proportion*				52	54	52	48	43	44	39	36	38	
Access to bank credit	*proportion*				17	18	15	15	15	17	14	18	15	
Sales surface	*proportion*				14	12	16	11	11	9	9	10	11	
Storage capacity	*proportion*				17	31	19	14	8	11	9	8	11	
Competition in own sector	*proportion*				49	54	62	54	54	56	58	49	59	
Intentions of placing orders														
Total: future tendency	*balance*				9	25	23	20	-10	27	30	26	-10	
Domestic: future tendency	*balance*				14	25	29	25	-5	22	28	20	-8	
Foreign: future tendency	*balance*				-23	-7	-11	-6	-15	3	3	16	-13	
Stocks														
Level	*balance*				3	12	11	24	18	19	18	16	13	
Selling prices														
Tendency	*balance*				73	56	53	75	69	64	56	58	58	
Rate of increase: tendency	*balance*				20	3	4	26	21	14	7	-1	1	
Future tendency	*balance*				80	56	59	73	63	62	62	54	52	
Rate of increase: future tendency	*balance*				20	-1	8	14	-3	-5	-5	5	3	
Employment														
Future tendency	*balance*				-25	-27	-29	-12	-7	-4	-12	-8	-11	
Financial situation														
Tendency	*balance*				-9	-23	4	38	36	-18	11	27	16	

1995										1996			
Mar	Apr	May	Jun	Jul	Aug	Sep	Oct	Nov	Dec	Jan	Feb	Mar	

ENQUÊTES DE CONJONCTURE - COMMERCE DE DÉTAIL
État des affaires

Tendance	*solde*
Perspectives	*solde*
Concurrence dans le secteur : tendance	*solde*

Limites de l'amélioration des affaires

Aucune	*proportion*
Demande insuffisante	*proportion*
Approvisionnement	*proportion*
Coût de la main d'oeuvre	*proportion*
Coût de financement	*proportion*
Accès aux crédits bancaires	*proportion*
Surface de vente	*proportion*
Capacités de stockage	*proportion*
Concurrence dans le secteur	*proportion*

Commandes : intentions

Total : perspectives	*solde*
Fournisseurs nationaux : perspectives	*solde*
Fournisseurs étrangers : perspectives	*solde*

Stocks

Niveau	*solde*

Prix de vente

Tendance	*solde*
Taux d'augmentation : tendance	*solde*
Perspectives	*solde*
Taux d'augmentation : perspectives	*solde*

Emploi

Perspectives	*solde*

Situation financière

Tendance	*solde*

ROMANIA

		1993				1994				1995				1996
		Q1	Q2	Q3	Q4	Q1	Q2	Q3	Q4	Q1	Q2	Q3	Q4	Q1
BUSINESS SURVEYS - MANUFACTURING														
Business situation														
Tendency	*balance*		-27	18	23	29	12	10	18	14	22	22	25	25
Future tendency	*balance*		-15	6	0	-4	10	7	13	12	27	15	24	23
Order books / Demand														
Total: level	*balance*	-6	-34	-30	-25	-32	-45	-43	-28	-27	-23	-23	-12	-10
Total: future tendency	*balance*		33	11	10	17	18	12	13	23	37	19	28	38
Export: future tendency	*balance*	39	33	20	16	19	27	22	22	36	53	27	28	45
Production														
Tendency	*balance*	4	19	22	-1	13	2	-2	3	19	22	20	21	23
Future tendency	*balance*	23	31	10	5	6	18	10	16	22	38	27	31	32
Current capacity	*balance*	38	42	27	31	29	31	39	32	35	35	29	28	27
Limits to production														
None	*proportion*		1	1	2	2	1	1	1	1	1	1	2	3
Insufficient domestic demand	*proportion*		17	19	19	18	19	20	20	19	20	19	19	20
Insufficient foreign demand	*proportion*		12	12	11	10	10	10	9	8	8	7	8	10
Shortage of skilled labour	*proportion*		1	1	1	1	0	0	0	1	1	10	10	3
Shortage of raw materials	*proportion*	9	17	15	16	14	14	12	13	14	15	15	13	15
Lack of appropriate equipment	*proportion*		5	4	4	4	4	4	4	5	4	4	6	
Shortage of energy	*proportion*	14	4	1	1	3	2	1	1	1	2	1		3
Financial problems	*proportion*	0	33	40	42	42	44	45	44	45	42	43	42	45
Stocks														
Finished goods: level	*balance*	21	18	8	2	16	21	26	13	9	11	4	1	0
Selling prices														
Future tendency	*balance*		90	88	93	91	94	78	78	74	81	75	70	85
Employment														
Future tendency	*balance*	-49	-33	-36	-39	-43	-49	-48	-46	-42	-36	-39	-32	-32
Fixed investment														
Intentions	*proportion*				4	8		12			32		31	
Type of fixed investment														
Replacement of old equipment	*proportion*				18	27		26			26		27	
Extending prod. capacity w/unchanged product range	*proportion*				4	5		5			5		5	
Extending prod. capacity w/extended product range	*proportion*				7	10		9			7		9	
Automation of production process	*proportion*				10	15		14			15		15	
New production techniques	*proportion*				10	14		16			15		15	
Energy saving	*proportion*				8	10		10			11		11	
Pollution control	*proportion*				6	9		10			11		9	
Safety measures	*proportion*				5	7		7			7		7	
Other	*proportion*				32	3		3			4		1	
Limits to fixed investment														
Insufficient demand	*proportion*				4	6		6			6		6	
High cost of capital	*proportion*				29	46		43			45		46	
Insufficient profits	*proportion*				8	11		16			14		16	
Insufficient credit guarantees	*proportion*				20	33		31			32		32	
Technical factors	*proportion*				1	0		1			1		1	
Other	*proportion*				38	4		3			4		2	

1995										1996		
Mar	Apr	May	Jun	Jul	Aug	Sep	Oct	Nov	Dec	Jan	Feb	Mar

ENQUÊTES DE CONJONCTURE - INDUST. MANUFACTUR.

État des affaires

Tendance — *solde*

Perspectives — *solde*

Carnets de commandes / Demande

Total : niveau — *solde*

Total : perspectives — *solde*

Exportations : perspectives — *solde*

Production

Tendance — *solde*

Perspectives — *solde*

Capacité actuelle — *solde*

Limites de la production

Aucune — *proportion*

Demande intérieure insuffisante — *proportion*

Demande extérieure insuffisante — *proportion*

Pénurie de main-d'oeuvre qualifiée — *proportion*

Pénurie de matières premières — *proportion*

Manque d'équipement approprié — *proportion*

Pénurie d'énergie — *proportion*

Problèmes financiers — *proportion*

Stocks

Produits finis : niveau — *solde*

Prix de vente

Perspectives — *solde*

Emploi

Perspectives — *solde*

Investissements fixes

Intentions — *proportion*

Type d'investissement fixe

Remplacement d'équipements anciens — *proportion*

Invest. de capacité: même gamme de produits — *proportion*

Invest. de capacité: gamme de produits élargie — *proportion*

Automatisation du procédé de production — *proportion*

Nouvelles techniques de production — *proportion*

Économies d'énergie — *proportion*

Lutte contre la pollution — *proportion*

Mesures de securité — *proportion*

Autres — *proportion*

Limites de l'investissement

Demande insuffisante — *proportion*

Coût élevé du capital — *proportion*

Profits insuffisants — *proportion*

Garanties insuffisantes pour crédits — *proportion*

Facteurs techniques — *proportion*

Autres — *proportion*

ROMANIA (continued)

		1993				1994				1995				1996
		Q1	Q2	Q3	Q4	Q1	Q2	Q3	Q4	Q1	Q2	Q3	Q4	Q1
BUSINESS SURVEYS - CONSTRUCTION														
Business activity														
Future tendency	*balance*				-25	-16	60	44	-6	-1	77	61	12	-19
Duration of work in hand	*months*				5	5	8	6	6	7	7	7	7	7
Orders / Demand														
Future tendency	*balance*				-22	-9	55	31	-1	8	69	56	14	-17
Limits to production activity														
Insufficient demand	*proportion*				16	18	51	0	50	56	54	42	46	41
Shortage of skilled labour	*proportion*				9	7	8	0	10	6	12	11	10	7
Shortage of raw materials	*proportion*				9	5	11	55	8	5	8	6	10	6
Cost of financing	*proportion*				12	13	34	12	33	40	42	29	32	30
Access to bank credit	*proportion*				21	23	78	44	70	62	59	56	50	56
Price expectations														
Future tendency	*balance*				95	96	98	84	83	81	83	91	86	90
Employment														
Future tendency	*balance*				-50	-38	15	-4	-45	-32	37	30	-21	-34
Financial situation														
Tendency	*balance*				17	5	-15	11	26	16	-3	14	17	-1
Client delays in payment: private	*balance*				17	16	4	11	21	-1	1	1	12	33
Client delays in payment: public	*balance*				55	50	52	52	53	54	41	28	54	57
BUSINESS SURVEYS - RETAIL TRADE														
Business situation														
Tendency	*balance*					53	41	26	29	34	28	42	49	62
Future tendency	*balance*					0	0	0	0	0	0	44	58	9
Limits to improvement in business situation														
None	*proportion*					10	2	4	2	7	6	7	5	5
Insufficient demand	*proportion*					21	31	37	30	34	34	32	31	18
Access to bank credit	*proportion*					20	18	16	13	16	14	11	16	6
Competition in own sector	*proportion*					11	17	16	22	16	20	21	23	24
Intentions of placing orders														
Future tendency	*balance*					27	31	18	41	21	58	57	65	14
Stocks														
Level	*balance*					-12	-4	-5	-16	-11	2	3	-2	2
Employment														
Future tendency	*balance*					-15	-23	-37	-30	5	-18	-22	-14	-21

1995										1996		
Mar	Apr	May	Jun	Jul	Aug	Sep	Oct	Nov	Dec	Jan	Feb	Mar

ENQUÊTES DE CONJONCTURE - CONSTRUCTION

Activité de l'entreprise

Perspectives — *solde*

Durée des travaux commandés — *mois*

Commandes / Demande

Perspectives — *solde*

Limites de la production

Demande insuffisante — *proportion*

Pénurie de main-d'oeuvre qualifiée — *proportion*

Pénurie de matières premières — *proportion*

Coût de financement — *proportion*

Accès aux crédits bancaires — *proportion*

Pronostic sur les prix

Perspectives — *solde*

Emploi

Perspectives — *solde*

Situation financière

Tendance — *solde*

Retards de paiement de la clientèle : privé — *solde*

Retards de paiement de la clientèle : public — *solde*

ENQUÊTES DE CONJONCTURE - COMMERCE DE DÉTAIL

État des affaires

Tendance — *solde*

Perspectives — *solde*

Limites de l'amélioration des affaires

Aucune — *proportion*

Demande insuffisante — *proportion*

Accès aux crédits bancaires — *proportion*

Concurrence dans le secteur — *proportion*

Commandes : intentions

Perspectives — *solde*

Stocks

Niveau — *solde*

Emploi

Perspectives — *solde*

SLOVAK REPUBLIC

		1993				1994				1995				1996
		Q1	Q2	Q3	Q4	Q1	Q2	Q3	Q4	Q1	Q2	Q3	Q4	Q1
BUSINESS SURVEYS - MANUFACTURING[1]														
Business situation														
Tendency	balance	-39	-20	-9	0	-2	5	-2	-1	-1	15	-1	-6	6
Future tendency	balance	-25	-20	11	9	6	19	14	11	35	23	22	21	32
Order books / Demand														
Domestic: tendency	balance	-24	-32	0	28	-2	13	-6	20⁺	-9	11	-5	-14	-18
Export: tendency	balance	1	0	4	46	28	4	-3	17	5	6	-5	-12	-14
Domestic: future tendency	balance		-32	29	21	15	11	21	24	44	8	49	17	68
Export: future tendency	balance	22	15	18	28	48	20	56	38	39	8	48	-1	79
Production														
Tendency	balance	-20	-1	4	28	14	1	-2	39	12	7	-13	-6	26
Future tendency	balance	9	-6	34	28	34	15	35	44	67	20	43	26	57
Current capacity	balance			34	23	23	24	14	14	12	5	10	1	9
Rate of capacity utilisation	%	68	71	73	76	77	78	76	77	74	75	74	76	78
Limits to production														
Insufficient domestic demand	proportion	22	19	22	21	18	19	18	20	15	15	13	17	17
Insufficient foreign demand	proportion	18	13	14	13	12	15	16	14	13	10	9	11	14
Competitive imports	proportion	10	8	10	6	8	6	7	6	9	8	9	9	9
Shortage of raw materials	proportion									9	7	6	5	6
Financial problems	proportion	13	19	21	22	27	25	22	23	21	19	19	19	17
Uncertainty in the economic environment	proportion	24	21	16	16	14	15	15	14	16	19	20	19	16
Stocks														
Finished goods: level	balance	-7	5	39	27	37	34	37	33	20	22	25	25	34
Selling prices														
Future tendency	balance	3	8	68	62	60	43	48	61	48	56	40	33	55
Rate of increase: future tendency	balance												-32	-28
Employment														
Future tendency	balance	-50	-59	-45	-47	-38	-37	-29	-23	-19	-11	-20	-17	-7
Fixed investment														
Intentions	proportion				96			100	96				98	
Future tendency	balance				-22			4	-14				24	
Type of fixed investment														
Replacement of old equipment	proportion				30				22				30	
Extending prod. capacity w/unchanged product range	proportion				20				15				12	
Extending prod. capacity w/extended product range	proportion				5				12				12	
Automation of production process	proportion				11				12				13	
New production techniques	proportion				12				14				12	
Energy saving	proportion				14				14				17	
Pollution control	proportion				2				8				3	
Safety measures	proportion				6				3				1	
Other	proportion				0				0				0	
Limits to fixed investment														
Insufficient demand	proportion				43				21				39	
High cost of capital	proportion				32				25				11	
Fear of indebtedness	proportion				0				3				1	
Insufficient credit guarantees	proportion				9				32				29	
Insufficient profits	proportion				11				16				14	
Technical factors	proportion				5				3				6	
Other	proportion				0				0				0	

(1) Prior to January 1995, survey covered managers in total industry; since January 1995, only managers in the manufacturing sector are surveyed.

1995										1996					
Mar	Apr	May	Jun	Jul	Aug	Sep	Oct	Nov	Dec	Jan	Feb	Mar		
													ENQUÊTES DE CONJONCTURE - INDUST. MANUFACTUR.[1]	
													État des affaires	
7	19	14	13	-2	-2	2	-3	-7	-8	6	8	3	Tendance	*solde*
29	22	25	21	25	22	20	22	17	24	21	42	34	Perspectives	*solde*
													Carnets de commandes / Demande	
-11	17	11	4	-8	-8	2	-4	-12	-26	-21	-15	-19	Intérieures : tendance	*solde*
58	5	10	2	-12	-4	1	-6	-13	-16	-17	-11	-14	Exportations : tendance	*solde*
27	23	3	-3	64	60	22	31	0	19	65	83	56	Intérieures : perspectives	*solde*
31	19	2	3	66	58	20	-5	-9	11	85	82	69	Exportations : perspectives	*solde*
													Production	
69	-35	66	-9	-63	14	11	26	3	-46	28	13	38	Tendance	*solde*
61	77	-18	2	39	22	68	34	13	32	50	56	64	Perspectives	*solde*
9	8	0	6	12	9	9	3	4	-5	6	9	12	Capacité actuelle	*solde*
75	74	75	75	72	75	76	76	76	76	78	78	79	Taux d'utilisation des capacités	*%*
													Limites de la production	
12	13	14	18	14	15	11	14	17	19	24	13	15	Demande intérieure insuffisante	*proportion*
9	9	9	11	9	9	8	11	13	9	17	12	12	Demande extérieure insuffisante	*proportion*
8	9	7	8	9	8	9	9	10	8	7	10	10	Importations compétitives	*proportion*
10	8	7	7	6	5	6	7	6	1	5	5	9	Pénurie de matières premières	*proportion*
21	21	20	17	18	21	18	20	20	18	18	15	18	Problèmes financiers	*proportion*
19	21	18	19	17	25	19	20	17	21	16	16	17	Environnement économique incertain	*proportion*
													Stocks	
24	8	24	33	31	18	27	29	23	22	39	46	17	Produits finis : niveau	*solde*
													Prix de vente	
55	76	46	47	45	47	28	37	20	41	52	54	60	Perspectives	*solde*
							-31	-31	-33	-15	-27	-41	Taux d'augmentation : perspectives	*solde*
													Emploi	
-18	-21	-12	-1	-20	-20	-21	-21	-23	-7	-8	-4	-8	Perspectives	*solde*
													Investissements fixes	
													Intentions	*proportion*
													Perspectives	*solde*
													Type d'investissement fixe	
													Remplacement d'équipements anciens	*proportion*
													Invest. de capacité: même gamme de produits	*proportion*
													Invest. de capacité: gamme de produits élargie	*proportion*
													Automatisation du procédé de production	*proportion*
													Nouvelles techniques de production	*proportion*
													Économies d'énergie	*proportion*
													Lutte contre la pollution	*proportion*
													Mesures de securité	*proportion*
													Autres	*proportion*
													Limites de l'investissement	
													Demande insuffisante	*proportion*
													Coût élevé du capital	*proportion*
													Crainte d'endettement	*proportion*
													Garanties insuffisantes pour crédits	*proportion*
													Profits insuffisants	*proportion*
													Facteurs techniques	*proportion*
													Autres	*proportion*

1) Avant janvier 1995, l'enquête était effectuée auprès des chefs d'entreprise dans l'ensemble de l'industrie; depuis janvier 1995, seuls les chefs d'entreprise du secteur manufacturier sont enquêtés.

SLOVAK REPUBLIC *(continued)*

		1993				1994				1995				1996
		Q1	Q2	Q3	Q4	Q1	Q2	Q3	Q4	Q1	Q2	Q3	Q4	Q1
BUSINESS SURVEYS - CONSTRUCTION														
Business activity														
Tendency	*balance*	-43	-25	-20	-3	-12	-2	-6	-10	6	35	20	8	4
Duration of work in hand	*months*			7	11	2	10	12	10	11	10	9	9	9
Orders / Demand														
Total: level	*balance*			-75	-75	-84	-74	-87	-66	-49	-44	-53	-36	-33
Domestic: level	*balance*	-70		-77	-76	-85	-79	-88	-69	-56	-56	-55	-41	-36
Foreign: level	*balance*	-51		-59	-71	-77	-77	-77	-67	-37	-47	-35	-50	-66
Total: future tendency	*balance*	-2	-26	10	-50	-15	26	-1	-23	13	19	1	-23	1
Technical capacity														
With regard to expected demand: tendency	*balance*			37	20	16	25	15	19	35	30	15	7	15
Limits to production activity														
None	*proportion*	0	0	0	0	0	0	0	0	2	3	5	4	4
Insufficient demand	*proportion*	41	48	34	36	38	36	36	33	20	20	23	23	22
Weather conditions	*proportion*			0	5	3	0	1	5	5	3	2	12	20
Shortage of skilled labour	*proportion*	1	0	1	1	1	1	1	1	1	1	2	2	2
Shortage of raw materials	*proportion*	1	1	1	0	0	0	0	0	0	0	0	0	0
Cost of materials	*proportion*	6	2	4	4	3	3	2	3	7	13	10	8	7
Lack of appropriate equipment	*proportion*	0	0	1	1	1	1	1	2	1	3	4	4	8
Cost of financing	*proportion*			8	8	7	9	14	10	18	12	11	9	8
Access to bank credit	*proportion*			13	12	14	17	16	16	17	15	15	11	8
Competition in own sector	*proportion*	6	8	12	13	14	13	10	14	21	24	22	20	16
Price expectations														
Future tendency	*balance*	55	28	33	36	35	38	36	32	40	31	13	14	32
Employment														
Future tendency	*balance*	-52	-57	-60	-69	-34	4	-29	-49	7	15	-14	-49	1
Financial situation														
Tendency	*balance*	-44	-25	-20	3	-12	-2	-6	-10	-18	2	15	20	25
Client delays in payment: total	*balance*	62	70	67	66	65	52	74	63	46	26	24	20	14
Client delays in payment: private	*balance*			36	36	50	44	50	48	37	20	11	16	14
Client delays in payment: public	*balance*			67	66	61	52	73	62	44	28	22	29	34
BUSINESS SURVEYS - RETAIL TRADE														
Business situation														
Tendency	*balance*			-36	-25	-21	-30	-22	-22	-9	-28	-17	-14	1
Future tendency	*balance*			10	-17	15	18	23	-12	29	25	25	23	28
Competition in own sector: tendency	*balance*			54	42	40	43	46	58	36	38	46	61	50
Limits to improvement in business situation														
None	*proportion*			0	0	0	0	0	0	0	0	0	0	2
Insufficient demand	*proportion*			31	30	32	31	30	32	32	34	29	30	25
Supply	*proportion*			1	1	1	1	3	2	1	0	1	1	2
Cost of labour	*proportion*			1	0	0	0	0	1	0	0	0	1	0
Cost of financing	*proportion*			23	24	20	20	21	22	19	22	23	21	22
Access to bank credit	*proportion*			11	13	11	11	11	11	10	11	8	10	7
Sales surface	*proportion*			2	2	3	4	5	4	6	3	2	3	10
Storage capacity	*proportion*			1	0	0	0	0	1	1	0	1	1	0
Competition in own sector	*proportion*			27	26	30	30	27	27	30	28	32	31	29
Other	*proportion*			2	4	4	2	2	1	1	2	4	1	2
Intentions of placing orders														
Total: future tendency	*balance*												2	26
Domestic: future tendency	*balance*			9	-13	28	28	27	7	8	19	12	-3	21
Foreign: future tendency	*balance*			-15	-25	-19	-5	4	-3	0	-2	-3	-7	13
Stocks														
Level	*balance*			21	20	15	12	8	19	22	4	8	10	1
Selling prices														
Tendency	*balance*			29	40	31	14	43	16	33	15	36	34	22
Rate of increase: tendency	*balance*			-28	-1	-34	-24	-38	-14	-32	-30	-39	-21	-5
Future tendency	*balance*			54	43	50	54	57	41	55	50	56	54	34
Rate of increase: future tendency	*balance*			-51	-38	-50	-49	-51	-30	-53	-36	-46	-36	-23
Employment														
Future tendency	*balance*			-63	-69	-60	-53	-59	-59	-42	-16	-48	-20	-29
Financial situation														
Tendency	*balance*			5	8	-2	15	0	0	1	16	8	6	21

1995										1996				
Mar	Apr	May	Jun	Jul	Aug	Sep	Oct	Nov	Dec	Jan	Feb	Mar		
													ENQUÊTES DE CONJONCTURE - CONSTRUCTION	
													Activité de l'entreprise	
33	26	33	45	15	30	15	10	17	-3	-1	-6	20	Tendance	*solde*
11	9	11	9	9	10	9	9	9	9	9	9	9	Durée des travaux commandés	*mois*
													Commandes / Demande	
-37	-58	-52	-21	-53	-62	-45	-45	-42	-20	-20	-51	-28	Total : niveau	*solde*
-52	-61	-55	-51	-54	-63	-48	-49	-33	-40	-39	-47	-23	Intérieures : niveau	*solde*
-31	-52	-56	-34	-41	-25	-39	-36	-66	-48	-49	-69	-80	Extérieures : niveau	*solde*
27	24	4	28	13	-9	0	-36	-23	-11	-32	9	26	Total : perspectives	*solde*
													Capacité technique	
39	38	33	20	9	27	10	8	-2	16	16	18	11	Tendance compte tenu de la demande prévue	*solde*
													Limites de la production	
0	0	5	4	3	7	4	4	5	4	5	3	3	Aucune	*proportion*
16	19	23	17	22	21	25	22	24	23	23	23	21	Demande insuffisante	*proportion*
4	3	2	3	2	2	2	6	10	20	20	20	19	Intempéries	*proportion*
0	1	1	2	1	2	2	2	1	2	2	2	2	Pénurie de main-d'oeuvre qualifiée	*proportion*
0	0	0	0	1	0	0	0	0	0	0	0	0	Pénurie de matières premières	*proportion*
12	13	14	12	11	11	9	10	10	5	5	7	8	Coût des matériaux	*proportion*
1	1	4	4	5	2	5	5	1	7	7	8	9	Manque d'équipement approprié	*proportion*
18	16	8	12	13	10	11	10	9	8	7	9	8	Coût de financement	*proportion*
17	16	15	15	14	16	14	12	14	8	8	8	7	Accès aux crédits bancaires	*proportion*
21	25	23	23	22	25	20	24	20	16	16	17	16	Concurrence dans le secteur	*proportion*
													Pronostic sur les prix	
11	61	19	14	9	15	14	9	6	28	28	35	32	Perspectives	*solde*
													Emploi	
3	6	23	17	-2	-5	-36	-43	-55	-49	-47	15	36	Perspectives	*solde*
													Situation financière	
-32	-32	21	18	7	21	18	8	8	43	43	15	18	Tendance	*solde*
65	50	14	15	7	32	32	22	35	3	3	25	14	Retards de paiement de la clientèle : total	*solde*
53	44	12	3	16	12	6	8	25	14	14	15	12	Retards de paiement de la clientèle : privé	*solde*
63	49	32	4	4	31	31	24	38	24	23	44	35	Retards de paiement de la clientèle : public	*solde*
													ENQUÊTES DE CONJONCTURE - COMMERCE DE DÉTAIL	
													État des affaires	
0	-18	-25	-42	-24	-21	-7	-36	-20	14	8	-2	-4	Tendance	*solde*
30	37	25	12	24	33	17	49	31	-10	-7	51	40	Perspectives	*solde*
52	47	35	31	42	50	46	60	56	66	67	51	31	Concurrence dans le secteur : tendance	*solde*
													Limites de l'amélioration des affaires	
0	0	0	0	0	0	1	1	0	0	0	3	3	Aucune	*proportion*
33	34	34	34	27	28	32	28	30	33	32	20	24	Demande insuffisante	*proportion*
0	0	0	1	0	1	1	1	1	1	1	4	1	Approvisionnement	*proportion*
0	0	0	1	0	0	0	0	3	0	0	0	0	Coût de la main d'oeuvre	*proportion*
20	20	17	30	27	23	18	22	20	22	21	26	20	Coût de financement	*proportion*
13	11	15	6	7	5	13	12	11	6	7	7	7	Accès aux crédits bancaires	*proportion*
1	1	7	0	4	1	1	1	0	8	7	13	10	Surface de vente	*proportion*
0	0	0	1	0	3	0	3	0	0	0	1	0	Capacités de stockage	*proportion*
32	32	25	26	33	31	33	30	33	30	32	24	32	Concurrence dans le secteur	*proportion*
1	2	2	1	2	8	1	2	2	0	0	2	3	Autres	*proportion*
													Commandes : intentions	
							9	-15	12	4	37	36	Total : perspectives	*solde*
21	17	13	27	25	0	12	16	-16	-9	-13	35	41	Fournisseurs nationaux : perspectives	*solde*
2	-2	-4	-1	10	-6	-12	-8	-24	11	5	19	16	Fournisseurs étrangers : perspectives	*solde*
													Stocks	
22	1	5	5	0	16	8	10	13	8	9	-3	-2	Niveau	*solde*
													Prix de vente	
21	-13	13	45	47	31	30	38	29	34	32	22	13	Tendance	*solde*
-20	-24	-16	-50	-48	-33	-35	-22	-10	-32	-27	16	-4	Taux d'augmentation : tendance	*solde*
46	51	51	47	47	65	56	75	60	27	23	32	46	Perspectives	*solde*
-40	-49	-38	-22	-41	-46	-52	-38	-40	-29	-28	-20	-21	Taux d'augmentation : perspectives	*solde*
													Emploi	
-43	-20	-23	-6	-45	-46	-54	-26	-30	-5	-10	-31	-47	Perspectives	*solde*
													Situation financière	
7	-16	34	30	30	3	-8	-12	-7	37	29	26	7	Tendance	*solde*

BELARUS

		1993				1994				1995				1996
		Q1	Q2	Q3	Q4	Q1	Q2	Q3	Q4	Q1	Q2	Q3	Q4	Q1
BUSINESS SURVEYS - MANUFACTURING														
Order books / Demand														
Total: level	*balance*						-54	-43	-32	-40	-75	-72	-67	-76
Export: level	*balance*						-29	-24	-25	-29	-45	-37	-36	-43
Export: future tendency	*balance*						3	8	8	8	-1	2	-3	3
Production														
Tendency	*balance*						-70	-47	-15	-14	-42	-44	-11	-35
Future tendency	*balance*						-33	-17	-22	-4	-16	-23	-7	-3
Current capacity	*balance*						16	29	19	26	36	44	37	49
Rate of capacity utilisation	*%*						53	51	54	55	51	46	50	47
Limits to production														
None	*proportion*						1	2	3	4	0	0	0	0
Insufficient domestic demand	*proportion*						38	30	23	21	68	68	24	76
Labour shortage	*proportion*						0	0	1	1	2	2	1	3
Lack of appropriate equipment	*proportion*						8	3	7	5	6	3	1	3
Financial problems	*proportion*						75	73	75	77	77	69	70	71
Other	*proportion*						50	39	41	47	20	18	6	20
Stocks														
Finished goods: level	*balance*						27	1	-10	-11	33	34	20	23
Selling prices														
Future tendency	*balance*						84	83	94	92	55	15	42	50
Employment														
Future tendency	*balance*						-44	-23	-25	-23	-36	-43	-28	-29

1995										1996			
Mar	Apr	May	Jun	Jul	Aug	Sep	Oct	Nov	Dec	Jan	Feb	Mar	

ENQUÊTES DE CONJONCTURE - INDUST. MANUFACTUR.	
Carnets de commandes / Demande	
Total : niveau	*solde*
Exportations : niveau	*solde*
Exportations : perspectives	*solde*
Production	
Tendance	*solde*
Perspectives	*solde*
Capacité actuelle	*solde*
Taux d'utilisation des capacités	*%*
Limites de la production	
Aucune	*proportion*
Demande intérieure insuffisante	*proportion*
Pénurie de main d'oeuvre	*proportion*
Manque d'équipement approprié	*proportion*
Problèmes financiers	*proportion*
Autres	*proportion*
Stocks	
Produits finis : niveau	*solde*
Prix de vente	
Perspectives	*solde*
Emploi	
Perspectives	*solde*

RUSSIAN FEDERATION

		1993				1994				1995				1996
		Q1	Q2	Q3	Q4	Q1	Q2	Q3	Q4	Q1	Q2	Q3	Q4	Q1
BUSINESS SURVEYS - MANUFACTURING														
Order books / Demand														
Total: level	balance	-31	-39	-49	-76	-86	-83	-77	-73	-73	-83	-79	-89	-91
Export: level	balance	-32	-28	-31	-35	-37	-38	-36	-34	-32	-36	-34	-37	-41
Export: future tendency	balance		5	4	4	-3	-9	-4	3	1	3	-1	0	-1
Production														
Tendency	balance		-17	-31	-35	-48	-53	-47	-21	-20	-26	-16	-23	-37
Future tendency	balance	8	-10	-9	-26	-34	-41	-21	-7	-7	-6	5	-7	4
Current capacity	balance		13	29	31	32	50	40	39	36	36	33	40	42
Rate of capacity utilisation	%		66	60	59	56	54	48	49	48	47	47	46	44
Limits to production														
None	proportion		7	3	3	1	3	1	3	1	0	0	1	1
Insufficient demand	proportion		32	29	66	78	80	82	69	58	55	59	54	62
Insufficient foreign demand	proportion										11	12	8	13
Competitive imports	proportion										11	12	7	10
Shortage of labour	proportion		16	27	23	19	17	20	16	12	15	19	10	8
Lack of appropriate equipment	proportion		5	5	5	7	6	3	4	10	6	6	5	4
Shortage of raw materials	proportion										33	31	31	19
Shortage of energy	proportion										3	5	7	4
Stocks														
Finished goods: level	balance	23	20	23	39	46	37	14	1	1	11	6	19	24
Selling prices														
Future tendency	balance	88	90	90	86	89	60	66	79	83	73	74	55	46
Employment														
Future tendency	balance		-20	-33	-28	-51	-59	-45	-32	-23	-33	-20	-25	-28
BUSINESS SURVEYS - CONSTRUCTION														
Business activity														
Duration of work in hand	months				5	6	5	5	4	4	5	4	3	3
Orders / Demand														
Total: future tendency	balance					-6	7	-4	-53	-27	12	-8	-64	-39
Limits to production activity														
None	proportion				4	5	2	4	3	3	1	1	0	0
Insufficient demand	proportion				12	18	19	18	25	40	32	26	33	40
Weather conditions	proportion				5	3	1	2	7	3	0	1	2	2
Cost of materials	proportion										13	17	16	12
Financial problems	proportion				64	29	32	37	44	69	60	62	66	64
Shortage of skilled labour	proportion				16	13	8	10	6	5	6	6	4	1
Lack of appropriate equipment	proportion				3	1	2	3	1	2	2	3	2	3
Shortage of raw materials	proportion				7	8	7	5	3	5	6	4	4	3
Competition in own sector	proportion					3	3	3	6	3	5	1	1	1
Price expectations														
Future tendency	balance				44	47	44	41	14	57	57	55	45	44
Employment														
Future tendency	balance				-23	-18	-6	-14	-29	-25	-8	-17	-46	-43

1995										1996					
Mar	Apr	May	Jun	Jul	Aug	Sep	Oct	Nov	Dec	Jan	Feb	Mar			

ENQUÊTES DE CONJONCTURE - INDUST. MANUFACTUR.
Carnets de commandes / Demande

Mar	Apr	May	Jun	Jul	Aug	Sep	Oct	Nov	Dec	Jan	Feb	Mar	Description		
-75	-78	-86	-84	-80	-78	-80	-87	-91	-89	-90	-90	-94	Total : niveau	*solde*	
-33	-32	-41	-36	-34	-34	-34	-32	-39	-40	-39	-41	-44	Exportations : niveau	*solde*	
													Exportations : perspectives	*solde*	

Production

-20	-30	-24	-24	-24	-15	-9	-16	-28	-26	-39	-43	-29	Tendance	*solde*
-7	-5	-3	-9	2	10	3	-4	-13	-5	-1	6	6	Perspectives	*solde*
													Capacité actuelle	*solde*
													Taux d'utilisation des capacités	*%*

Limites de la production

													Aucune	*proportion*
													Demande insuffisante	*proportion*
													Demande extérieure insuffisante	*proportion*
													Importations compétitives	*proportion*
													Pénurie de main-d'oeuvre	*proportion*
													Manque d'équipement approprié	*proportion*
													Pénurie de matières premières	*proportion*
													Pénurie d'énergie	*proportion*

Stocks

1	7	13	12	5	3	10	13	19	26	28	22	22	Produits finis : niveau	*solde*

Prix de vente

79	80	66	73	75	78	70	67	51	47	51	44	44	Perspectives	*solde*

Emploi

Perspectives — *solde*

ENQUÊTES DE CONJONCTURE - CONSTRUCTION
Activité de l'entreprise
Durée des travaux commandés — *mois*
Commandes / Demande
Total : perspectives — *solde*
Limites de la production
Aucune — *proportion*
Demande insuffisante — *proportion*
Intempéries — *proportion*
Coût des matériaux — *proportion*
Problèmes financiers — *proportion*
Pénurie de main-d'oeuvre qualifiée — *proportion*
Manque d'équipement approprié — *proportion*
Pénurie de matières premières — *proportion*
Concurrence dans le secteur — *proportion*
Pronostic sur les prix
Perspectives — *solde*
Emploi
Perspectives — *solde*

Manufacturing industry survey

Harmonised questions

Business situation: tendency
Assessment of present business situation:
good (+), sufficient (=), bad (-)

Business situation: future tendency
Expected business situation six months from now:
better (+), same (=), worse (-)

Order books / Demand Total: level
Assessment of total demand/order books (present level):
above normal (+), normal (=), below normal (-)

Order books / Demand Export: level
Assessment of demand from abroad/export order books (present level):
above normal (+), normal (=), below normal (-)

Order books / Demand Total: future tendency
Expected total demand in the next 3-4 months:
up (+), unchanged (=), down (-)

Order books / Demand Export: future tendency
Export expectations for the next 3-4 months:
up (+), unchanged (=), down (-)

Production: tendency
Assessment of production activities in the last month (quarter):
up (+), unchanged (=), down (-)

Production: future tendency
Production activities for the next 3-4 months:
up (+), unchanged (=), down (-)

Production: current capacity
Assessment of current production capacity (with regard to expected demand in the next 12 months):
more than sufficient (+), sufficient (=), not sufficient (-)

Production: rate of capacity utilisation
Current level of capacity utilisation (in per cent of normal capacity utilisation).

Limits to production
Limits to production (present situation):
– none
– insufficient domestic demand
– insufficient foreign demand
– competitive imports
– shortage of labour
– shortage of skilled labour
– lack of appropriate equipment
– shortage of semi-finished goods
– shortage of raw materials
– shortage of energy
– financial problems (e.g. insolvency, credits)
– unclear economic laws

– uncertainty of the economic environment
– others, please specify

Stocks Finished goods: level
Assessment of stocks of finished goods (present level):
above normal (+), normal (=), below normal (-)

Selling prices: future tendency
Selling price expectations for the next 3-4 months:
increase (+), remain stable (=), decrease (-);

Selling prices Rate of increase: future tendency
if increase:
increase at a higher rate (+)
increase at about the same rate (=)
increase at a lower rate (-)

Employment: future tendency
Employment expectations for the next 3-4 months:
up (+), unchanged (=), down (-)

Fixed investment: intentions
Do you plan fixed investment for this year (next year):
yes (+1), no (0)

Fixed investment: future tendency
If fixed investment (machinery, buildings etc.) is planned will investment for this year (next year) compared to last year (current year) be:
higher (+), about the same (=), lower (-)

Type of fixed investment
If fixed investment is planned for next year, what type of investment will it be primarily:
– replacement of old equipment
– investment aimed at extending production capacity
    - with an unchanged product range
    - so as to extend the product range
– rationalisation investment
    - mechanisation/automation of existing production process
    - introduction of new production techniques
    - energy saving
– other motives
    - pollution control
    - safety measures
– others, please specify

Limits to fixed investment
Factors limiting planned investments for the next year:
– insufficient demand
– cost of capital too high
– credit guarantees insufficient
– insufficient profits
– fear of indebtedness
– technical factors
– other

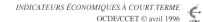

Departures from harmonised questions

Estonia

The assessment of total/export demand is measured in terms of a change in demand between the current and previous quarter.

In the question on limits to production, only a subset of the alternatives is included.

Hungary

The comparison period for production: future tendency and employment expectations is six months.

Selling price expectations are measured in seven intervals expressing per cent changes transformed to a qualitative three point scale (increase/remain stable/decrease) and with a comparison period of six months.

In limits to production, the alternative "shortage of energy" is not included.

Expected total/export demand refer to the volume of sales and the comparison period is six months.

Poland

The assessment of total/export demand is measured as changes between the current and previous month.

The comparison period for future production and for future selling price expectations is one month.

Investment intentions refer to the value of fixed investment expenditure in the current quarter as compared to the previous quarter.

The comparison period for the expected business situation is three months.

Romania

The comparison period for the expected business situation is three months.

Slovak Republic

The assessment of total/export demand is measured in terms of the change between the current and previous month.

Answers to limits to production are restricted to a maximum of five possibilities.

The assessment of the business situation is measured as the change between current and previous period.

The comparison period of the expected business situation is three months.

Construction survey

Harmonised questions

Business activity: tendency
Assessment of business activity compared to last month (quarter)
up (+), unchanged (=), down (-)

Business activity: duration of work in hand
With normal working hours, the work in hand and work already contracted will account for approximately .... months operating time.

Order books / Demand: level
Assessment of order books or production schedules for domestic/foreign contracts
total: above normal (+), normal (=), below normal (-)
domestic: above normal (+), normal (=), below normal (-)
foreign: above normal (+), normal (=), below normal (-)

Orders / Demand Total: future tendency
Orders (contracts) expectations for the next 3-4 months
up (+), unchanged (=), down (-)

Technical capacity with regard to expected demand: tendency
Assessment of technical capacity (amount and quality of equipment) with regard to expected demand in the next 12 months
more than sufficient (+), sufficient (=), not sufficient (-)

Limits to production
Limits to production (present situation)
– none
– demand
– weather conditions
– cost of materials
– cost of labour
– cost of finance (e.g. interest rates)
– access to bank credit
– shortage of skilled labour
– lack of equipment
– shortage of materials
– competition in own sector
– others, please specify

Price expectations: future tendency
Price expectations for next 3-4 months
increase (+), remain stable (=), decrease (-);

Price expectations Rate of increase: future tendency
if increase:
increase at a higher rate (+)
increase at about the same rate (=)
increase at a lower rate (-)

Employment: future tendency
Employment expectations for the next 3-4 months
up (+), unchanged (=), down (-)

Financial situation: tendency
Assessment of financial situation compared to last month (quarter)
better (+), same (=), worse (-)

Financial situation: client delays in payment
Delays in payment by public/private clients compared to last month (quarter)
total: more widespread (+), unchanged (=), less widespread (-)
private: more widespread (+), unchanged (=), less widespread (-)
public: more widespread (+), unchanged (=), less widespread (-)

Departures from harmonised questions

Hungary

Business activity is measured in comparison with a normal situation in terms of an appreciation of the level of activity.

The employment expectations and price expectations refer to the situation in six months.

Poland

The assessment of order books is measured as the change between the current and previous quarter.

The assessment of technical capacity with regard to demand is measured in terms of the change in capacity in the form of a comparison between the last quarter and future 3-4 months.

Retail trade survey

Harmonised questions

Business situation: tendency
Assessment of present business situation
good (+), satisfactory (normal for season) (=), bad (-)

Business situation: future tendency
Expected business situation six months ahead
better (+), same (=), worse (-)

Competition in own sector: tendency
Assessment of competition in own sector compared to last month (quarter)
up (+), unchanged (=), down (-)

Limits to improvements in business situation
Factors limiting improvements to the present business situation
– none
– demand
– supply
– cost of labour
– cost of finance (e.g. interest rates)
– access to bank credit
– sales surface
– storage capacity
– competition in own sector
– others, please specify

Intentions of placing orders: future tendency
Expectations on orders placed with domestic/foreign suppliers in the next 3-4 months
total: up (+), unchanged (=), down (-)
domestic: up (+), unchanged (=), down (-)
foreign: up (+), unchanged (=), down (-)

Stocks: level
Assessment of stocks
too large (+), adequate (normal for season) (=), too small (-)

Selling prices: tendency
Selling prices compared with the last month (quarter)
increase (+), remain stable (=), decrease (-), in absolute terms

Selling prices Rate of increase: tendency
if increase
increase at a higher rate (+)
increase at about the same rate (=)
increase at a lower rate (-)

Selling prices: future tendency
Selling price expectations for the next 3-4 months
increase (+), remain stable (=), decrease (-), in absolute terms

Selling prices Rate of increase: future tendency
If increase
increase at a higher rate (+)
increase at about the same rate (=)
increase at a lower rate (-)

Employment: future tendency
Employment expectations for the next 3-4 months
up (+), unchanged (=), down (-)

Financial situation: tendency
Assessment of financial situation compared to last month (quarter)
better (+), same (=), worse (-)

Departures from harmonised questions

Poland

The assessment of stocks is measured as the change between the current and previous quarter.

Romania

The expected business situation refers to the situation three months in the future.

Slovak Republic

The expected business situation refers to three months in the future.

The assessment of financial situation refers to the incapacity to pay or delays in payment by the firm or company.

Enquête sur l'industrie manufacturière

Questions harmonisées

Etat des affaires: tendance
Appréciation portée sur la situation des affaires:
bonne (+), passable (=), mauvaise (-)

Etat des affaires: perspectives
Perspectives sur la situation des affaires dans six mois:
meilleur (-), identique (=), pire (-)

Carnets de commandes / Demande total: niveau
Appréciation portée sur la demande totale/les carnets de commandes (niveau actuel):
supérieur (+), égal (=), inférieur (-) à la normale

Carnets de commandes / Demande à l'export: niveau
Appréciation portée sur la demande de l'étranger/les carnets de commandes d'exportation (niveau actuel):
supérieur (+), égal (=), inférieur (-) à la normale

Carnets de commandes / Demande total: perspectives
Demande totale prévue pour les 3 ou 4 prochains mois:
en hausse (+), sans changement (=), en baisse (-)

Carnets de commandes / Demande à l'export: perspectives
Exportations: pronostics pour les 3 ou 4 prochains mois:
en hausse (+), sans changement (=), en baisse (-)

Production: tendance
Appréciation portée sur les activités de production du mois (trimestre) écoulé :
en hausse (+), sans changement (=), en baisse (-)

Production: perspectives
Activités de production prévues pour les 3 ou 4 prochains mois:
en hausse (+), sans changement (=), en baisse (-)

Production: capacité actuelle
Appréciation portée sur la capacité de production actuelle (compte tenu de la demande prévue pour les 12 prochains mois):
plus que suffisante (+), suffisante (=), insuffisante (-)

Production: taux d'utilisation des capacités
Niveau actuel de l'utilisation des capacités (en pourcentage de leur utilisation normale).

Limitations à de la production
Limitations à la production (situation actuelle):
– aucune
– demande intérieure insuffisante
– demande extérieure insuffisante
– importations compétitives
– pénurie de main-d'oeuvre
– pénurie de main-d'oeuvre qualifiée
– manque d'équipement approprié
– pénurie de produits semi-finis
– pénurie de matières premières
– pénurie d'énergie
– problèmes financiers (par exemple insolvabilité, crédits)

- législation économique peu claire
- environnement économique incertain
- autres (veuillez préciser)

Stocks de produits finis: niveau
Appréciation portée sur les stocks de produits finis (niveau actuel):
supérieur (+), égal (=), inférieur (-) à la normale

Prix de vente: perspectives
Prix de vente: perspectives pour les 3-4 prochains mois:
ils augmenteront (+), resteront stables (=), baisseront (-)

Prix de vente taux d'augmentation: perspectives
En cas d'augmentation, ils:
augmenteront à un taux plus élevé (+)
augmenteront à peu près au même taux (=)
augmenteront à un taux plus faible (-)

Emploi: perspectives
Emploi: perspectives pour les 3 ou 4 prochains mois:
en hausse (+), sans changement (=), en baisse (-)

Investissements fixes: intentions
Projetez-vous des investissements fixes pour cette année (pour l'an prochain):
oui (+1), non (0)

Investissements fixes: perspectives
Si des investissements fixes (machines, bâtiments, etc.) sont prévus, les investissements seront-ils cette année (l'an prochain), par rapport à l'an dernier (l'année en cours):
supérieurs (+), à peu près les mêmes (=), inférieurs (-)

Type d'investissement fixe
Si des investissements fixes sont prévus pour l'an prochain, de quel type d'investissement s'agira-t-il principalement:
- remplacement d'équipements anciens
- investissements de capacité
  . avec une gamme de produits inchangée
  . afin d'élargir la gamme de produits
- investissements de rationalisation
  . mécanisation/automatisation du procédé de production existant
  . introduction de nouvelles techniques de production
  . économies d'énergie
- autres motifs
  . lutte contre la pollution
  . mesures de sécurité
- autres (veuillez préciser)

Limitations à l'investissement
Facteurs limitant les investissements prévus pour l'an prochain:
- demande insuffisante
- coût du capital trop élevé
- garanties insuffisantes pour les crédits
- profits insuffisants
- peur de l'endettement
- facteurs techniques
- autres

Différences par rapport aux questions harmonisées

Estonie

L'appréciation concernant le niveau actuel de la demande totale et celui de la demande à l'export est donnée sous la forme d'une variation par rapport au trimestre précédent.

La question sur les limitations à la production ne prévoit qu'un sous-ensemble des choix énumérés dans la question harmonisée.

Hongrie

La période de prévision applicable aux perspectives de production et à l'évolution de l'emploi est de six mois.

Les prévisions relatives aux prix de vente sont d'abord exprimées au moyen de sept fourchettes de pourcentages de variation, puis reportées sur une échelle qualitative à trois degrés (ils augmenteront/resteront stables/baisseront), la période de prévision étant de six mois.

Parmi les limitations à la production, la réponse "pénurie d'énergie" ne figure pas.

Les questions sur l'évolution probable de la demande totale et de la demande d'exportations s'appliquent au volume des ventes, et la période de prévision est de six mois.

Pologne

L'appréciation concernant le niveau actuel de la demande totale et celui de la demande d'exportations est donnée sous la forme d'une variation par rapport au mois précédent.

La période de prévision applicable aux perspectives de production et aux prix de vente futurs est d'un mois.

Les intentions d'investissement sont exprimées sous la forme d'une comparaison de la valeur des dépenses d'immobilisation pour le trimestre en cours à celle du trimestre précédent.

La période de prévision applicable à l'état des affaires est de trois mois.

Roumanie

La période de prévision applicable à l'état des affaires est de trois mois.

République slovaque

L'appréciation relative au niveau actuel de la demande totale et de la demande d'exportations est donnée sous la forme d'une variation par rapport au mois précédent.

Le nombre des réponses possibles quant aux limitations à la production sont réduites à cinq au maximum.

L'appréciation portée sur l'état des affaires est donnée sous la forme d'une variation par rapport à la période précédente.

La période de prévision applicable à l'état des affaires est de trois mois.

Enquête sur le secteur de la construction

Questions harmonisées

Activité de l'entreprise: tendance
Appréciation portée sur l'activité de l'entreprise par rapport au mois (trimestre) écoulé
en hausse (+), sans changement (=), en baisse (-)

Activité de l'entreprise: durée des travaux commandés
Avec des horaires de travail normaux, les travaux en cours, y compris ceux déjà commandés représenteront approximativement ... mois d'exploitation.

Carnets de commandes / Demande: niveau
Appréciation portée sur les carnets de commandes ou le programme d'exécution des travaux concernant les marchés intérieurs/étrangers
totaux: supérieurs (+), égaux (=), inférieurs (-) à la normale
intérieurs: supérieurs (+), égaux (=), inférieurs (-) à la normale
étrangers: supérieurs (+), égaux (=), inférieurs (-) à la normale

Carnets de commandes / Demande: perspectives
Commandes (marchés conclus): pronostics pour les 3 ou 4 prochains mois
en hausse (+), sans changement (=), en baisse (-)

Capacité technique par rapport à la demande prévue: tendance
Appréciation portée sur la capacité technique (volume et qualité de l'équipement) compte tenu de la demande prévue pour les 12 prochains mois
plus que suffisante (+), suffisante (=), insuffisante (-)

Limitations à la production
Limites de la production (situation actuelle)
– aucune
– demande
– intempéries
– coût des matériaux
– coût de la main-d'oeuvre
– coût du financement (par exemple taux d'intérêt)
– accès au crédit bancaire
– pénurie de main-d'oeuvre qualifiée
– manque d'équipement
– pénurie de matériaux
– concurrence dans le secteur
– autres (veuillez préciser)

Pronostics sur les prix: perspectives
Prix: pronostics pour les 3 ou 4 prochains mois
ils augmenteront (+), resteront stables (=), baisseront (-)

Pronostics sur le taux d'augmentation des prix
En cas d'augmentation, ils:
augmenteront à un taux plus élevé (+)
augmenteront à peu près au même taux (=)
augmenteront à un taux plus faible (-)

Emploi: perspectives
Emploi: perspectives pour les 3 ou 4 prochains mois
en hausse (+), sans changement (=), en baisse (-)

Situation financière: tendance

Appréciation portée sur la situation financière par rapport au mois (trimestre) écoulé

meilleure (+), identique (=), pire (-)

Situation financière: retard de paiement de la clientèle

Retards de paiement de la clientèle publique/privée par rapport au mois (trimestre) écoulé

totale: plus fréquents (+), sans changement (=), moins fréquents (-)

privée: plus fréquents (+), sans changement (=), moins fréquents (-)

publique: plus fréquents (+), sans changement (=), moins fréquents (-)

Différences par rapport aux questions harmonisées

Hongrie

Le niveau d'activité de l'entreprise est apprécié par rapport à une situation normale.

Les prévisions relatives à l'emploi et aux prix ont trait à la situation six mois plus tard.

Pologne

L'appréciation portée sur l'état actuel des carnets de commandes est donnée sous la forme d'une variation par rapport au trimestre précédent.

L'appréciation portée sur la capacité technique compte tenu de la demande est exprimée sous la forme d'une variation, entre le trimestre écoulé et les 3 ou 4 mois à venir.

Enquête sur le commerce de détail

Questions harmonisées

Etat des affaires: niveau
Appréciation portée sur l'état actuel des affaires
bon (+), satisfaisant (normale pour la saison) (=), mauvais (-)

Situation des affaires: perspectives
Situation probable des affaires dans six mois
meilleure (+), identique (=), pire (-)

Etat des affaires, concurrence dans le secteur: tendance
Appréciation portée sur la concurrence dans le secteur par rapport au mois (trimestre) écoulé
en hausse (+), sans changement (=), en baisse (-)

Limitations à l'amélioration des affaires
Facteurs limitant l'amélioration de l'état actuel des affaires
– aucun
– demande
– approvisionnement
– coût de la main-d'oeuvre
– coût du financement, par example: taux d'intérêt
– accès au crédit bancaire
– surface de vente
– capacité de stockage
– concurrence dans le secteur
– autres (veuillez préciser)

Intentions de commandes placées: perspectives
Evolution prévue des commandes placées auprès des fournisseurs nationaux/étrangers au cours des trois ou quatre prochains mois
ensemble: en hausse (+), sans changement (=), en baisse (-)
nationaux: en hausse (+), sans changement (=), en baisse (-)
étrangers: en hausse (+), sans changement (=), en baisse (-)

Stocks: niveau
Appréciation portée sur les stocks
trop importants (+), satisfaisants (normaux pour la saison) (=), trop faibles (-)

Prix de vente: tendance
Prix de vente par rapport au mois (trimestre) écoulé
Ils augmenteront (+), resteront stables (=), baisseront (-), en valeur absolue

Prix de vente taux d'augmentation: tendance
En cas d'augmentation, ils
augmenteront à un taux plus élevé (+)
augmenteront à peu près au même taux (=)
augmenteront à un taux plus faible (-)

Prix de vente: perspectives
Prix de vente pour les 3-4 prochains mois
Ils augmenteront (+), resteront stables (=), baisseront (-), en valeur absolue

Prix de vente taux d'augmentation: perspectives
En cas d'augmentation, ils
augmenteront à un taux plus élevé (+)
augmenteront à peu près au même taux (=)
augmenteront à un taux plus faible (-)

Emploi: perspectives
Emploi: pronostic pour les trois ou quatre prochains mois
en hausse (+), sans changement (=), en baisse (-)

Situation financière: tendance
Appréciation portée sur la situation financière par rapport au mois (trimestre) écoulé
meilleure (+), identique (=), pire (-)

Différences par rapport aux questions harmonisées

Pologne

L'appréciation portée sur le niveau actuel des stocks est exprimée sous la forme d'une variation par rapport au trimestre précédent.

Roumanie

L'état probable des affaires est celui qui est prévu pour trois mois plus tard.

République slovaque

L'état actuel des affaires se réfère à un horizon de trois mois.

L'appréciation portée sur la situation financière concerne l'incapacité de paiement ou les retards de paiement de l'entreprise ou de la société.

PUBLISHED SUPPLEMENTS AND ANNEXES

—

ANNEXES ET SUPPLÉMENTS PUBLIÉS

Sources and definitions — Sources et définitions

Title — Titre	Issue — Numéro
Short-term Economic Indicators: Transition Economies, Sources and Definitions Indicateurs Économiques à court terme : Économies en transition, Sources et définitions	2/1996
	2/1995
	3/1994
	2/1993

Subject annexes — Annexes par sujet

Title — Titre	Issue — Numéro
Labour market indicators — Indicateurs du marché du travail	1/1996
	3/1995
	1/1995
	4/1994
Business surveys — Enquêtes de conjoncture	2/1996
	2/1995

Historical supplements — Suppléments rétrospectifs

Title — Titre	Issue — Numéro
Republic of Slovenia — République de Slovénie	2/1995
Ukraine — Ukraine	1/1994
Lithuania — Lituanie	3/1993
Latvia — Lettonie	2/1993
Estonia — Estonie	2/1993

Historical publications — Publications rétrospectives

Short-term Economic Statistics: Commonwealth of Independent States 1980-1993 — Statistiques Économiques à court terme : Communauté des États Indépendants 1980-1993 1993

Short-term Economic Statistics: Central and Eastern Europe (Bulgaria, CSFR, Hungary, Poland, Romania) 1980-1991— Statistiques Économiques à court terme : Europe centrale et orientale (Bulgarie, RFTS, Hongrie, Pologne, Roumanie) 1980 à 1991 1992

MAIN SALES OUTLETS OF OECD PUBLICATIONS
PRINCIPAUX POINTS DE VENTE DES PUBLICATIONS DE L'OCDE

ARGENTINA – ARGENTINE
Carlos Hirsch S.R.L.
Galería Güemes, Florida 165, 4° Piso
1333 Buenos Aires   Tel. (1) 331.1787 y 331.2391
Telefax: (1) 331.1787

AUSTRALIA – AUSTRALIE
D.A. Information Services
648 Whitehorse Road, P.O.B 163
Mitcham, Victoria 3132   Tel. (03) 9210.7777
Telefax: (03) 9210.7788

AUSTRIA – AUTRICHE
Gerold & Co.
Graben 31
Wien I   Tel. (0222) 533.50.14
Telefax: (0222) 512.47.31.29

BELGIUM – BELGIQUE
Jean De Lannoy
Avenue du Roi 202 Koningslaan
B-1060 Bruxelles   Tel. (02) 538.51.69/538.08.41
Telefax: (02) 538.08.41

CANADA
Renouf Publishing Company Ltd.
1294 Algoma Road
Ottawa, ON K1B 3W8   Tel. (613) 741.4333
Telefax: (613) 741.5439

Stores:
61 Sparks Street
Ottawa, ON K1P 5R1   Tel. (613) 238.8985
12 Adelaide Street West
Toronto, ON M5H 1L6   Tel. (416) 363.3171
Telefax: (416)363.59.63

Les Éditions La Liberté Inc.
3020 Chemin Sainte-Foy
Sainte-Foy, PQ G1X 3V6   Tel. (418) 658.3763
Telefax: (418) 658.3763

Federal Publications Inc.
165 University Avenue, Suite 701
Toronto, ON M5H 3B8   Tel. (416) 860.1611
Telefax: (416) 860.1608

Les Publications Fédérales
1185 Université
Montréal, QC H3B 3A7   Tel. (514) 954.1633
Telefax: (514) 954.1635

CHINA – CHINE
China National Publications Import
Export Corporation (CNPIEC)
16 Gongti E. Road, Chaoyang District
P.O. Box 88 or 50
Beijing 100704 PR   Tel. (01) 506.6688
Telefax: (01) 506.3101

CHINESE TAIPEI – TAIPEI CHINOIS
Good Faith Worldwide Int'l. Co. Ltd.
9th Floor, No. 118, Sec. 2
Chung Hsiao E. Road
Taipei   Tel. (02) 391.7396/391.7397
Telefax: (02) 394.9176

**CZECH REPUBLIC –
RÉPUBLIQUE TCHÈQUE**
Artia Pegas Press Ltd.
Narodni Trida 25
POB 825
111 21 Praha 1   Tel. (2) 242 246 04
Telefax: (2) 242 278 72

DENMARK – DANEMARK
Munksgaard Book and Subscription Service
35, Nørre Søgade, P.O. Box 2148
DK-1016 København K   Tel. (33) 12.85.70
Telefax: (33) 12.93.87

EGYPT – ÉGYPTE
Middle East Observer
41 Sherif Street
Cairo   Tel. 392.6919
Telefax: 360-6804

FINLAND – FINLANDE
Akateeminen Kirjakauppa
Keskuskatu 1, P.O. Box 128
00100 Helsinki
Subscription Services/Agence d'abonnements :
P.O. Box 23
00371 Helsinki   Tel. (358 0) 121 4416
Telefax: (358 0) 121.4450

FRANCE
OECD/OCDE
Mail Orders/Commandes par correspondance :
2, rue André-Pascal
75775 Paris Cedex 16   Tel. (33-1) 45.24.82.00
Telefax: (33-1) 49.10.42.76
Telex: 640048 OCDE
Internet: Compte.PUBSINQ @ oecd.org
Orders via Minitel, France only/
Commandes par Minitel, France exclusivement :
36 15 OCDE
OECD Bookshop/Librairie de l'OCDE :
33, rue Octave-Feuillet
75016 Paris   Tel. (33-1) 45.24.81.81
(33-1) 45.24.81.67

Dawson
B.P. 40
91121 Palaiseau Cedex   Tel. 69.10.47.00
Telefax : 64.54.83.26

Documentation Française
29, quai Voltaire
75007 Paris   Tel. 40.15.70.00

Economica
49, rue Héricart
75015 Paris   Tel. 45.78.12.92
Telefax : 40.58.15.70

Gibert Jeune (Droit-Économie)
6, place Saint-Michel
75006 Paris   Tel. 43.25.91.19

Librairie du Commerce International
10, avenue d'Iéna
75016 Paris   Tel. 40.73.34.60

Librairie Dunod
Université Paris-Dauphine
Place du Maréchal-de-Lattre-de-Tassigny
75016 Paris   Tel. 44.05.40.13

Librairie Lavoisier
11, rue Lavoisier
75008 Paris   Tel. 42.65.39.95

Librairie des Sciences Politiques
30, rue Saint-Guillaume
75007 Paris   Tel. 45.48.36.02

P.U.F.
49, boulevard Saint-Michel
75005 Paris   Tel. 43.25.83.40

Librairie de l'Université
12a, rue Nazareth
13100 Aix-en-Provence   Tel. (16) 42.26.18.08

Documentation Française
165, rue Garibaldi
69003 Lyon   Tel. (16) 78.63.32.23

Librairie Decitre
29, place Bellecour
69002 Lyon   Tel. (16) 72.40.54.54

Librairie Sauramps
Le Triangle
34967 Montpellier Cedex 2   Tel. (16) 67.58.85.15
Tekefax: (16) 67.58.27.36

A la Sorbonne Actual
23, rue de l'Hôtel-des-Postes
06000 Nice   Tel. (16) 93.13.77.75
Telefax: (16) 93.80.75.69

GERMANY – ALLEMAGNE
OECD Publications and Information Centre
August-Bebel-Allee 6
D-53175 Bonn   Tel. (0228) 959.120
Telefax: (0228) 959.12.17

GREECE – GRÈCE
Librairie Kauffmann
Mavrokordatou 9
106 78 Athens   Tel. (01) 32.55.321
Telefax: (01) 32.30.320

HONG-KONG
Swindon Book Co. Ltd.
Astoria Bldg. 3F
34 Ashley Road, Tsimshatsui
Kowloon, Hong Kong   Tel. 2376.2062
Telefax: 2376.0685

HUNGARY – HONGRIE
Euro Info Service
Margitsziget, Európa Ház
1138 Budapest   Tel. (1) 111.62.16
Telefax: (1) 111.60.61

ICELAND – ISLANDE
Mál Mog Menning
Laugavegi 18, Pósthólf 392
121 Reykjavik   Tel. (1) 552.4240
Telefax: (1) 562.3523

INDIA – INDE
Oxford Book and Stationery Co.
Scindia House
New Delhi 110001   Tel. (11) 331.5896/5308
Telefax: (11) 332.5993

17 Park Street
Calcutta 700016   Tel. 240832

INDONESIA – INDONÉSIE
Pdii-Lipi
P.O. Box 4298
Jakarta 12042   Tel. (21) 573.34.67
Telefax: (21) 573.34.67

IRELAND – IRLANDE
Government Supplies Agency
Publications Section
4/5 Harcourt Road
Dublin 2   Tel. 661.31.11
Telefax: 475.27.60

ISRAEL – ISRAËL
Praedicta
5 Shatner Street
P.O. Box 34030
Jerusalem 91430   Tel. (2) 52.84.90/1/2
Telefax: (2) 52.84.93

R.O.Y. International
P.O. Box 13056
Tel Aviv 61130   Tel. (3) 546 1423
Telefax: (3) 546 1442

Palestinian Authority/Middle East:
INDEX Information Services
P.O.B. 19502
Jerusalem   Tel. (2) 27.12.19
Telefax: (2) 27.16.34

ITALY – ITALIE
Libreria Commissionaria Sansoni
Via Duca di Calabria 1/1
50125 Firenze   Tel. (055) 64.54.15
Telefax: (055) 64.12.57
Via Bartolini 29
20155 Milano   Tel. (02) 36.50.83

Editrice e Libreria Herder
Piazza Montecitorio 120
00186 Roma   Tel. 679.46.28
                          Telefax: 678.47.51

Libreria Hoepli
Via Hoepli 5
20121 Milano   Tel. (02) 86.54.46
                          Telefax: (02) 805.28.86

Libreria Scientifica
Dott. Lucio de Biasio 'Aeiou'
Via Coronelli, 6
20146 Milano   Tel. (02) 48.95.45.52
                          Telefax: (02) 48.95.45.48

JAPAN – JAPON
OECD Publications and Information Centre
Landic Akasaka Building
2-3-4 Akasaka, Minato-ku
Tokyo 107   Tel. (81.3) 3586.2016
                          Telefax: (81.3) 3584.7929

KOREA – CORÉE
Kyobo Book Centre Co. Ltd.
P.O. Box 1658, Kwang Hwa Moon
Seoul   Tel. 730.78.91
                          Telefax: 735.00.30

MALAYSIA – MALAISIE
University of Malaya Bookshop
University of Malaya
P.O. Box 1127, Jalan Pantai Baru
59700 Kuala Lumpur
Malaysia   Tel. 756.5000/756.5425
                          Telefax: 756.3246

MEXICO – MEXIQUE
OECD Publications and Information Centre
Edificio INFOTEC
Av. San Fernando no. 37
Col. Toriello Guerra
Tlalpan C.P. 14050
Mexico D.F.
             Tel. (525) 606 00 11 Extension 100
                          Fax : (525) 606 13 07

Revistas y Periodicos Internacionales S.A. de C.V.
Florencia 57 - 1004
Mexico, D.F. 06600   Tel. 207.81.00
                          Telefax: 208.39.79

NETHERLANDS – PAYS-BAS
SDU Uitgeverij Plantijnstraat
Externe Fondsen
Postbus 20014
2500 EA's-Gravenhage   Tel. (070) 37.89.880
Voor bestellingen: Telefax: (070) 34.75.778

NEW ZEALAND –
NOUVELLE-ZÉLANDE
GPLegislation Services
P.O. Box 12418
Thorndon, Wellington   Tel. (04) 496.5655
                          Telefax: (04) 496.5698

NORWAY – NORVÈGE
NIC INFO A/S
Bertrand Narvesens vei 2
P.O. Box 6512 Etterstad
0606 Oslo 6   Tel. (022) 57.33.00
                          Telefax: (022) 68.19.01

PAKISTAN
Mirza Book Agency
65 Shahrah Quaid-E-Azam
Lahore 54000   Tel. (42) 353.601
                          Telefax: (42) 231.730

PHILIPPINE – PHILIPPINES
International Booksource Center Inc.
Rm 179/920 Cityland 10 Condo Tower 2
HV dela Costa Ext cor Valero St.
Makati Metro Manila   Tel. (632) 817 9676
                          Telefax : (632) 817 1741

POLAND – POLOGNE
Ars Polona
00-950 Warszawa
Krakowskie Przedmieácie 7   Tel. (22) 264760
                          Telefax : (22) 268673

PORTUGAL
Livraria Portugal
Rua do Carmo 70-74
Apart. 2681
1200 Lisboa   Tel. (01) 347.49.82/5
                          Telefax: (01) 347.02.64

SINGAPORE – SINGAPOUR
Gower Asia Pacific Pte Ltd.
Golden Wheel Building
41, Kallang Pudding Road, No. 04-03
Singapore 1334   Tel. 741.5166
                          Telefax: 742.9356

SPAIN – ESPAGNE
Mundi-Prensa Libros S.A.
Castelló 37, Apartado 1223
Madrid 28001   Tel. (91) 431.33.99
                          Telefax: (91) 575.39.98

Mundi-Prensa Barcelona
Consell de Cent No. 391
08009 – Barcelona   Tel. (93) 488.34.92
                          Telefax: (93) 487.76.59

Llibreria de la Generalitat
Palau Moja
Rambla dels Estudis, 118
08002 – Barcelona
               (Subscripcions) Tel. (93) 318.80.12
               (Publicacions) Tel. (93) 302.67.23
                          Telefax: (93) 412.18.54

SRI LANKA
Centre for Policy Research
c/o Colombo Agencies Ltd.
No. 300-304, Galle Road
Colombo 3   Tel. (1) 574240, 573551-2
                  Telefax: (1) 575394, 510711

SWEDEN – SUÈDE
CE Fritzes AB
S–106 47 Stockholm   Tel. (08) 690.90.90
                          Telefax: (08) 20.50.21

Subscription Agency/Agence d'abonnements :
Wennergren-Williams Info AB
P.O. Box 1305
171 25 Solna   Tel. (08) 705.97.50
                          Telefax: (08) 27.00.71

SWITZERLAND – SUISSE
Maditec S.A. (Books and Periodicals - Livres
et périodiques)
Chemin des Palettes 4
Case postale 266
1020 Renens VD 1   Tel. (021) 635.08.65
                          Telefax: (021) 635.07.80

Librairie Payot S.A.
4, place Pépinet
CP 3212
1002 Lausanne   Tel. (021) 320.25.11
                          Telefax: (021) 320.25.14

Librairie Unilivres
6, rue de Candolle
1205 Genève   Tel. (022) 320.26.23
                          Telefax: (022) 329.73.18

Subscription Agency/Agence d'abonnements :
Dynapresse Marketing S.A.
38 avenue Vibert
1227 Carouge   Tel. (022) 308.07.89
                          Telefax: (022) 308.07.99

See also – Voir aussi :
OECD Publications and Information Centre
August-Bebel-Allee 6
D-53175 Bonn (Germany)   Tel. (0228) 959.120
                          Telefax: (0228) 959.12.17

THAILAND – THAÏLANDE
Suksit Siam Co. Ltd.
113, 115 Fuang Nakhon Rd.
Opp. Wat Rajbopith
Bangkok 10200   Tel. (662) 225.9531/2
                          Telefax: (662) 222.5188

TUNISIA – TUNISIE
Grande Librairie Spécialisée
Fendri Ali
Avenue Haffouz Imm El-Intilaka
Bloc B 1 Sfax 3000   Tel. (216-4) 296 855
                          Telefax: (216-4) 298.270

TURKEY – TURQUIE
Kültür Yayinlari Is-Türk Ltd. Sti.
Atatürk Bulvari No. 191/Kat 13
Kavaklidere/Ankara
                  Tel. (312) 428.11.40 Ext. 2458
                          Telefax: (312) 417 24 90
Dolmabahce Cad. No. 29
Besiktas/Istanbul   Tel. (212) 260 7188

UNITED KINGDOM – ROYAUME-UNI
HMSO
Gen. enquiries   Tel. (171) 873 8242
Postal orders only:
P.O. Box 276, London SW8 5DT
Personal Callers HMSO Bookshop
49 High Holborn, London WC1V 6HB
                          Telefax: (171) 873 8416
Branches at: Belfast, Birmingham, Bristol,
Edinburgh, Manchester

UNITED STATES – ÉTATS-UNIS
OECD Publications and Information Center
2001 L Street N.W., Suite 650
Washington, D.C. 20036-4922 Tel. (202) 785.6323
                          Telefax: (202) 785.0350

Subscriptions to OECD periodicals may also be
placed through main subscription agencies.

Les abonnements aux publications périodiques de
l'OCDE peuvent être souscrits auprès des
principales agences d'abonnement.

Orders and inquiries from countries where Distribu-
tors have not yet been appointed should be sent to:
OECD Publications Service, 2, rue André-Pascal,
75775 Paris Cedex 16, France.

Les commandes provenant de pays où l'OCDE n'a
pas encore désigné de distributeur peuvent être
adressées à : OCDE, Service des Publications,
2, rue André-Pascal, 75775 Paris Cedex 16, France.

1-1996

OECD PUBLICATIONS, 2, rue André-Pascal, 75775 PARIS CEDEX 16
PRINTED IN FRANCE
(07 96 02 3) ISBN 92-64-04744-1 – No. 48750 1996
ISSN 1019-9829